Cultural Diversity and the Curriculum

Volume 2

Cultural Diversity and the Curriculum

Volume 2

Cross-Curricular Contexts, Themes and Dimensions in Secondary Schools

Edited by

G.K. Verma and P.D. Pumfrey

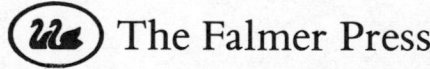 **The Falmer Press**

(A member of Taylor & Francis Group)
London • Washington D.C.

UK   The Falmer Press, 4 John Street, London WCIN 2ET
USA   The Falmer Press, Taylor & Francis Inc., 1900 Frost Road, Suite 101, Bristol, PA 19007

© G.K. Verma and P.D. Pumfrey 1993

First published 1993

Library of Congress Cataloging-in-Publication data are available on request

A catalogue record for this book is available from the British Library

ISBN 075070 141 2
ISBN 075070 142 0 (Paperback)

Jacket design by Caroline Archer

Typeset in 10/12pt Bembo by
Graphicraft Typesetters Ltd., Hong Kong

Printed in Great Britain by Burgess Science Press, Basingstoke on paper which has a specified pH value on final paper manufacture of not less than 7.5 and is therefore 'acid free'.

Contents

Contents

Preface

In May 1992, once again, the sociological tinder box of Los Angeles exploded literally and metaphorically. The idealistic concept of the USA as a 'melting pot', in which differing groups establish mutually acceptable *modus vivendi*, was once more challenged. The feelings aroused amongst black communities following the verdict in the trial of four police officers charged with assaulting Rodney King, at which an amateur video-recording of his arrest was presented, can well be understood. Was the subsequent rioting, looting, arson and murder justified? Was nothing learned from the Watts riots of twenty seven years before? There are crucial lessons for individuals and institutions to be learned from this latest manifestation of minority group alienation by *all* members of society. No country, no ethnic, religious or social group can afford to adopt a 'holier than thou' attitude. The riots in Manchester, London, Bristol, Liverpool and Leeds during the 1980s and the ethnic, religious and social tensions that exist in the 1990s show the fragilities inherent in our own social cohesion. They underline the importance of multicultural education if the concept of 'one nation' is to be approached.

This is the second in a series of four books. Volumes 1 and 2 concern secondary schools. Parallel volumes 3 and 4 concern primary schools. Volumes 1 and 3 address the implications of the National Curriculum foundation subjects and religious education in relation to cultural diversity at the secondary and primary-school levels, respectively. Volumes 2 and 4 consider the implications of cross-curricular elements in relation to cultural diversity at the secondary and primary-school levels.

This series of four books serves two major purposes. The first is to describe and discuss cultural diversity and the curriculum from various curricular perspectives. The second is to consider how the legitimate educational concerns of minority ethnic groups, and the aspirations of larger proups, can be constructively addressed within the framework of the National Curriculum and those equally important aspects of the curriculum subsumed under the broader headings of the 'basic' and 'whole' curriculum respectively. To this end, specialists in the key components of the curriculum have considered some of the challenges and describe promising practices in a number of specific subjects and cross-curricular fields.

Each contributor in each of the four volumes comments under three headings on that aspect of the curriculum in which the contributor has specialist experience and expertise, in relation to cultural diversity. The headings used by all contributors are identified as 'Context', 'Challenges' and 'Responses'. The views expressed, the analyses of contexts, the identification of challenges and the suggestions for responses represent the considered opinions of the individual contributors.

The series begins with two volumes devoted to the secondary school. The editors deliberately chose to start with the secondary stage of education. Much remains undecided concerning the structure, content, pedagogy and assessment of many components of the secondary-school curriculum. Despite these considerations, and virtually irrespective of the decisions reached concerning them, the multicultural nature of the population and of schools will develop. Demographic data presented in Volume 1, Chapter 3 and in Chapter 2 of this volume, confirm this point and provide indications of the demographic changes that are likely to take place in the future. These demographic changes, and their educational implications, must be considered if the educational system is to respond adequately and fairly. We have deliberately ventured into this controversial field whilst the 'rules of the curricular game' in state secondary schools are still being negotiated in relation to certain aspects of the curriculum. We do so because of the importance with which we view the increasing ethnic diversity of the school population and of the country. Janus-faced, that ethnic diversity represents both problems and opportunities for all parties involved. To deny either would be a disservice to the pupils and the communities that the educational system exists to serve. It would also limit the chances that an education meeting the requirements of the Education Reform Act 1988 would ever be provided.

It has been argued that cross-curricular elements, of which an extensive number can be listed, make a major contribution to the personal and social education of pupils. Such elements 'are ingredients which tie together the broad education of the individual and augment what comes from the basic curriculum' (NCC, 1990, p. 2). The NCC has distinguished three aspects of cross-curricular elements: dimensions; skills; and themes. Dimensions include a commitment to the provison of *equal opportunities* for all pupils, coupled with recognition that 'preparation for life in a multicultural society is relevant to all pupils' and should permeate the entire curriculum (ibid., p. 2). Cultural diversity, gender and special educational needs are identified by the NCC as three key considerations. There are others. Because of their salience, we have selected four further dimensions of particular importance in a multicultural school, society and world. There are also many cross-curricular skills. These include:

- communication skills (receptive and expressive aspects of language);
- numeracy skills;

- study skills;
- problem-solving skills;
- personal and social skills; and
- information technology skills.

Cross-curricular themes refer to five major facets of any curriculum that are considered by the NCC to be essential parts of the whole curriculum.

Volume 2 is in three parts. Part 1 comprises three chapters written to establish the importance to all schools and all pupils, of the overall interacting theme of cultural diversity and a range of cross-curricular aspects of the curriculum. These chapters set the scene for subsequent contributions. Part 2 comprises chapters on each of the five major cross-curricular themes specified in the publications of the National Curriculum Council, which are concerned with:

- education for economic and industrial awareness;
- careers education and guidance;
- health education;
- education for citizenship; and
- environmental education.

In addition to these important cross-curricular themes, we have identified a further seven cross-curricular dimensions that merit attention, these are presented in Part 3:

- countering racism in British education;
- personal and social education: a black perspective;
- gender issues in education for citizenship;
- children with special educational needs;
- European community understanding;
- cultural differences and staff development; and
- accountability and the local management of schools.

Our contributors are drawn from various cultural, ethnic and professional backgrounds. Consequently, their respective philosophical and theoretical stances vary. To have sought only individuals operating from a single agreed ideological, philosophical, or theoretical position concerning the nature and curricular implications of cultural diversity, would have implied that the editors considered such a position existed and was the most tenable. Irrespective of the authors' respective ideological, philosophical and theoretical positions, all are clearly concerned with ensuring that the National Curriculum is effectively delivered in our multicultural society. The claim that good practice can help to drive out poor theory, has something to commend it. A belief in the importance of the curricular implications and practices deriving from cultural diversity unites our contributors.

List of Tables and Figures

List of Abbreviations

AIMER	Access to Information on Multicultural Education Resources
AIMS	Art and Design in a Multicultural Society
AMA	Association of Metropolitan Authorities
APU	Assessment of Performance Unit
ARE	Anti-Racist Education
AREAI	Association of Religious Education Advisers and Inspectors
ARTEN	Anti-Racist Teacher Education Network
AT	Attainment Targets
ATEM	Association of Ethnic Minority Teachers
BCBP	British Council for Physical Education
BNP	British National Party
BTEC	Business and Technical Education Council
CARM	Campaign Against Racism in the Media
CATE	Council for the Accreditation of Teacher Education
CBI	Confederation of British Industry
CDT	Craft, Design and Technology
CILT	Centre for Information on Language Teaching
CPD	Continuing Professional Development
CPVE	Certificate of Pre-Vocational Education
CRE	Commission for Racial Equality
CSE	Certificate of Secondary Education
CTA	Caribbean Teachers Association
DES	Department of Education and Science
DFE	Department for Education
DoE	Department of Employment
EEC	European Economic Community
EFL	English as a Foreign Language
EFTA	European Free Trade Association
EIU	Economic and Industrial Understanding
EMAG	Ethnic Minority Advisory Groups
EMS	European Monetary System

EPIC	Education Policy Information Centre
ERA	Education Reform Act 1988
ERM	Exchange Rate Mechanism
ESF	European Social Fund
ESG	Education Support Grant
ESHA	European Secondary Heads Association
ESL/E2L	English as a Second Language
ESRC	Economic and Social Science Research Council
GCSE	General Certificate of Secondary Education
GEST	Grants for Educational Support and Training
GLC	Greater London Council
GRIST	Grant Related In-service Training
HE	Higher Education
HMI	Her Majesty's Inspectorate
HMSO	Her Majesty's Stationery Office
ILEA	Inner London Education Authority
INSET	In-service Education for Teachers
IT	Information Technology
ITT	Initial Teacher Training
KS	Key Stages (of the National Curriculum)
LEA	Local Education Authority
LMS	Local Management of Schools
LMSS	Local Management of Special Schools
MCE	Multi-Cultural Education
MFLWG	Modern Foreign Languages Working Group
NAHT	National Association of Head Teachers
NAME	National Antiracist Movement in Education
NC	National Curriculum
NCC	National Curriculum Council
NCDP	National Curriculum Development Plan
NCDS	National Child Development Study
NCMT	National Council for the Mother Tongue
NEPTUNE	New European Programme for Technology Utilisation in Education
NERIS	National Educational Resources Information Service
NFER	National Foundation for Educational Research
NSC	National Science Curriculum
OPCS	Office of Population Censuses and Surveys
PC	Profile Components
PoS	Programme of Study
PSE	Personal and Social Education
RAT	Racism Awareness Training
RE	Religious Education
RI	Religious Instruction
RoA	Records of Achievement

RT	Runnymede Trust
SACRE	Standing Advisory Council on Religious Education
SAIL	Staged Assessments in Literacy
SEAC	School Examinations and Assessment Council
SCDC	School Curriculum Development Committee
SEN	Special Educational Needs
SoA	Statements of Attainment
SSD	Social Services Department
TACADE	Teachers Advisory Council on Alcohol and Drug Education
TGAT	Task Group on Assessment and Testing
TUC	Trades Union Congress
TVE	Technical and Vocational Education
TVEI	Technical and Vocational Education Initiative
UKCEE	The UK Centre for European Education
UNEP	United National Environment Programme
UNESCO	United Nations Educational, Scientific and Cultural Organisation

Educational Equality and Cultural Pluralism in Secondary Education: Cross-curricular Perspectives

Chapter 1

Educational Equality?

Gajendra K. Verma and Peter D. Pumfrey

Context

Is there equality of educational opportunities? Is the aspiration 'pie in the sky', 'idealistic nonsense', 'a waste of time'? Or is it an ideal that must be at the heart of our educational system and society? Is it a concept without which the National Curriculum will wither on the vine of vindictiveness? The Swann report rightly asserts that if educational equality is to be attained, it must address the needs and aspirations of both minority and majority groups (DES, 1985). It must educate the ethnic-majority group to enable the minority group to achieve access to educational, social, and political equality as full citizens of the society.

The *Shorter Oxford Dictionary* defines equality as 'the condition of being equal in quantity, amount, value, intensity, etc . . . the condition of being equal is dignity, privileges, power'. According to this definition provision for ethnic minority groups in most British schools can hardly yet be said to be equal. Educational equality means uniformity of esteem and opportunity for all ethnic and cultural groups in all that relates to the common core of knowledge, skills, attitudes and experiences.

In the United Kingdom today if we ask any group of pupils to say whatever comes into their heads when they think of Africa, Asia or any region in the so-called 'Third World' or 'developing countries', then the vast majority of them would come up with some predictable images: famine, poverty, disease, ignorance and so on, which would probably be high on their list of descriptions. If these issues were explored further with them, those ills would be attributed to the size of the population (overpopulated), infertile lands, the weather conditions (too hot or too much rain), poor husbandry, primitive surroundings, illiteracy etc. This would be the view of certain sections of the adult population as well.

A study was conducted with 11 to 12-year-old pupils in two middle schools to test the veracity of the above statement (Verma and Mallick, 1984). The discussion with pupils was directed to include the images they had of the Third World countries, the inhabitants of those countries, their economy and their lifestyles. The findings showed that people from the Third World were perceived as inhabitants of an undeveloped continent who were primitives, battling unsuccessfully against their environment. They were described as 'weird', 'exotic', 'dark-skinned'. These perceptions and images are created through literature, textbooks and the medias, especially television, which have been found to embody 'stereotyping', 'ethnocentrism' and 'tokenism' (Verma and Darby, 1990). The role of popular television clearly stands above that of other forms of mass media. Its influence may be both crude and direct (such as the TV programme 'Till death us do part') or subtle and indirect.

It is quite obvious what differing impacts these will have on ethnic-minority pupils. It is a blow to the self-concept of these pupils when they see the main images of people from Africa and Asia on 'Oxfam' and 'Save the Children' posters, in subordinate positions in the media and in other situations. British television's coverage of the Third World fosters 'mythic reactions' and is typically opposed to historical explication of complex social reality, by evoking irony, scepticism and fascination. Having examined coverage of the developments in South Africa, terrorism in Europe and race relations in Britain, one is forced to conclude that television coverage is constrained by its structural limitations as a medium (Verma, 1988). The images of other countries and their people are presented to us through a culture filter, that is to say, through the commentaries that accompany the images. The images themselves are also filtered, in terms of the selection of events covered. Thus, what is presented to us on the television is a second-hand reality. We are also dependent, in large measures, on the commentary, which, if well-informed, can draw our attention to important and significant points. Furthermore, the images are subject to still further filtering as we react to them. This reaction is part of the acculturation process, based on our previous experience.

Most pupils come to school with little understanding of how their cultures and lifestyles are unique and different from those of other cultural groups. Pupils knowing very little about other societies and cultures, usually respond to them in terms of superficial generalizations and stereotypes. Such a learning output is not based on individual imagination but is culturally derived. A culture uninformed by a sensitive appreciation of others will judge them in terms of its own norms. Thus, pupils taught to look at the world only from the perspective of their own culture, without having been exposed to other cultures, are very likely to reject or misinterpret all that cannot resemble the narrow categories of their own way of perceiving the world. When ethnic minority pupils are constantly exposed to an ethnocentric curriculum that presents their cultures and communities in a biased and unflattering way, they can hardly avoid being alienated and developing a sense of inferiority.

We are all prisoners of our experiences. The children of English missionaries brought up in South Africa returned to the UK. After some time in secondary school, the art teacher took the class outside to observe a field of tall grass and wild flowers. On their return to the classroom, the pupils were asked to paint a picture of some aspect of the field they had just seen. The two children born and raised in South Africa drew very attractive representations *but the grass was coloured yellow*. Despite the evidence of their senses, their perceptions were determined by their prior experiences. We do well to remember that this is true of all of us unless we reflect on our experiences.

Challenges

Perhaps the most pressing problem facing British education is how to respond to the compelling fact of cultural diversity in the 1990s and beyond. The fabric of British society is irreversibly pluralist with dozens of different religions, hundreds of languages and dialect groups and various ethnic groups. In order to begin the analysis of challenges these present in education, it would seem appropriate to pose four key questions:

1 What are the fundamental issues which underpin the contribution that education is making?
2 What contribution is education making towards creating a society in which life chances of all citizens are fairly distributed?
3 What contribution is education making towards creating a society in which individuals can go about their lives in dignity and freedom?
4 What contribution is education making towards the creation of a society in which individual differences in lifestyle can prosper without detriment or prejudice to the individual or to that of others?

Few would disagree that the education system is a powerful force in moulding the individual and the society it serves, because of the knowledge it transmits (see Chapter 3 in this volume for further analysis). However, what is regarded as knowledge is not an unbiased and impartial collection of facts and cumulation of an individual's and a group's total collective experiences. Knowledge is primarily subjective, value-laden, imprecise and uncertain. It evolves and is transmitted over time. Education functions not only as a powerful vehicle for transferring knowledge but also for communicating cultural and social values of the dominant ideologies. In the UK, it is primarily a western, if not a European conceptualization of what it is presumed others ought to know (Ladmiral and Lipiansky, 1989).

The translation of the deep structures of knowledge into behavioural objectives is one of the main causes of the distortion of knowledge in schools. The filtering of knowledge, through an analysis of objectives, gives the school an authority and power over its students by setting arbitrary limits to speculation and by defining arbitrary solutions to unresolved problems of knowledge. 'This translates the teacher from the role of the student of a complex field of knowledge to the role of the master of the schools' agreed version of that field' (Stenhouse, 1975). A good example is ways in which learning technology in the European communities can so easily be constrained by an implicit set of values. The culture of learning technology is supplementary to, and perhaps a reflection of, the culture of society. Culture encompasses almost every aspect of human life; it is more or less consistent 'patterns' of thoughts, feelings and actions, and it is structured (Verma and Entzinger, 1992). This mechanism of knowledge and the transmission of knowledge, with its emphasis on the product rather than the process, carries with it the threat of uniformity rather than recognition of differences. This danger is implicit and has been made explicit in the development of history, geography, RE, music and other core and foundation subjects in the National Curriculum (for a more detailed discussion see Volume 1).

Education in a plural society ought to teach people to feel comfortable with differences — in fact, to expect these as a normal and agreeable fact of life. Viewed from a broader perspective, it is the differences in various features and dimensions that make an individual stand apart from other individuals. Differences provide the identifying markers around individuals and render them unique and distinct. Education helps people to become aware of this distinguishing process and teaches them to become sensitive and more receptive to differences. Properly understood, this does not conflict with, but rather complements its function in facilitating a cohesive national identity as a legitimate aim of education.

The Education Reform Act 1988 (NCC, 1988) was a neglected opportunity to develop a National Curriculum for schools that would have recognized differences. It could have made a more positive contribution to the development of diversity within a framework of national unity than appears to be the case. Regrettably it was an opportunity that was missed. Many commentators believe that the National Curriculum denies the values of other cultures. Is this assertion valid?

A traditional but widely accepted view of education is that it aims to cultivate such human capacities as critical reflection, imagination, self-criticism, the ability to reason, argue, weigh up endings and to form independent judgments of one's own. It is often assumed that as a result of acquiring such capacities, individuals will be able to live a life free from ignorance, prejudice, superstition and dogma, and one in which they can freely choose their beliefs and plan their pattern of life. Education should aim to familiarize pupils with the great intellectual, moral, religious, and other achievements of the human race. It is also supposed to initiate them not merely into the cultural capital of their own community but also that of other groups. In this way the function of education would be to humanize rather than merely to socialize. They are to be taught the languages, history, geography, culture, social structures, religion and so on of other communities in order that they can learn to appreciate the unity and diversity of mankind. Unfortunately, the reality falls short of this theory in western societies.

Unless secondary-school staff consciously consider equality issues, nothing will happen to redress the imbalanced images indicated earlier in this paper.

Responses

The National Curriculum in England and Wales does not challenge the fundamental perspectives of education, and measures for change are largely considered within the existing educational framework. It does not attempt to pursue an ethos committed to diversity by challenging schools' traditional role as the transmitters of the dominant culture.

Another element, which has a crucial role in making the formal National Curriculum changes 'real', is the hidden curriculum. The formal changes are likely to come from the curriculum process which may 'teach' the knowledge, but the hidden curriculum has a part to play in bringing about the changes in the affective domain ('hearts and minds') to complete the process of change. The hidden curriculum should be complementary to the formal curriculum: easy words; hard to achieve; but essential! Few educators would disagree that the hidden curriculum is not the easiest aspect of schooling to understand and manipulate whatever formal structures may be in place. This is because of the important contribution of peer-group influences that are brought to bear (also outside influences especially of older siblings, friends, parents and neighbourhood). The school cannot counter all of these since they are beyond their direct sphere of influence. However, an awareness of the nature, extent and impact of the hidden curriculum on pupils (and staff) is important to schools. Schools need to attempt to influence as many aspects of the hidden curriculum as is feasible. There is further scope for interventions through the personal and social-development education programme, community-work programmes and so on. These types of activity can help increase experience of cultural diversity as opposed to knowledge of curriculum development, its concomitant.

There is no constitution which can override Acts of Parliament. There is presently no Bill of Rights, but this does not mean that there are no firmly rooted principles which can challenge arbitrary action by government officials. Magna Carta and its consequences are not meaningless. However, there are no legal class actions which entitle redress for entire groups of people. Consequently, there have been increasing calls for a Bill of Rights which would provide a legal framework to protect the rights of individuals and groups in society. Some argue that such a bill is unnecessary because the law already affords adequate protection to the individual. But it may be said that the law in its present form is largely concerned only to define what is not permissible. By its very nature, it has little to say about what is desirable. However, the advantage of a Bill of Rights would be in its positive statement legitimating social, cultural and ethnic differences. Such a bill could change the context of the debate from one being primarily concerned with attacking educational inequality to one which investigates the best means of promoting equality of opportunity. It would transform the task which lies ahead i.e., proactive thinking and actions could supercede reactive ones.

This must be seen in the context of the extraordinary changes that have been taking place in Europe. A report commissioned by the European Commission warns of the risk of a social time-bomb unless steps are rapidly taken to improve the rights of ethnic minority groups following the collapse of eastern-European States and the rise of Islam as a force to be reckoned with. The report warns of the possibility of millions of migrants each year moving into western Europe.

The American legislation and the Canadian Human Rights Codes and Commissions show gaps in European provision. In Britain, the political climate over the past quarter of a century has not been very conducive to the development of educational policies which would lead to educational equality for all members of society, irrespective of their backgrounds. However, unlike the American and the Canadian situation the 1976 Race Relations Act in the United Kingdom is, in some respects, more protective of minority students. The 1976 Act, unlike the 1965 and 1968 Acts, specifically includes education as a protected activity. It makes clear that discrimination in education can happen both at the time of admission and in the provision of services (see Appendices 1 and 3 in this volume).

In the past two decades a variety of policy initiatives and programmes have appeared, both at the national and international levels. These have been based on the explicit premise of providing equality in employment, education, housing and public life in general. Successive governments have expressed their commitment to this broad objective. Policies have been developed which have promised to tackle various forms of direct and indirect discrimination and to promote 'equality of opportunity'. These policy documents have also promised to deal with social disadvantages suffered by ethnic minority communities in British society. Research findings have shown that, in practice, the impact of public policy in this field had been limited. Studies also show that equality policies in the field of education have had little effect, if any (Brown and Gay, 1985; Jenkins and Solomos, 1989).

There has been much written on the implications of the Education Reform Act 1988, both in academic and non-academic publications. What is however very noticeable is the distinct lack of literature looking specifically at what impact the 1988 Act will have on cultural diversity in schools. Cultural development is seen by the Education Reform Act (document 1) as being essential both for each individual pupil and for society as a whole. It is within the framework of this concern for the cultural identity development of individuals and of society that official documents stress the importance of 'positive attitudes to cultural diversity' and 'multicultural perspectives' (National Curriculum Council in documents 5 and 6), and 'embracing the opportunities offered by diversity'. Schools will now, under the Act, have a free hand to set up their procedures for ensuring equal opportunity. Initial indicators show that equal opportunity policies are unlikely to be on the primary agenda of many schools, in part because of the financial constraints.

The consequences of this failure are twofold. First, and currently, it means that pupils and students of ethnic minority origins are being deprived of opportunities which their indigenous peers take as their natural rights. These may be summarized as the reinforcement of their cultural identities and the acquisition of life skills that will serve them well in their future careers. Second, and perhaps more speculatively, it creates the circumstances in which the traditional fabric of British society is artificially preserved for a little longer at the expense of an avoidable and violent realignment in the future.

The question is: Can the 1988 Education Reform Act change gross inequalities, which have been an endemic feature of the British education system for decades? The responses to this central challenge will throw light on the four key questions posed earlier in this paper.

References

BROWN, C. and GAY, P. (1985) *Racial Discrimination: 17 Years After the Act*, London, Policy Studies Institute.

DEPARTMENT OF EDUCATION AND SCIENCE (1985) *Education for All*: Report of the Committee of Inquiry into the Education of Children from Ethnic Minority Groups (The Swann Report), Cmnd., 9453, London, HMSO.

JENKINS, R. and SOLOMOS, J. (1989) (Eds) *Racism and Equal Opportunity Policies in the 1980s*, Cambridge, Cambridge University Press, 2nd ed.

LADMIRAL, J.R. and LIPIANSKY, E.M. (1989) *La Communication Interculturelle*, Paris, Armand Colin.

NATIONAL CURRICULUM COUNCIL (1990) *The Whole Curriculum, Curriculum Guidance No. 3*, York, NCC.

NATIONAL CURRICULUM COUNCIL (1988) *Introducing the National Curriculum Council*, York, NCC.

STENHOUSE, L. (1975) *An Introduction to Curriculum Research and Development*, London, Heinemann.

VERMA, G.K. (1988) 'Attitudes, Race Relations and Television', in TWITCHIN, J. (Ed.) *The Black and White Media Book*, Stoke-on-Trent, England, Trentham Books.

VERMA, G.K. and DARBY, D. (1990) 'Race Relations and the Media', in PUMFREY, P. D. and VERMA, G.K. (Eds) *Race Relations and Urban Education: Contexts and Promising Practices*, London, The Falmer Press.

VERMA, G.K. and ENTZINGER, H. (1992) 'Transferring Knowledge in a Cross-Cultural Perspective', in *Learning Technology in the European Communities*, proceedings of the Delta Conference on Research and Development, The Hague, Kluwer Academic Publishers.

VERMA, G.K. and MALLICK, K. (1984) 'Children's Books and Ethnic Minorities', in VERMA, G.K. and BAGLEY, C. (Eds) *Race Relations and Cultural Differences*, London, Croom Helm.

Chapter 2

Cross-curricular Elements and the National Curriculum: Contexts Challenges and Responses

Peter D. Pumfrey

Context

'Only connect' is a maxim that has much to commend it. The National-Curriculum Council foundation subjects and religious education represent but a part of the 'whole curriculum' (see below). Important as these foundation subjects are, by themselves they cannot provide the experiences from which secondary school students will be enabled to acquire the range of skills, knowledge and attitudes required to function effectively in a culturally diverse community such as the United Kingdom and also the wider European and world communities. The boundaries between the subjects in a curriculum are often artificial and arbitrary. The importance of integrative cross-curricular dimensions, skills and themes, within the 'entitlement' curriculum required by the Education Reform Act 1988, is widely accepted for all pupils (NCC, 1989b; 1990a; Hargreaves, 1991).

Under the provisions of Section 1 of the Education Reform Act 1988, all maintained schools are expected to provide 'a balanced and broadly based curriculum which: promotes the spiritual, moral, cultural, mental and physical development of pupils at the school and of society; and prepares such pupils for the opportunities, responsibilities and experiences of adult life'.

The four components of the 'whole curriculum' are listed in Table 2.1.

Table 2.1: Components of the Whole Curriculum

- Religious Education
- Subjects additional to the three core subjects and the further seven foundation subjects in the National Curriculum
- A range of cross-curricular elements
- Extra-curricular activities

The aspirations of the ERA are commendable. Can the present educational system help students within our increasingly culturally diverse nation attain them? The authors consider that the answer is an unequivocal 'Yes'. The enormity of the challenge this presents to teachers must be recognized. It is important to be realistic. Prejudice, racism and racialism millitate against the delivery of the entitlement curriculum. All secondary school teachers have the responsibilities presented by their subject specialisms, in addition to any additional duties they may have for developing cross-curricular elements. In the face of such daunting demands, it is wise to bear in mind the adage 'No person ever made a greater mistake than one who did nothing merely because to do everything was impossible'.

Dealing constructively with ethnic diversity through the cross-curricular elements (dimensions, skills and themes) may lose out to the demands for the delivery of subject-specific aspects of the school curriculum. The importance of a clearly articulated and resourced school policy in the cross-curricular field is a key requirement, if such a consequence is to be avoided. The roles of the governors and the headteacher in giving such endeavours the coverage merited, is crucial. An ever-present danger is that cross-curricular elements, deemed to be the concern of all teachers, can be overlooked unless specific responsibilities are identified and collectively accepted by a staff. All too easily, what is accepted 'in principle' as the collective responsibility of all members of staff can become 'in practice' that of no one. Policy papers proliferate: promising practices perish. Beware!

Delivery of the curriculum to which all pupils attending state schools are entitled, requires an appreciation of the natures of prejudice, racism and racialism, and their interrelationships. Prejudice refers to either favourable or unfavourable attitudes, feelings and beliefs that have been formed without prior knowledge, understanding or reason. In essence, prejudice is irrational. We all acquire varied prejudices through the socialization processes of the family, school, neighbourhood and society. Who can claim to be without prejudice? When groups are struggling or in competition for power and influence, the potential for prejudices to flourish is high. Positive prejudices are largely focused on whichever group has the individual's allegiance; unfavourable prejudices are directed at others.

Racism involves the combination of prejudice with the ability or power to subordinate other individuals or groups, consciously or otherwise. It has been argued that minority ethnic groups in Britain have virtually no power. Hence such minority ethnic groups may be prejudiced, but cannot be racist. Whether all minority ethnic groups in the country are personally or institutionally powerless is open to question. It does not follow that all members of minority ethnic groups are necessarily non-racist. However, even if some members of ethnic minority groups are racist, they are not currently in a position to affect significantly the life chances of the majority group.

In neither England, Wales nor Scotland does the term 'racism' appear in statute law. The law restricts itself to addressing particular manifestations of racism. Under the provisions of the Race Relations Act 1976, it is unlawful to discriminate on grounds of colour, race, nationality, or ethnic or national origins. Additionally, incitement to racial hatred is illegal. Thus any individual who 'publishes or distributes written matter which is threatening, abusive or insulting, or when he uses in any public place or at any public meeting words which are threatening, abusive or insulting' has committed such incitement. To be charged with racism is indeed a serious matter. Libel cases have been brought where the use of the term is claimed to be defamatory (Pumfrey, 1988; Pumfrey and Verma, 1990). The statements reported to have been made in 1991 in Manchester Town Hall by Dr Kalim Saddiqui were considered actionable under the Race Relation Act by a number of commentators. His comments concerning Salman Rushdie, author of the book *Satanic Verses*, and on the Ayatollah Khomeini's death sentence on Rushdie, aroused considerable public attention and concern, both locally and nationally, as did the subsequently launched (non-elected) 'Muslim Parliament' (see Volume 1). In the event, no legal action ensued. This country's law of blasphemy protects only the Christian religion. In 1985 the Law Commissioners favoured the abolition of the blasphemy law. It is argued that the law should either be abolished or extended to protect other non-Christian religions (CRE, 1991). The religious sensitivities involved are potentially highly divisive.

In March 1992 the union of Muslim organizations held its winter conference at the University of Manchester Institute of Science and Technology. It is reported that a call was made for electoral reform in order to 'ensure equal treatment of Britain's two million Muslims'. Whilst laws exist to protect members of all ethnic groups, the Muslims considered that there were no laws to protect them as a religious minority. Dr Pasha, the organizer of the conference, stated 'It is essential for Muslims to be recognised as a religious community who have the right to preserve their religious and cultural identity.' At the same conference, Moeen Yaseen, a representative of the Islamic Schools Trust called for independent Muslim schools to be accorded the same voluntary-aided status as other denominational schools. In 1992 there were some 4,936 Anglican, 2,245 Roman Catholic, thirty-one Methodist and twenty-two Jewish voluntary-aided schools. To date, the government has refused to provide voluntary-aided status to the twenty-six independent Muslim schools. There are indications that this situation may change.

In Newham, the 'Campaign for Muslim Schools' aims to launch 'opting-out' campaigns in those local schools that have a majority of Muslim pupils on their rolls. In November 1991 it was reported that five schools had been identified as targets for the movement. Plashet Grove Comprehensive School is one of these. It is reported that 90 per cent of the current staff would resign if the school opted-out of the state system. What is seen by some of the individuals involved as 'opting-out' is viewed by others as 'opting-in to Islam'.

Under the provisions of the Education Reform Act 1988, grant-maintained status gives governors and parents control over the school, subject to certain conditions. That a majority of parents want grant-maintained status is a necessary but not sufficient condition for it to be given. If most of a school's parents and pupils are Muslim, a way is apparently open for the establishment of state-funded Muslim schools. Such grant-maintained schools are not allowed to change their character within five years. There are some salutary lessons for parents, teachers, school governors and the then Department of Education and Science in the following case.

Stratford School is a grant-maintained secondary school in East London. At the time of writing, its headteacher is a Mrs A. Snelling. The chairman of the governors, Ghulam Shaida, and a teacher-governor, Harbhajan Singh, have been in serious dispute with the headteacher concerning aspects of the running of the school, which is predominantly attended by Muslim pupils and taught by predominantly non-Muslim teachers. Relationships between the headteacher and a number of the governors became increasingly acrimonious. At the time of writing conflicts remain even though the chairman has resigned. Three votes of 'no confidence' in the teacher-governors have been passed by the staff of the school, to no apparent effect. At one point the headteacher was suspended by the governors and then reinstated after pressure from the Secretary of State for Education and Science. The acrimony reached such a degree that the Secretary of State for Education appointed two eminent educationists as governors: Mr E. Bolton, former Chief HMI, and Ms D. Gould, a former headteacher for seventeen years at Mulberry School in Tower Hamlets. Their removal from the seventeen-strong governing body is being pressed by one faction of governors. In this they are backed by the 'London Collective of Black Governors'. Numerous writs, private summonses and injunctions are being brought by the parties involved. One gets the feeling that the only individuals benefiting from this sorry situation are the legal advisors. The school has been informed that the Secretary of State for Education would remove funding from the school if the unsuitable conduct of the parties involved continued (Rafferty, 1992). In March 1992 the possibility of legal action against the governing body by the National Association of Headteachers on behalf of Mrs Snell was publicly mooted.

'Only connect' was our starting point. Or is the following quotation from Yeates more apposite?

Turning and turning in the widening gyre
The falcon cannot hear the falconer;
Things fall apart; the centre cannot hold;
Mere anarchy is loosed upon the world,
The blood-dimmed tide is loosed, and everywhere
The ceremony of innocence is drowned;
The best lack all conviction, while the worst
Are full of passionate intensity.
(The Second Coming)

In the interests of all citizens, the 'centre' must hold; but what is it? And how can identifying it help minimize the damage to all involved in events such as those at Stratford School?

The Race Relations Act 1976 lays upon local authorities two major responsibilities concerning the services that they provide. Firstly, unlawful racial discrimination must be eliminated. Secondly, they must provide equality of opportunity and encourage good relations between members of different racial and ethnic groups. The major public services of education, social services and the National Health Service and the police services must address the issues of race relations. A valuable guide to provisions of the Race Relations Act 1976 entitled *Racial Discrimination* is available (Home Office, 1987). Every school should have a copy. (See also Appendix 1).

There are always overt and covert power struggles ongoing in any nation or community, including its schools. These struggles are often less visible when a country has the space and resources such that its citizens are not in stressful competition for the necessities of life. When opportunities for education, housing and work are readily available, where tolerance of differences exists, interindividual and group tensions and stresses within a society are reduced. When economic and social pressures produce high levels of competition for limited resources, where intolerance dominates and scapegoats are sought, racism is often manifested in its most violent forms. All too easily the evils of nationalism and xenophobia flourish under such conditions.

The assumption that Britain is a tolerant society has been questioned in a recent book entitled *A Tolerant Country? Immigrants, Refugees and Minorities in Britain* (Holmes, 1990). He portrays a sombre picture. It is not difficult to find in Britain hostile attitudes towards many minorities. Not all of these minorities are distinguishable by skin colour. Despite this analysis, the race-relations legislation that is in place cannot be bettered anywhere in Europe, or is such a statement a sign of anglocentric complacency?

The Wider Scene

The rise of extreme right-wing political organizations in certain countries within the EEC is a cause of concern to many citizens. The current resurgence of neo-facism in Europe and in the UK probably involves relatively small numbers of individuals. Despite this, their potential for harm to the social cohesion of various countries must not be overlooked. A reunified Germany has underlined the point. On the first anniversary of reunification, a wave of attacks on 'Guest-workers' took place. In November 1991 some 1,200 illegally uniformed neo-Nazi activists attended a 'Remembrance-Day' ceremony in a forest near to Berlin. Alongside local and state politicians, they laid wreaths at a war memorial. In the same country, a hostel, where victims of the Chernobyl disaster were receiving medical treatment, was attacked.

The opening of the borders with eastern Europe resulted in an influx of families into Austria. As foreigners are not entitled to a municipal flat, most live in substandard housing. The breakup of Yugoslavia led to many families fleeing to adjacent countries. Many Croatians sought refuge in Austria. In the autumn of 1991 a number of schools in the socio-economically deprived areas of Vienna had very high proportions of non German-speaking pupils. Over the past ten years, the percentage of foreign children in classes in Vienna has doubled from about 15 to 30 per cent. A tendency for certain Austrian parents to move their children away from schools that educate mainly immigrant children has been noted. Already a right-wing reaction has manifested itself. Jorg Haider is the leader of the radical 'Freedom' party. It is small numerically, but its influence is increasing. Its anti-immigrant policies have resulted in electoral gains in provincial elections. In Vienna, the party's election slogan was 'Give our children a chance'. There is a call for immigration to be ended until jobs, housing and education are guaranteed for Austrians. A compulsory course in the German language is demanded for non German-speaking children of refugees before the start of school. The 'Freedom' party wants the numbers and percentage of foreign pupils in Vienna's schools markedly reduced. One wonders how this might be achieved. The ruling Social Democrats charge opposition parties with playing the antiimmigration card in order to gain political advantage.

Intergroup tensions in Sri Lanka, Fiji, Nicaragua, Canada, the United States, Australia, New Zealand, South Africa, Afghanistan, India and Pakistan (to mention but a few) underline the point that the phenomenon of intergroup battles for power is not one involving only European countries. The forced exodus from certain East-African countries of many Asians was but one of myriad examples. The exodus of Muslims from Burma to Bangladesh is another. The current anti-immigrant movements in France, Germany and the UK represent a cultural context that cannot be ignored. In Sweden, for so long held up as an example of ethnic tolerance, racist-inspired shootings took place in February 1992. Foreigners and gypsies have also been attacked by neo-Fascist youths in Czechoslovakia, France, Italy, Hungary, Poland and Romania.

Ethnic-group identities, religious and political allegiances are typically highly valued by members of such groups. These group identities and affinities can be causes of friction between groups. In the UK, Welsh, Scottish and Irish nationalism represent tendencies that can either be unnecessarily politically polarized as the saving of distinctive cultures, or as the sacrifice of the unity of Great Britain. The Balkan scenario can repeat itself virtually anywhere in the world where differing ethnic groups coexist. However, the citizens of England, Scotland and Wales are not minorities within their respective countries. In addition, they are all citizens of the United Kingdom of Great Britain and Northern Ireland. Fortunately, there are more than two polarized ways of construing the challenges presented by ethnic diversity in a community.

Where members of any ethnic group of any size feel threatened for what-ever reasons, the security afforded by ethnic-group membership and shared values is heightened and increasingly used to identify groups and classify individuals. Religion, politics and economics play key roles in such processes. So too does education. Where an ethnic-minority group is clearly visible through, for example, skin colour and/or language, racism manifests itself all too easily. This is particularly marked when the pressures on the resources in a community increase as in times of economic difficulties. When a minority ethnic and/or religious group is particularly successful in any country in terms of increasing its influence either numerically and/or financially, antagonisms can arise. Anti-semitism remains a worldwide phenomenon.

How can teachers help pupils to avoid the restricted and egocentric positions characterized by extremists and/or fundamentalists to whom the words 'compromise' and 'tolerance' are construed as 'betrayal'? Is the mission impossible? The sentiment expressed in at least two of the New Testament Gospels make the point 'He that is not with me is against me'. Even more forcibly, in St Paul's 'Letters to the Romans', we are told 'If God be for us, who can be against us?' Such ideas are common and very powerful. They are not the preserve of any single group, ethnic, religious or otherwise. Neither are they geographically nor socially restricted. They represent potent con-tributors to group coherence. They have a long tradition and are not going to disappear in the face of any reconstructionist plea for compromise and tolerance.

Fortunately less polarizing positions, antithetical to intolerances of all types can also be found in religious texts. 'Let he who is without fault cast the first stone' challenges all individuals and groups. Sadly, the predisposition to devote energy and time to casting metaphorical stones by allocating to others 'blame' for any event, rather than to ask 'What can we jointly do to improve the situation?', appears to have a great appeal to many individuals and groups.

A central dilemma faces individuals and society. Group identities, ethnic, cultural or otherwise, can peacefully coexist provided that there are larger groups holding values with which the smaller groups can identify: ones within which a diversity of smaller groups can be incorporated (i.e., in the body of) yet neither assimilated nor integrated. The system must also be perceived by a majority as 'fair' in its dealings with all citizens. Membership of a democratic society is one such overarching cohesive concept, whether of the family, the class, the school or the nation. Elected democracies, their institutions and processes, are far from perfect but the alternatives have even less to commend them.

Recently a television programme was shown of a Yorkshire school at which the vast majority of pupils were from families of Indian origins. The headteacher asked the assembled pupils to raise their hands if they were British. *All* of them did so. He then asked those who were 'Yorkshire' to raise their hands. Only the very small minority of Yorkshire-born white

Table 2.2:   Population of Great Britain by Ethnic Group in 1988

Indian	814,000
West Indian	468,000
Pakistani	428,000
Mixed	328,000
Chinese	136,000
African	122,000
Bangladeshi	91,000
Arab	66,000
Other	184,000
All ethnic minority groups	2,687,000
White	51,632,000
Not stated	472,000
All ethnic groups	54,662,000

Source: (Adapted from Haskey, 1990)

pupils did so. The headteacher saw the challenge of multicultural education as ensuring that, in the future, all pupils attending the school would acknowledge themselves as having *Both* English and Yorkshire allegiances, irrespective of ethnic group or colour.

Certain boundaries between ethnic groups are artificial, arbitrary and avoidable. Others are real and robust. Fundamentalist Christianity and Islam have a longstanding history of antagonism. Both sets of boundaries must be reciprocally acknowledged by the various ethnic groups comprising the population. Irrespective of their many differences, all citizens in an elected democracy have an important communality of interests. The contributions of ethnic diversity to that communality can be identified and fostered through the cross-curricular dimensions, skills and themes included within the National Curriculum and also within the broader 'whole curriculum'. However, without the goodwill and cooperation of the many groups whose youngsters comprise a school and its community, that communality of interests cannot be fostered.

The incidence and distribution of differing ethnic groups within the UK provides an essential backcloth to using that diversity constructively in relation to all aspects of the curriculum. The Office of Population Censuses and Surveys (OPCS) is one major source of such demographic information in the United Kingdom. Currently it is estimated that there are 2,577,000 members of minority ethnic groups in Great Britain. Table 2.2 summarizes the situation as estimated in 1988.

Cultural diversity is here to stay and is virtually certain to increase. Analyses of the distribution of the above ethnic groups by age show that the majority of most of these are at the younger age levels. From this it follows that the ethnic minority groups will form an increasingly larger proportion of

Table 2.3: Estimated Size of Total Ethnic-minority Population in Great Britain, 1951–1990

	1951	1961	1971	1981	1984–6	1986–8	1988–90
N (thousands)	200	500	1,200	2,100	2,432	2,557	2,624
% of total population	0.4	1.0	2.3	3.9	4.5	4.7	4.8

Source: Shaw, 1988, Table 2; Haskey, 1990, Table 1; Haskey, 1992.

the total population over time. Currently, the estimated average annual increase in the ethnic minority population is 'just over 80 thousand per year' (Haskey, 1991). The ethnic minority groups with the oldest age profiles have been resident in the UK for longer than those groups with the younger age profiles. Irrespective of minority ethnic group, the younger the individual, the greater the probability that they were born in the UK. Over 90 per cent of the ethnic-minority children under the age of 5 years have been born in the UK.

Concern about an increasing rate of immigration to the UK led to the introduction of the Asylum Bill in the UK in 1991. The Bill was designed to reduce the number of 'economic migrants' to the UK. It is a politically controversial issue and is opposed by representatives of most minority ethnic groups, as well as by the two major opposition parties in Parliament. On 24 March 1992 a leader in *The Times* discussed the dangers to social cohesion that arise when population movements occur too rapidly: 'Modern democracies with highly developed social market economies are likely to experience a permanent tension between an economic need for cheap labour and a social resistance to rising dependency rates. There is always likely to be a critical level of immigration above which sharp resistance is generated in the host community. Restraining movement below that level is an unavoidable obligation of government and one that governments of all parties have accepted in Britain since (and before) the war. Controlling migration, whether in France or Britain or in the European Community as a whole is not racist. The racist cause is helped only by pretending the opposite.'

The distribution of minority ethnic groups across Great Britain shows concentrations in certain parts of the country. The largest concentrations of minority ethnic-group members are found in the major conurbations. Estimates of these distributions analysed by ethnic group and geographical area have been presented in Volume 1 (Haskey, 1991).

It is estimated by the OPCS that 267,000 individuals migrated to the United Kingdom in 1990, more than in any other year since 1964, the first year when such figures were collected. The figure includes returning British citizens. The emigration of 231,000 indicated that the UK population increased by 36,000. There was a net inflow in 1990 of 66,000 non-British citizens and a net outflow of 30,000 British citizens. Almost a third of the migrants who entered the UK had been born here and were returning after a time spent overseas. Approximately a half of migrants to and from the UK were aged between 15 and 29 years. For the resident UK population this figure was less than 25 per cent (OPCS, 1992, ibid.). Statistics can inform decision-making but it is the way in which the figures are interpreted that is of the utmost importance.

The 1991 Census data are now available. A series of seminars is being organized by the 'Census Analysis Group' to help potential users utilize the available data effectively. Powys County Council has developed PC-based software for analysing the 1991 Census data (OPCS, 1992). Each LEA and each school will be able to dispel ignorance concerning the variety of ethnic groups in the country and in its own area or intake.

Inevitably, the number of children of mixed ethnic-group parentages is increasing. The related issue of whether transracial adoption is desirable raises many questions concerning identity formation (Tizard and Phoenix, 1989). It is known that self-identity can be threatened by the 'marginality' that this can bring. A recent study of fifty-eight young people aged 15 to 16 years, each of whom had one white and one Afro-Carribean or African parent elaborates the point. Just under half of the group considered themselves as 'black'. The others considered themselves as 'coloured', 'brown' or 'half and half'. Most also described themselves as of 'mixed race' and 'half-caste'. Some two-thirds were positive about their racially-mixed parentage. At earlier stages in their lives, about a half of them had wished that they were another colour (Tizard, 1992). The effects of racism in our society and the adverse implications of being neither clearly white nor black and thus different from both, created problems of racial identity more so than in either black or white groups. The issue of identity formation is central to the education of *all* pupils. Its facilitation requires cross-curricular elements. It is to the nature of these elements that we now turn.

Challenges

A common curricular language, whereby all teachers and parents can communicate more effectively, is at the heart of the National Curriculum (see Volume 1). Knowing and using that vocabulary is an important challenge. Here the concepts central to cross-curricular elements are considered in more detail. Cross-curricular elements are described as having three major facets: dimensions; skills; and themes.

Dimensions

Dimensions include a commitment to providing equal opportunities for all pupils. Preparation for life in a multicultural society is important to all, and 'should permeate every aspect of the curriculum' (NCC, 1990a, p. 2). Central to the notion of equal opportunities is the importance of enabling all pupils to

Table 2.4: Cross-curricular Skills

- Communication
- Numeracy
- Study skills
- Problem-solving
- Personal and social skills
- Information-technology skills

fulfil their potential, irrespective of sex and social, cultural or linguistic background. The National Curriculum is an entitlement curriculum. The creation of a common curriculum for all pupils, by minimizing premature restriction of subjects, enhances access to the curriculum for all.

Pupils from certain minority ethnic groups may require language support. At the time of writing, Section 11 funding is one means whereby this can be provided. Changes in administrative and financial arrangements for such resources are under scrutiny (see Appendix 3). The equally important concern for identifying pupils with special educational needs, and with making arrangements to alleviate these, is addressed in 'Curriculum Guidance 2' *A Curriculum for All* (NCC, 1989b). These concerns demand 'whole-school' policies in which all staff subscribe to the value of, and aim to develop, positive attitudes towards 'gender equality, cultural diversity and special needs of all kinds' (ibid., p. 3). The words are more easily uttered than the actions that are required, performed. Acknowledging this point, preparing pupils for life in a multicultural, multilingual Europe and world, is not a luxury. It is essential (Lynch, 1991).

Skills

Skills can be developed coherently throughout the curriculum, subject to teachers accepting the 'principle of shared responsibility'. The National Curriculum requires that these skills be systematically and consciously fostered across the whole curriculum. Such skills are listed in Table 2.4.

Themes

Cross-curricular themes have been defined in the National Curriculum Council Circular No. 6 as 'elements that enrich the educational experience of pupils . . . [They] are more structured and pervasive than any other cross-curricular provision . . . They include a strong component of knowledge and understanding in addition to skills. Most can be taught through other subjects as well as through themes and topics' (NCC, 1989a). The NCC identified five major cross-curricular themes. In 1990, curriculum guidance concerning the whole curriculum was published in March (NCC, 1990a). Between April and November in the same year, curriculum guidance in each of the five

Table 2.5: NCC Cross-curricular Themes

- Education for Economic and Industrial Understanding (NCC, 1990b) (April)
- Health Education (NCC, 1990c) (July)
- Careers Education and Guidance (NCC, 1990d) (August)
- Environmental Education (NCC, 1990e) (October)
- Education for Citizenship (NCC, 1990f) (November)

cross-curricular themes was published (see Table 2.5). These are without question important themes. Each is addressed by specialists in the field of secondary education in the present volume (Chapters 4–8). In each cross-curricular theme the context is set within which ethnic diversity is to be utilized in achieving the central objectives of the Education Reform Act 1988. Challenges are identified and responses to these discussed.

However, there are other cross-curricular dimensions that are probably equally important. A selected number of these are included in this volume (Chapters 9–15). What are the challenges to their implementation in the curriculum? If the curriculum is, in part, preparation for life as a citizen of the United Kingdom, the European Community and the world, their inclusion is essential.

The sheer rate of change that is taking place in education is unprecedented. The volume of paper reaching schools and requiring responses is daunting, even to the most committed professional. In a day in which there are only twenty-four hours, priorities have to be established. The 'core' and other foundation subjects are currently centre-staged. Unless teachers and schools are vigilant, the benefits of the cross-curricular themes could be adversely affected.

At present, the National Curriculum is far from fully in place in schools. The way in which various subjects and cross-curricular themes have been introduced into the secondary-school syllabus has not been of the highest order. Too little preparation and consultation have led to controversial changes. The working party on music in the National Curriculum was but one whose considered recommendations suffered serious damage at the hands of the then Secretary of State for Education (see Volume 1, Chapter 10).

A somewhat different challenge to be faced by secondary schools in particular, is that presented by the British National Party (BNP). It is reported as having under 2,000 members, but with an appeal to a considerably larger number (Klein, 1992). In part, this is achieved by the BNP through its magazine and its music. The movement offers to alienated and disaffected youth a shared identity and an ideology that provides a focus for discontent. Minorities such as the Jews, Blacks and Asians are presented as depriving the majority ethnic groups of work and of the material and personal benefits that derive from the former. How can the activities of the BNP be constructively addressed by teachers? The issue is not a new one; nor are there any simple solutions available. However, there is considerable

Table 2.6:   Cross-curricular Materials Produced by the City of Manchester LEA Inspection and Advisory Service

---

1. Economic and Industrial Awareness (Ramsay, M., Savori, A. and Fuller, S.)   (1991)
2. Health Education (Ramsay, M. and Savori, A.)   (1991)
3. Careers Education (Rogers, W. and Wickham, D.)   (1991)
4. Environmental Education (Greenhough, P., Hyde, M., Kirby, B. and Murray, P.)   (1991)
5. Education for Citizenship (Cooke, D., King, D., Rushforth, C. and Steiner, M.)   (1991)

---

expertise and experience available. Guidelines and details of promising practices whereby potentially damaging effects can be combatted are available (Shaw, Nordlie and Shapiro, 1987; Pumfrey and Verma, 1990).

Responses

Cross-curricular Development

What can be done to ensure that the opportunities embodied in cross-curricular work are realized? The NCC has given some advice, but more valuable sources of ideas, materials and approaches that owe much to 'grass-roots' involvement are available. One of the foremost LEAs in developing cross-curricular materials has been the City of Manchester. Manchester is a multicultural community and rightly proud of the fact. Even before the Education Reform Act had received the Royal Assent, the education department of the City of Manchester had established a collaboration between a wide range of professionals including teachers, advisers, inspectors, support services and members of organizations having links with industry. Because the Manchester team was concerned with pupils at all key stages, there is a considerable amount of material of value to both secondary and primary-school teachers.

Themes and Models of Delivery

This massive cross-curricular development project was led by Diane King of the City of Manchester Inspection and Advisory Service. Three years' intensive work led to the publication in November 1991 of a pack of six loose-leaf folders. The first of these provides an overview of the project. It indicates strategies for implementing cross-curricular themes, identifies models of delivery, provides exemplars and case-studies and gives examples of planning guides for cross-curricular activities (King, 1991a). The remaining five provide cross-curricular theme-specific advice and guidance (see Table 2.6).

The Manchester team identified and considered seven models for the delivery of cross-curricular development. Schools differ markedly in their curricular organization and priorities, despite the common list of cross-curricular themes, subjects, Programmes of Study, Attainment Targets and Standard Assessment Tasks comprising the National Curriculum (see Table 2.7).

Table 2.7:   Cross-curricular Theme-delivery Models (Manchester LEA)

- Permeating the whole curriculum
- As part of a separately timetabled personal and social education programme
- As a separately timetabled space
- As part of a pastoral/tutorial programme
- Long-block timetabling
- Through opportunities arising from after-school initiatives/activities
- Through using resources within the LEA.

In October 1992 the Manchester Inspection and Advisory Service held a conference at which Strategies for implementing the secondary phase of their project were discussed.

Acknowledging the importance of the multicultural aspects of the messages embodied in a school curriculum, both the Rampton and Swann reports recommended that teachers should review the books and materials used in schools (Committee of Inquiry 1981; 1985). This objective is easily stated, but less readily accomplished by many practising teachers. The changes taking place in education as a consequence of the Education Reform Act 1988 are themselves extremely time demanding, and the ongoing and inexorable demands of educating pupils must not be neglected. The flood of materials produced within LEAs, by other statutory bodies, quasi-autonomous non-governmental, and by many other voluntary organizations continues to grow (Pumfrey and Verma, 1990; Wolfendale, 1991). Appendix 2 reinforces this point.

AIMER
Because of its general importance in relation to all aspects of multicultural education at all levels, a short description of AIMER is included here. A similar description is presented in Volume 1, Chapter 3. The establishment of a clearing house for such materials was proposed in 1982. With the support of the Commission for Racial Equality, a project was mounted at Bulmershe College. It is known by the acronym 'AIMER' (Access to Information on Multicultural Education Resources). It offers 'students, teachers, advisers and others information on multicultural anti-racist teaching materials'. By virtue of the interest shown by teachers and others in the project, the Department of Education and Science made a three-year grant covering the period 1987–1990. This enabled a full-time resource-development officer to be appointed. In 1989 the amalgamation of Bulmershe College with the University of Reading Faculty of Education and Community Studies took place. Eighty six LEAs were the major users of the service.

The AIMER database is available on the National Educational Resources Information Service (NERIS). NERIS itself was established in 1987 to help teachers, and others, efficiently locate information about teaching materials and other resources. It is an electronic database, run by a non profit-making trust and funded by the Department of Trade and Industry through its industry–education unit. NERIS is also supported by the DES (now DFE), NCC, SEAC, CCW (Wales), NICC (Northern Ireland), SCCC (Scotland) and the Training Agency. NERIS is based at:

> Maryland College,
> Leighton Street,
> Woburn,
> Milton Keynes,
> Buckinghamshire.

The AIMER database is available to institutions with access to NERIS either on-line and/or by CD-ROM.

AIMER itself provides a postal enquiry service. It can be contacted at the following address:

> AIMER,
> Faculty of Education and Community Studies,
> The University of Reading,
> Bulmershe Court,
> Earley,
> Reading, RG6 1HV.

AIMER's postal-enquiry form covers the following fields:

- professional issues;
- language/communication;
- humanities;
- personal/social education;
- science/mathematics technology;
- arts - performing/creative;
- religious studies;
- home economics;
- business studies;
- games and sport; and
- other enquiries.

(At the time of writing, the AIMER postal-enquiry form is being revised).

As from 1992 an additional service is offered. Resource lists, updated twice yearly, will be published on a wide range of different topics. These are likely to include the subjects outlined in Table 2.8.

The continuing updating of the AIMER database is labour intensive. Currently, although it continues to receive many requests for information on multicultural teaching materials, the service is under threat because of lack of resources. Its future as a self-funding system will depend on the income that it can generate from subscribers and users. It would be a national tragedy if the service did not continue. Is your LEA a subscribing member? Does your school use the service?

Table 2.8: AIMER 1992 Topics

History	Geography	Environmental studies
Economics	Careers	Health education
Race awareness	Materials in Bengali	Materials in Gujarati
Materials in Panjabi	Materials in Chinese	Materials in Italian
Home–school links	Assessment and testing	Physics
Chemistry	Life sciences	Maths
Technology	Music	Dance
Arts and crafts	Oral and written literature	
Religious studies	Home economics	Business studies
Games, sports and toys	English for adults	English for beginners
Language support	Professional development and in-service	

Source: From Volume 1-Table 3.11

The Open University

The Open University has developed a course entitled 'Race, Education and Society' (ED 356). Three particularly helpful books have been specially prepared. Their respective titles and contents are consonant with a number of the concerns addressed in the present series: *Racism and Antiracism: Inequalities, Opportunities and Policies* (Braham, Rattansi and Skellington, 1992); *Race, Culture and Difference* (Donald and Rattansi, 1992); *Racism and Education: Structures and Strategies* (Gill, Mayor and Blair, 1991).

Communication and the National Curriculum

Britain is a multicultural, multiethnic society. As indicated in Tables 2.2 and 2.3 it is becoming increasingly so. It has been estimated that pupils in schools speak a range of over 200 different languages other than English. The following question summarizes an important curricular concern. 'How can the values of ethnic and linguistic diversity, and the social cohesion represented by a common language, be reconciled?'

This central educational issue has been addressed in *Bilingual Pupils and the National Curriculum: Overcoming Difficulties in Teaching and Learning* (Cline and Frederickson, 1991). To be bilingual is to be fluent in two different languages. At its highest level, the individual is able to think in each language. There is no need laboriously to translate from the less familiar language into the one in which one is competent. In this 1991 publication, 'bilingual' is used to refer to 'individuals who have to alternate between the use of two languages, *whatever their level of proficiency* in each of the two. Pupils whose parents are not native speakers of English 'face particular challenges at school because they are exposed to a variant of English at home and in their community'.

Communication is central to community. Verbal language matters. The building of the Tower of Babel was not a success. Readers who have visited a country and were either ignorant of its language, or had only an elementary knowledge of it, will well appreciate the increasing difficulties that can arise as verbal communication between individuals reduces. Isolation and alienation of the individual unable to communicate effectively in the majority language is likely to increase. In Britain, not to be able to communicate effectively and efficiently in English carries high social and economic costs. Is this no more than an expression of an Anglocentric linguistic imperialism, or is it a legitimate concern in a democratic society? The aspiration of building a multicultural, democratic, metaphorical equivalent of Jerusalem in this green and pleasant land, including its less than salubrious deprived urban areas, is facilitated by the use of a common language. Or is it?

Apart from the current minority ethnic groups in the United Kingdom, there have been, and still are, marked divisions between various subgroups within the native majority, the English-speaking community. Regional and social-class differences are but two. With reference to the first, a paper entitled 'The Image of Wales and Problems of Assimilating Newcomers' was presented at a meeting in October 1991 (Bellin, 1991). Integration, pluralism and multicultural education probably take longer.

The social class divisions within the English language community are well documented. Their nature is, in part, exemplified by the current dispute involving Crest Homes at their property development on the Woodlands Estate near to East Grinstead. Some individuals, who thought that they were purchasing houses on a private development, subsequently found that one part of the estate was to be sold as non-private rented accommodation. At the time of writing, a group of private purchasers were considering taking legal action against the developers under the Property Misdescriptions Act. The social phenomenon whereby 'Birds of a feather flock together', occurs in most countries and communities. If the ethnic and social-group stratifications in this country are to be constructively addressed, their existence, extent and evolution must be publicly acknowledged.

This section was written a week before the 1992 general election in Britain. The protagonists used (mainly) English. Speakers for each of the major parties communicated in a common language, insofar as syntax was concerned. The message often conveyed to the listener was all too frequently a mutual mistrust between the speakers. Social Darwinism is clearly manifest in any struggle for political and economic power. Exchanges are characterized by assertions without evidence, fundamentalism without facts and rhetoric without reason. This underlines the point that competence and skilled performance in a common language is a necessary but not sufficient condition for constructive communication. Such communication requires an underpinning of values and attitudes in common, such as beliefs in equal opportunities, social justice and tolerance. There are many sound ideas as to how this desirable situation can be approached (Pumfrey and Verma, 1990). Education for citizenship is of the essence. Let us consider one key aspect of the linguistic divides within our multicultural society.

In 1992, the two largest minority ethnic groups in Great Britain are from India and Pakistan. The third largest minority ethnic group is pupils of parents of Afro-Caribbean origins. The issue of non-standard dialects is different from that facing bilingual children. For those concerned about the former, an annotated reading list on 'British Black English' is provided at the end of the materials by Cline and Frederickson (pp. 241–2).

Do many British-born bilingual children of parents whose mother tongue is not English fail to fulfil their potential in the educational system? If this is the case, is it, at least in part, a consequence of the demands of bilingualism and of perceptions of the minority culture and language held by members of the majority group of native English speakers? What are the implications for that subset of bilingual pupils who have learning difficulties? On the positive side, the benefits of bilingualism can be considerable. 'Additive' and 'subtractive' bilingualism are interestingly explored. Understanding the nature of bilingualism amongst minority ethnic groups and its educational and social implications are crucial to the development of a multicultural democracy.

The above set of learning resource materials has drawn on the experiences of a wide range of educational psychologists, teachers and other professionals working mainly in LEAs in London, the Home Counties and the North of England. It is based on the following three assumptions:

- institutional racism can affect the educational achievements of many pupils from minority ethnic and linguistic groups;
- the needs of bilingual pupils and their families would best be served by teachers and educational psychologists who share the clients' first language; and
- current professional practice has many weaknesses, but there are promising practices that can be developed and disseminated.

The materials have been developed for use by local study groups. The initial focus is on the individual's learning objectives in joining a study group. Such groups can be either professionally homogeneous or multidisciplinary. The purpose of the materials is to help teachers and educational psychologists improve their knowledge, understanding and skills in relation to work with bilingual children in general and with those considered to have learning difficulties, in particular. The system is extremely flexible. This is exemplified in the three examples of study-group plans that were developed by different groups (ibid., pp. 8–10). A distinction is drawn between such children's special needs and their special educational needs. The former are construed as existing in any social group whose 'circumstances or backgrounds are different from those of most of the school population' (p. 89). This is an extremely broad concept. Language, culture, overt racism and socio-economic disadvantage are given as examples. The authors list three aims:

- to 'raise awareness of current thinking and practice in the education of bilingual pupils';
- to 'inform the selection of methods and material for assessment and teaching when children with limited English proficiency appear to show learning difficulties'; and
- to 'assist staff in devising suitable methods and materials in response to individual needs'. (ibid., p. 1)

The materials come in a sturdy ring folder. They comprise an introductory chapter on how to use the materials, plus a 'menu' of five substantial units and one smaller unit, respectively, on:

- language and community;
- language development;
- cognitive development and learning difficulties;
- the National Curriculum in multilingual schools;
- multiprofessional assessment of special educational needs; and
- additional resources.

What a cornucopia! Each of the five major units has a similar structure. Each begins with an overview and a coordinator's guide. Then follow a number of discussion papers, plus group exercises. The number of words in each of the readings, plus an estimated reading time, is provided. In total, there are seventeen discussion papers and thirteen group exercises. A questionnaire has been specially designed to help users identify their key interests and priorities. This helps in planning a training programme.

The materials will be helpful to all professionals concerned with education. The structure is clear and the contents coherently presented, focusing on an important series of multicultural cross-curricular elements. Suggestions presented for group and individual activities are neither conceptual nor ideological straightjackets. The illustrative situations used as stimuli to discussion have the 'ring of truth'. The vignettes presented are recognizable, professionally challenging and to which there are no straightforward or simple answers. Unit 4 is entitled 'The National Curriculum in Multilingual Schools'. The aims of this section are to help users to:

- consider the educational opportunities and challenges facing multilingual schools;
- evaluate options for enhancing the quality of education of bilingual pupils in the context of the Education Reform Act and the National Curriculum; and
- work towards making effective use of additional support for bilingual pupils with learning difficulties who are in ordinary classrooms. (ibid., p. 107)

(The use of 'mainstream' rather than 'ordinary' would, in the writer's opinion, have been preferable).

The approaches to assessment presented in Unit 5 draw on the work of Cummins, a Canadian psychologist, concerning the nature of bilingualism. A hypothesis-testing model developed in Surrey and the use of curriculum-related assessment are two stimulating and complementary papers. The curriculum-related assessment of bilingual children was considered in more detail in an earlier publication edited by the same two authors (Cline and Frederickson, 1990). It includes a section containing six examples of curriculum-related assessment with bilingual children. Although these are focused on NC levels 1, 2 and 3, the ideas can be adapted for use at higher levels. These two most helpful publications by Cline and Frederickson provide materials whereby schools can systematically consider a range of cross-curricular elements. Together with policies and practices selected from the sources and suggestion included in the 'Responses' section of this and other chapters, a 'tailored' programme of cross-curricular considerations can be devised. In conjunction with the related curricular responses in Volume 1 of this series, these can be integrated into the NCC-recommended three-step curriculum-planning cycle of curriculum audit (Step 1), production of whole-curriculum development plan (Step 2) and implementation of the plan (Step 3) in your secondary school (NCC, 1990a).

Respect for the cultural backgrounds of pupils drawn from minority ethnic backgrounds is enhanced when teachers:

- value different cultures by drawing on their pupils' knowledge, experiences and understandings in a planned manner;
- accept pupils' competence in a range of dialects and languages; and
- provide positive images and role models from a range of cultures.

References

ALIBHAI, Y. and BROWN, C. (1991) *Racism*, London, Wayland.

BELLIN, W. (1991) 'The Image of Wales and Problems of Assimilating Newcomers', Paper presented at the Annual Conference of the Education Section of the British Psychological Society, Carmarthen, Dyfed, September.

BRAHAM, P., RATTANSI, A. and SKELLINGTON, R. (1992) *Racism and Antiracism: Inequalities, Opportunities and Policies*, London, Sage in association with Open University Press.

CLINE, A. and FREDERICKSON, N. (1991) *Learning Resource Materials — Bilingual Pupils and the National Curriculum: Overcoming Difficulties in Teaching and Learning*, London, University College.

COMMISSION FOR RACIAL EQUALITY CRE (1991) *Second Review of the Race Relations Act 1976*, London, CRE.

COMMITTEE OF INQUIRY INTO THE EDUCATION OF CHILDREN FROM MINORITY ETHNIC GROUPS (1981) *Interim Report: West Indian Children in our Schools*, London, HMSO.

Committee of Inquiry into the Education of Children from Minority Ethnic Groups (1985) *Education for All*, London, HMSO.

Cooke, D., King, D., Rushforth, C. and Steiner, M. (1991) *Implementing the Whole Curriculum: Cross Curricular Themes — Education for Citizenship*, Manchester, Manchester City Council Education Department.

Donald, J. and Rattansi, A. (1992) *Race, Culture and Difference*, London, Sage in association with the Open University Press.

Greenhough, P., Hyde, M., Kirby, B. and Murray, P. (1991) *Implementing the Whole Curriculum: Cross Curricular Themes — Environmental Education*, Manchester, Manchester City Council Education Department.

Gill, D., Mayor, B. and Blair, M. (1991) *Racism and Education: Structures and Strategies*, London, Sage in association with the Open University Press.

Haskey, J. (1990) 'The ethnic minority populations of Great Britain: estimates by ethnic group and country of birth', *Population Trends*, 60, pp. 35–8.

Hargreaves, D.H. (1991) 'Coherence and manageability: reflections on the National Curriculum and Cross-curricular provision', *The Curriculum Journal*, 2, 1, pp. 33–41.

Haskey, J. (1991) 'The ethnic minority populations resident in private households — estimates by county and metropolitan district of England and Wales', *Population Trends*, 63, pp. 22–35.

Holmes, C. (1990) *A Tolerant Country? Immigrants, Refugees and Minorities in Britain*, London, Faber.

Home Office (1987) *Racial Discrimination: A Guide to the Race Relations Act 1976*, Circular 7/87 London, HMSO.

King, D. (1991a) *Implementing the Whole Curriculum: Cross Curricular Themes, Skills and Dimensions*, Manchester, Manchester City Council Education Department.

King, D. (1991b) *Implementing the Whole Curriculum: Cross Curricular Themes — Careers Guidance*, Manchester, Manchester City Council Education Department.

Klein, R. (1992) 'Blood and Honour', *Times Educational Supplement*, 28 February, p. 29.

Lynch, J. (1991) *Education for Citizenship in a Multi-Cultural Society*, London, Cassell.

McClean, B. (1991) *The Prejudice Book: Activities for the Classroom*, London, Common Ground.

National Curriculum Council (1989a) *Circular No. 6*, York, NCC.

National Curriculum Council (1989b) *A Curriculum for All — Special Educational Needs in the National Curriculum*, York, NCC, October.

National Curriculum Council (1990a) *The Whole Curriculum*, York, NCC, March.

National Curriculum Council (1990b) *Education for Economic and Industrial Understanding*, York, NCC, April.

National Curriculum Council (1990c) *Health Education*, York, NCC, July.

National Curriculum Council (1990d) *Careers Education and Guidance*, York, NCC, August.

National Curriculum Council (1990e) *Environmental Education*, York, NCC, October.

National Curriculum Council (1990f) *Education for Citizenship*, York, NCC, November.

Office of Population Censuses and Surveys (OPCS) (1992) *Census Newsletter*, 19, March.

Pumfrey, P.D. (1988) 'Racism awareness: training, education and accountability', in Verma, G.K. and Pumfrey, P.D. (Eds) *Educational Attainments: Issues and Outcomes in Multicultural Education*, Lewes, The Falmer Press, pp. 51–73.

PUMFREY, P.D. and VERMA, G.K. (1990) *Race Relations and Urban Education: Challenges and Responses*, London, The Falmer Press.

RAFFERTY, F. (1992) 'Writs fly furiously in Stratford', *Times Educational Supplement*, 3947, 21 February p. 6.

RAMSAY, M. and SAVORI, A. (1991) *Implementing the Whole Curriculum: Cross Curricular Themes — Health Education*, Manchester, Manchester City Council Education Department.

RAMSAY, M., SAVORI, A. and FULLER, S. (1991) *Implementing the Whole Curriculum: Cross Curricular Themes — Economic and Industrial Awareness*, Manchester, Manchester City Council Education Department.

ROGERS, W. and WICKHAM, D. (1991) *Implementing the Whole Curriculum: Cross Curricular Themes — Careers Education*, Manchester, Manchester City Council Education Department.

RUNNYMEDE TRUST (1991) *Racism and Anti-Racism in Schools: A summary of the Burnage Report*, London, Runnymede Trust.

SHAW, J.W., NORDLIE, P.G. and SHAPIRO, R.M. (1987) *Strategies for Improving Race Relations: the Anglo-American Experience*, Manchester, Manchester University Press.

Tizard, B. (1992) 'Young People of Mixed Race', *The Psychologist*, 5, 2, p. 51.

TIZARD, B. and PHOENIX, A. (1989) 'Black identity and transracial adoption', *New Community*, 15, pp. 427–37.

TROYNA, B. and HATCHER, R. (1992) *Racism in Children's Lives: A Study of Mainly White Primary Schools*, London, Routledge.

VERMA, G.K. (1989) *Education for All: A Landmark in Pluralism*, London, the Falmer Press.

WOLFENDALE, S. (1991) A Bibliography and Resource-Base on Anti-Racism and Multiculturalism: Foundations for a Categorised System, London, Psychology Department, Polytechnic of East London (3rd. edition).

Videos

1. Swingbridge Videos (1987) *White Lies*, Newcastle upon Tyne, Swingbridge Videos.

This video is intended for secondary-school pupils. It addresses fascism and racism in the north east of England, but is relevant to all areas. It is obtainable from:

Swingbridge Videos,
NordenHouse,
41 Stowell Street,
Newcastle upon Tyne,
NE1 4YB.

2. Yorkshire Television *No Pasaran*, Leeds, YTV.

This video is based on a play by David Holman set in Germany in the 1930s. It is suitable for top junior and secondary-school pupils (KS2, 3 and 4).

3. Yorkshire Television *The Longest Hatred*, Leeds, YTV.

This comprises a series of three videos dealing with the history of anti-semitism (KS3 and 4).

4. Yorkshire Television *World at War: The Final Solution — Auschwitz*, Leeds, YTV. (KS3 and 4).

Chapter 3

Cultural Diversity in Secondary Schools: Its Nature, Extent and Cross-curricular Implications

Gajendra K. Verma

Context

Over the past thirty to forty years, British society has experienced an accretion of people whose lifestyles and culture stand at varying degrees of divergence from what were considered 'British norms'. Britain is by no means alone in having such a challenge to meet. It is common to a number of other countries, particularly those in the so-called developed world.

In America, since the early years of the Republic, people from almost every culture, nationality, linguistic background and ethnic group have been able to become 'American' by conforming to the American democratic ideology. The price, of course, was cultural assimilation into the Anglo-Saxon dominated national culture (Banks, 1983). However, certain groups from Asia and Africa were not able to participate fully in American life because of their physical characteristics (ibid.). It is clear therefore that particular ideological, cultural and physical characteristics were perhaps prerequisite for a full American identity and total participation in the national life.

In Europe, contemporary recognition of linguistic, cultural and religious diversity is more recent. By the nineteenth century (the era of nationalism), cultural diversity in Europe was already marked in terms of differences in the religious, linguistic and cultural backgrounds of its inhabitants. In France, Britain and Germany in particular, great efforts were made to acculturate divergent cultural groups into the dominant culture and language. In spite of those efforts, the European nation states always retained within their political boundaries very substantial ethnic minorities, whose cultures varied significantly from that of the dominant state. The settlements made at the end of World War I attempted to establish culturally homogeneous nation states, insofar as their creation was consistent with the interests of the major powers. However, cultural diversity within individual states was not eliminated and, in some cases, their creation only served to accentuate it. Considerable differences in value orientation can still be found between the European countries. Nationalism, for instance, is still much stronger in some countries than in others.

In many western societies there has been fairly explicit concern in recent years about the pluralist nature of society. This has a marked impact on education, primarily because of the growing consciousness among ethnic-minority groups throughout the world that their identities were being eroded. This movement has asserted itself in most western countries and in Australia, and has manifested itself in political, social and educational life.

Nearly two decades ago, the 'Conference on Education and Teacher Education' for cultural diversity was held in Chicago. Its purpose was 'to take steps to make the cultural diversity that characterizes American society a major asset instead of being a problem or becoming a threat'.

One of the outcomes of this conference was a working definition of cultural pluralism:

> a state of equal coexistence in a mutually supportive relationship within the boundaries or framework of the nation of people of diverse cultures with significantly different patterns of beliefs, behaviour, colour and, in may cases, with different languages. To achieve cultural pluralism there must be unity with diversity. Each person must be aware of and secure in his own identity and be willing to extend to others the same respect and rights that he expects to enjoy himself. (Stent, Hazard and Rivlin, 1973)

In 1992 the concept of 'ethnic cleansing' used to justify, for example, the wars in the Balkans, highlight an ever present challenge to coexistence.

In Britain the relationship between cultural diversity and education has become an area of acute controversy since the 1960s (Verma, 1984). The context in which the debates and discussions have evolved could be seen under four overlapping dimensions: socio-economic and political; educational; national; and international. The range of situations and problems examined within these dimensions is wide. Collectively, such analyses have important implications for the ways in which society regulates itself — through legislation, social policy, educational provision and so on. Studies and reports (e.g., DES, 1981; 1985; Eggleston, 1986; Pumfrey and Verma, 1990) published so far have implications for the ways in which we perceive our society. They have contributed to the debate about the way society and its educational system are organized, the common values that should be upheld and the ways in which the past, present and future should be projected.

In a culturally and linguistically diverse society such a debate inevitably involves contentious issues of culture, language and ethnic relations. These issues have long been the source of considerable controversy in education, for the British have traditionally regarded formal schooling as the major institution for the transmission of society's core values and beliefs. Therefore, whenever disagreements over these values and beliefs have arisen, they have been reflected in the schools. Their impact over the last two decades has increased. This does not imply that all culturally pluralist societies have sought to mirror that diversity in education and that all societies are committed to democratic cultural pluralism. Only a few countries have attempted to implement policies of cultural diversity in education with explicit democratic ideals, e.g., Canada, The Netherlands.

Divergence from 'British norms' is exemplified in religious beliefs which brought conflict between home and schools of ethnic minority groups. This arose, for example, out of the issues relating to school uniform. The traditional rules on uniform contradicted the religio-cultural expectations of how certain ethnic minority boys and girls should dress; school cap against turban in the case of Sikh boys, skirts and socks against leggings or trousers for Asian girls, the wearing of jewellery and weapons (e.g., Sikh knives) of religious significance. There was also conflict over mixed education and religious beliefs relating to the modesty of adolescent girls. The application of rules relating to uniform to *all* pupils in individual schools without exception had been an increasing struggle for staff. Many ethnic minority youngsters and their parents found themselves caught in the cross-fire, as some schools clung blindly to unquestioned traditions.

Further conflict arose out of the requirement for schools under the 1944 Education Act to provide a daily Christian act of worship and religious instruction. Although the right of withdrawal on the grounds of religious beliefs had always been in place, this was a right that was largely ignored or discouraged within the framework of the individual school. The presence in schools of children from Muslim, Sikh, Hindu and other non-Christian faiths and an increasing awareness of the right of withdrawal again threatened to create a gulf between home and existing provision in schools.

Even though the passing years have seen the development of a far more sympathetic understanding and tolerance of (or grudging respect for) religious differences, there are other aspects of school life and the values it appears to support or condone, that are offensive to the views of the minority religious communities. This, in conjunction with provision that exists for governmental, financial support (through voluntary-aided status) of schools organized under particular religious denominations, such as Anglican and Roman-Catholic schools, has prompted demands for similar assistance to be given to create 'separate schools' for Muslim children. So far the DFE has resisted such demands. The issue of 'separate schools' was examined by the Swann committee and it came down against them on the grounds that separation was inconsistent with the concept of 'education for all'. The overall objective which Britain should be striving to attain was neatly summarized in its report:

> We would . . . regard a democratic pluralist society as seeking to achieve a balance between, on the one hand, the maintenance and

active support of the essential elements of the cultures and lifestyles
of all the ethnic groups within it, and, on the other, the acceptance
by all groups of a set of shared values distinctive of the society as a
whole. This then is our view of a genuinely pluralist society, as both
socially cohesive and culturally diverse. (DES, 1985)

As a consequence of various reports and initiatives, a body of ideas
which evolved out of pluralist approaches to education have been referred
to as multicultural and antiracist education. According to some writers
multicultural and antiracist education must be understood, in particular, as
part of the curriculum-reform movement that has developed in response to
ethnic minority groups' rejection of the conformist and assimilationist models
of the 1960s and 1970s. It also attempts to absorb ethnic minorities' specific
demands for the restructuring of knowledge and educational practices.

Modern societies expect their education system to prepare their young
for their expected roles and responsibilities in adult life. It also seeks to transmit knowledge, skills and attitudes that would enable them to operate
effectively as individuals and as members of society in the world of work,
community and in the transnational context. Thus, education serves three
interrelated functions. First, it seeks to foster an individual's development in
terms of the acquisition of skills and knowledge valued by society at large.
The second function centres on the needs and requirements of society as a
whole if it is to operate effectively. It is often the dominant ideologies that
determine the conception of such needs and requirements, and provide the
resources to achieve the objectives. The third educational function, not often
made explicit, sets the patterns and models of behaviour which young people
are expected to manifest in group settings in the school, in the world of work
and ultimately in the wider social setting. These include the development of
an identity which society seeks to justify. At the explicit level this process
may well involve the training of the individual to conform to the 'norms'
or 'rules' of that society. At the implicit level the information, values and
attitudes utilized in the transmission of knowledge and skills reflect the
cultural assumptions of that society. In a sense, therefore, education not only
tries to meet the present and future needs of society, but perpetuates the past.
A dynamic equilibrium between conflicting values and beliefs is maintained
when adaptation and accommodation occurs. Society chooses between evolution and revolution in effecting change. The education system in democratic
societies attempts to achieve these evolutionary purposes through the
implementation of the school curriculum. Thus, the school plays a mediating
role in this process.

In Britain, during the last decade or so, a number of policy documents
have been produced both locally and nationally, each with its statement of
broad curricular aims. There is general agreement that the purpose of
education on the one hand is to develop individuals' self-esteem, their growth
towards intellectual curiosity and a formulation of a reasoned set of beliefs,

attitudes and values. On the other hand, it is also the purpose of education to foster a respect for others and an informed appreciation of their beliefs, attitudes and values. Thus, the demands of the present and the future of the child as an individual and as a member of society must be kept in balance. Yet, the debate about the principles, practice and promise of a sound education has been largely conducted on an exclusive, narrow and ethnocentric basis.

It was not until 1985 that the Swann report made it explicit that a philosophy of education which drew on the principles of respect for individuals and their cultures should not halt that process at the boundaries of the nation state. It stated:

> In our view an education which seeks only to emphasize and enhance the ethnic group identity of a child, at the expense of developing both a national identity and indeed an international global perspective cannot be regarded as in any sense multicultural. (DES, 1985, p. 322)

Another reason advocated for incorporating a global perspective within the plural reality in education is that prejudice and discrimination are learnt by individuals as part of their personal experience and therefore cannot be restricted to national boundaries. Individuals and groups take their intellectual luggage with them. It must be seen and discussed both within European and international contexts.

In a paper on 'Cultural Democracy, Citizenship, Education and the American Dream', James Bank writes:

> 'While the school should not merely reinforce the parochial cultures of students, it should, however, try to avoid teaching students contempt for their primordial cultures and making them ashamed of their behaviour, values and world-views. In their eagerness to teach scientific views of the world, teachers often make students feel ashamed for holding sacred beliefs that defy scientific logic. Educators should have as one of their major aims teaching students the scientific, secular and universal culture of the nation-state, but should also realize that science and technology, despite their importance in modern life, cannot satisfy all of the important social and psychological needs of humans', writes Apter. '[Modernization] leaves what might be called a primordial space, a space people try to fill when they believe they have lost something fundamental and try to recreate it.' (Banks, 1983)

All children and adolescents are socialized in ethnic, religious and social groups. This enables them to develop certain values, attitudes, world-views, behaviour patterns and beliefs which differ and sometimes conflict with those of other groups. They are also citizens of a society acquiring certain national attributes. The argument is that if cultural, social, political and economic interconnections are such that any educational philosophy does not include these dimensions in an accurate and fair way, then it is narrow, parochial and incomplete in a pluralist context.

Thus, it is widely acknowledged that education for citizenship (see Chapter 7 in this volume) should help pupils to acquire the knowledge, skills and attitudes needed to make reflective public decisions: evolution, rather than revolution, has a major favourable cost–benefits ratio. The 'Reconstructionist' philosophy of education is based on the assumption that what is done in schools *can* affect the nature of society. On the other hand, schools reflect society, and can help to preserve and transmit values and certain orientations regarded as important by the dominant culture. The tensions between a 'Reconstructionist' philosophical stance and that of the 'Classical-humanist' and 'Progressive' positions bear on the ways in which the tensions associated with cultural diversity are both construed and resolved. In most schools, all three philosophies of education co-exist, but in very different proportions.

Challenges

The experience and aspirations of ethnic minority people in seeking an education that successfully moulds differing values and lifestyles with the realities and opportunities of a technological society illuminate the complex web of relationships that exist between cultural diversity and schooling, particularly in a multiethnic society. The issues of justice, equity, individual and collective rights, self-determination and social cohesion are on the agenda of any negotiation with ethnic minority groups. It is also true to say that ethnic minority groups accept the importance of a shared framework of societal and educational purposes, yet there are ambiguities and contradictions in the curriculum. There is sufficient evidence to suggest that these are currently being experienced in acute forms within the educational system. They arise largely because of the system's failure to strike an appropriate balance between the educational needs of ethnic minority groups on one hand, and those of the wider society on the other. Schools are expected to respond to such plurality and to contribute to the promotion of social and national cohesion.

As the literature in the field shows, many models and philosophies of pluralism have been advocated and even adopted by schools and LEAs on their own initiative (Verma, 1984). The latest philosophy as in the Swann report (DES, 1985) advocated that all children should be given a good and appropriate education if they are to be adequately prepared for life in a plural society. This relates closely to the National Curriculum as enshrined in the ERA of 1988 (DES, 1988).

The National Curriculum proposes that 'all pupils, regardless of sex, ethnic origin and geographical location will have access to broadly the same good and relevant curriculum' (NCC, 1988). The prescribed Programmes of Study in specified fields implies that all children should receive a common educational experience. If it is axiomatic to educational philosophy that all children should receive a common educational experience, then it is legitimate to raise questions such as 'What values and whose values are used — implicitly or explicitly — as the basis for constructing that common educational experience?' Answers to these questions are not easy. Knowledge acquisition does not take place in a vacuum. It has a bearing on real life and is essentially interactive. Issues of knowledge transmission can only be understood if social and cultural aspects are taken into account in designing the curriculum for a plural society. If society is to benefit from the development of a plural community, then social and cultural dimensions must be taken seriously. For the National Curriculum to have an impact on society it must adapt to meet, more adequately than is currently the case, the needs and aspirations of all cultural, social and ethnic groups.

No educational system exists in a historical and social vacuum. It is an integral part of a specific social structure by which it is shaped. This leads some writers to a consideration of the relationships between culture and social structure. Culture may be interpreted in terms of standards for living while social structure refers to the clustering of people in patterned ways (in this context, the educational system) which may or may not be consistent with ethnic minority norms and values. Furthermore, the knowledge transmitted by the values of the education system is not culturally neutral. Its intellectual content and orientation are permeated by the world-view characteristic of the dominant ideology. It cultivates specific values, attitudes and beliefs.

Tajfel (1981; 1982) stresses the social and historical, contextual influences on the individual's conceptions about himself as a member of an in-group versus the out-group others. The attitudes of the in-group towards the out-group are created within a historical, social context and then transferred to the individual members of the group. This means that, although an educational system may teach the ideals of objectivity, consensus, independent thinking, intellectual curiosity, creativity and so on, in actual practice it does little more than initiate its pupils into the dominant culture. The English state educational system is no exception with regard to its aims, contents, methods and assessment procedures. Despite the great variations between schools, it has a monocultural perspective, although such an orientation has become weaker during the last two decades. The monocultural orientation is still evident in the prescribed National Curriculum (see Volume 1).

The DES Circular 5/89 of 22 February 1989, quoting from the ERA 1988 (DES, 1988) points out that through the Act it 'is intended that the curriculum should reflect the culturally diverse society to which pupils belong and of which they will become adult members'. The next sentence includes a brief list of what is involved in adult life and experience. The list includes 'responsibilities as a citizen towards the community and society, nationally and internationally'.

The issues and concerns expressed by various writers with regard to core and foundation subjects in secondary education are the main theme of Volume 1 in this series (Pumfrey and Verma, 1992). It is clear from their analyses of specific subject areas within the framework of the National Curriculum that educational policy makers have failed to deal adequately and fairly with the central issues of equality and diversity. For example, underpinning the Educational Reform Act 1988 is the notion that parental choice is vital to ensure fairness and to improve the quality of education. If this choice is to be informed, then a key factor is the communication of information, particularly to those in our society for whom English is not their first language. Thus, it is necessary to establish more effective lines of communication between parents and teachers, but particularly for those parents whose children are not benefiting as fully as they should. This is now being done in some DFE publications for parents in which different languages are used.

Many social and cultural groups now strongly believe that without acquiring and employing the necessary political skills they will not succeed in effecting the changes they seek. This is hardly a new phenomenon, but its educational and social context and challenges have not been adequately addressed before in this country.

The present volume includes papers which focus on issues related to cross-curricular themes and dimensions. It is clear from their analysis (see Part 2 in the volume) that unless the debate about shared values and different values is resolved, the concept of cultural diversity remains rhetorical and ineffectual in the curriculum. How well we respond to these challenges is, of course, a matter for the future. No one today, however, can argue that the main issues of pluralist education have not become clear.

Responses

What can be done educationally to overcome egocentrism, groupcentrism and ethnocentrism? Few would disagree that the relationship between acknowledging biases and changing behaviour is complex. It is also true to say that biases, stereotypes and prejudices cannot be overcome simply by acknowledging their existence. It is important to ask what practices and history those stereotypes and prejudices support. We must insist on examining and revealing where racist ideas come from, and how they become translated into the everyday 'common sense' notions. The responses of democratic societies to the process of ethnic revitalization distinctly differed from each other. In Britain, only in very recent times have there been isolated attempts, particularly at local levels, to engage ethnic minorities in equal discourse as a means of resolving various conflicts.

One of the explicit educational objectives is to seek changes in the attitudes of the British towards each other. Most educators would agree that people could benefit from more information about different cultures, and perhaps some soul-searching about their attitudes towards those cultures. However, providing information about other cultures is unlikely to result in increased understanding and tolerance. This is because stereotypes of, and attitudes towards, other people have already been learned through parents, peers, teachers, books, toys, games, films, text books, television and through the observed social status of particular groups in society and globally. Unless these learnings are unravelled, new information can simply be organized to reinforce existing knowledge and understanding (Verma and Darby, 1990). The task of the teacher is to create a climate in the classroom where stereotypes and biased ideas can be exposed and critically examined. Institutional practices and procedures which are unfair need to be identified and attempts be made to put them right. Racism-awareness training is another strategy which has been adopted for improving relations between cultural/ethnic groups (Pumfrey, 1988; and Chapters 9 and 10 in this volume).

The ethnic minority groups find themselves in large part marginalized by mainstream groups, who, in turn, have yet to recognize the ways in which their actions and behaviour (whether intentional or unintentional) and their cultural assumptions contribute to that marginalization. Unless we match up to this responsibility, we run the risk of, at best, a pluralism that lacks cohesion and under which ethnic minority groups are forced to look increasingly inwards, because they find themselves excluded from a viable existence within mainstream society. The type of pluralist society for which we must strive is one that stresses core values but allows for diversity within an agreed framework (Verma, 1989).

Education has an important part to play in the process of the development of individuals — intellectually, affectively, physically, socially and morally — and through those individuals, of the commonwealth of the wider society. Thus, education, as a process, is of great importance even if it cannot be reduced to a neat scientific process which could offer guaranteed outcomes. The curriculum should reflect the reality that young people must function effectively both at the individual and societal levels. Education should also help develop pupils' capacity and willingness to resolve the conflicts that may arise from individuals functioning within the norms of the home and the community on one hand, and of the school and nation state on the other. The goals of that process find their expression, implicitly or explicitly, in the curriculum that is delivered. The extent to which the operationalization of the curriculum will achieve the desired goals will depend on the degree of their acceptance by those who deliver it and by those for whom it is intended.

The issues surrounding the degree of acceptance can be better illustrated by reference to the National Curriculum. The overt goals of the National Curriculum with regard to cross-curricular themes can be summarized as follows:

- to improve the quality of the education received by all children and adolescents in the maintained sector of schooling;
- to achieve a greater balance in the scope of the education received than previously offered; and
- to achieve a high degree of uniformity in the education as received in different areas in order that when families move or have to move, for whatever reason, there will be a higher degree of continuity than previously existed. (This point is equally valid for the curriculum as a whole.)

These goals would have a high degree of acceptance among the British population because they would seem to be common sense and fair to all. Schools have a key responsibility for ensuring that its members achieve a better understanding of the impact of the dynamics of culture upon us, if a pluralist philosophy is to emerge that will be relevant to British society both now and in the future.

Society is becoming increasingly complex. The issues raised in schools by the National Curriculum and its impact on cultural diversity cannot be dealt with by individual teachers alone. Joint efforts on the part of all teachers, who acknowledge a common responsibility and a commitment, are essential. They should:

- adopt a critical approach to identifying cultural bias, prejudice, racism and stereotyping in teaching strategies, and other teaching materials;
- approach all subjects in the curriculum in a way which combats ethnocentric views of the world;
- recognize the value of teaching which identifies and acknowledges effectively the aspirations of all pupils and students, and which seeks to enhance their chances of realizing their full potentials; and
- make use wherever possible of good professional practice.

How to do this in secondary schools is the focus of Volumes 1 and 2 in this series.

Education must find ways to teach people how to feel comfortable with diversity — in essence to expect it as a normal fact of life. It is the differences in the various dimensions that make an individual stand apart from other individuals. Without such differentiating characteristics, there may be nothing to distinguish and therefore nothing to perceive.

References

BANKS, J.A. (1983) 'Cultural Democracy, Citizenship Education and the American Dream', *Social Education*, March.

Gajendra K. Verma

DEPARTMENT OF EDUCATION AND SCIENCE (1981) West Indian Children in Our Schools, Committee of Inquiry into the Education of Children from Minority Ethnic Groups (The Rampton Report), Cmnd., 8273, London, HMSO.

DEPARTMENT OF EDUCATION AND SCIENCE (1985) Education for All, Report of the Committee of Inquiry into the Education of Children from Ethnic Minority Groups (The Swann Report), Cmnd., 9453, London, HMSO.

DEPARTMENT OF EDUCATION AND SCIENCE (1988) The Education Reform Act 1988, London, HMSO.

EGGLESTON, J. (1986) The Educational and Vocational Experience of 15–18-Year-Old Young People of Ethnic Minority Groups, Stoke, Trentham Books.

NATIONAL CURRICULUM COUNCIL (1988) Introducing the National Curriculum, York, NCC.

PUMFREY, P.D. (1988) 'Racism Awareness: Training, Education and Accountability', in VERMA, G.K. and PUMFREY, P.D. (Eds) Educational Attainments: Issues and Outcomes in Multicultural Education, London, The Falmer Press.

PUMFREY, P.D. and VERMA, G.K. (1990) Race Relations and Urban Education: Promising Practices, London, The Falmer Press.

PUMFREY, P.D. and VERMA, G.K. (1992) Cultural Diversity and the Curriculum: Volume 1. The Foundation Subjects and Religious Education in Secondary Schools, London, The Falmer Press.

STENT, M.D., HAZARD, W.R. and RIVLIN, H.N. (1973) Cultural Pluralism in Education: A Mandate for Change, New York, Appleton-Century-Crofts.

TAJFEL, H. (1981) Human Groups and Social Categories, Cambridge, Cambridge University Press.

TAJFEL, H. (1982) Social Identity and Intergroup Relations, Cambridge, Cambridge University Press.

VERMA, G.K. (1984) 'Multiculturalism and Education: Prelude to Practice', in VERMA, G.K. and BAGLEY, C. (Eds) Race Relations and Cultural Differences, London, Croom Helm.

VERMA, G.K. (1989) Education for All: A Landmark in Pluralism, London, The Falmer Press.

Part 2

National-Curriculum Cross-curricular Themes

Chapter 4

Economic and Industrial Understanding

Andy Forbes

Context

The Conservative governments of the 1980s were governments with a well-defined mission: to reassert the primacy of free-market economies over what was castigated as the 'creeping socialism' represented by state intervention in production and the expansion of the welfare state. In the field of education, this mission was carried out by a peculiar mixture of centralization, which aimed to uncouple school administration and curriculum from the control of Local Education Authorities overwhelmingly in the hands of those who believed in planned social intervention, and of a fierce ideological attack on educational approaches which were not sufficiently tailored to free-market ideologies and practices. This is not the place to rehearse the debates over 'trendy lefty' teachers and teaching; it is enough to note that this was the political soil for the growth of an almost entirely new curriculum area, 'Economic and Industrial Understanding', and to register that its rapid development into a significant aspect of the National Curriculum represents a direct response to the clear government demand for schools to make their curriculum more relevant to the 'real world' in general, and the 'enterprise culture' in particular.

No subject is entirely new, of course. Prior to the birth of 'Economic and Industrial Understanding' (which, for the sake of convenience, hereafter will be abbreviated to EIU), schools and LEAs would have identified aspects of the subject as cropping up in a variety of lessons under a variety of guises. In tutorials, especially under the influence of the 'active tutorial' approach, pupils would from time to time discuss career options, consumer issues and occasionally comment on topics such as unemployment, pay or welfare benefits. In personal and social education lessons, topics such as 'smoking', 'feminism' or 'pocket money' would often begin to touch on economic issues, albeit often in a relatively unstructured and tangential fashion. General studies syllabuses were often followed up to O and A level examinations, and again would contain broad and variegated mixtures of social and economic topics (alongside arts, politics and many others). It could be argued that in many standard subject lessons, depending on the syllabus, the materials used and the teacher's own inclinations, theory was illustrated by continuing references to the real world of production, consumption and exchange, although few would dispute that this constituted a highly fragmented and idiosyncratic introduction to economics or industrialism. Probably the most focused elements of EIU would have appeared in lessons on careers, and in the growing emphasis on work-experience placements for 15–17 year-old students in the 1970s and 1980s. Here again, significant numbers of school students received little or no formal careers curriculum, let alone work experience. In summary then, EIU was taught in an almost entirely piecemeal fashion in the vast majority of schools (DES, 1985b). This situation held true in schools of all types, whether secondary-modern, grammar, comprehensive or for that matter, direct-grant or independent.

The development of the National Curriculum led, for the first time, to a sustained discussion on how best to introduce pupils from 5–16 to a range of knowledge, understanding and skills about economic life. While no one disputed the relevance or importance of this, the problem was how to define the scope and content of a subject which had in practice been interpreted and delivered in such an unsystematic fashion previously. Here, the debate began to organize itself around a tension familiar to those involved in the debate around antiracist and multicultural education. On the one hand DES documents, influenced by the government's concern to make the curriculum more orientated to the enterprise culture, defined the subject in terms of preparation for work:

> Economic and Industrial Understanding aims to equip all young people with the knowledge, understanding and skills to meet the economic challenge of citizenship and employment. (DES, 1985b)

Rather as the references to multicultural education from the DES and National Curriculum Council have tended to emphasize the need for all pupils to assimilate to British norms and values, this definition points to a curriculum aimed at encouraging relatively uncritical participation in the British economy.

Broader definitions, emanating from the HMI and reflecting a more pupil-centred philosophy of education, introduce a more open-minded, critical approach:

> Economic and Industrial Understanding is concerned with helping pupils at all stages in their lives to make sense of the world in which they live and to participate fully in society as far as they are able or have the desire to do so. (DES, 1985c)

The vital difference between the first definition, and the one above which relates much more closely to antiracist perspectives within the multicultural education debate, is the sense of critical choices being made by pupils in relation to the economy and society, and the strong hint of support for a curriculum that allows individuals to evaluate economic issues in the light of their own experience and motivation. This is crucially important for those of us concerned with the development of a healthy multicultural curriculum, because it moves EIU away from any notions of accepting the status quo, with all its historical inequalities of opportunity, towards active discussion of individual and group options in the face of a status quo that may or may not be acceptable. In fact, the National Curriculum Council Draft Guidance document, Draft Guidance No. 4 steers a diplomatic course between the various interpretations and provides plenty of useful support for an evaluative, person-centred approach:

> Economic understanding means the ability to consider how an economy's scarce resource might best be used. An economically informed person has the skills, information and concepts necessary to assess the implications of the decisions people, organizations and governments make. (NCC, 1989)

The final version of the guidance document defines seven attitudes which should be developed across the four key stages. Several of these, such as 'concern for human rights, as they are affected by economic decisions', and 'respect for alternative economic viewpoints', open the way directly for a multicultural perspective to underpin teaching and learning in this aspect of the curriculum (NCC, 1990b).

The challenge then, within this more positive framework, is how to ensure that certain key issues of multicultural and antiracist education are woven into the fabric of the EIU curriculum in a way that validates the lived social and economic experience of children from a wide variety of cultural and ethnic backgrounds and provides them with evaluative tools to make choices about their economic life.

Challenges

Four major dimensions can be identified as areas where antiracist and multicultural education themes interact with themes relevant to EIU. Each poses a curriculum challenge, with practical implications for the way in which this aspect of the National Curriculum is taught within ethnically diverse classrooms.

Economic Success and Self-esteem

One of the pervading difficulties facing EIU is the persistence of strong socialclass differences in pupils' relationship to the economy and society. It may be that teachers have avoided taking certain issues because of the personal and group sensitivities caused by the divisiveness of social class patterns of economic life in the United Kingdom. Attempts to discuss career paths, pay rates, unionization, business organization, indeed, most of the topics relevant to EIU, have so easily touched on frustration, envy and hostility generated by the wide gulf that remains between the standard of living and lifestyle of professionals, manual workers and the unemployed (Hargreaves, 1982). Many school classrooms and playgrounds reflect this day-to-day tension in forms of abuse ('snobs', 'swot', 'thickos', 'low-lifes') and in the friendship groupings of pupils. It is not easy to manage an object-ive, calm and rational classroom discussion when the self-esteem of many pupils is still so wrapped up in attitudes to economic status and success.

Black and ethnic-minority immigrant groups within this country soon became embroiled in a form of social-class multiculturalism, with the majority finding themselves living and working in traditional working-class communities in northern mill towns, urban inner-city neighbourhoods and industrial ports such as Liverpool and Bristol. The pattern of post-war immig-ration to this country has led to a close association — geographically and economically at least — between ethnic-minority communities and working-class communities. Open hostility was often expressed by hard-pressed working-class 'host' communities towards ethnic-minority (and particularly black ethnic-minority) newcomers, who were seen as being in direct com-petition for jobs, housing and other scarce facilities (Fryer, 1984). Ethnic-minority citizens and their children faced the double burden of finding themselves at the lowest end of the British class system, and being regarded by English neighbours who were themselves economically disadvantaged, as somehow inferior or a threat because of skin colour and cultural differences. Ethnic-minority citizens were often trapped in very specific, often low-paid occupations, unable to get higher paid, more skilled employment because of direct and indirect discrimination. The dramatic rise in unemployment in the 1970s, 1980s and now the 1990s has often led to ethnic-minority workers being the first to lose jobs, and having the longest wait to re-enter the job market. In a cruel irony, they then run the risk of being labelled 'lazy', 'incompetent' or 'unambitious', because of their lack of economic success.

Any EIU teaching will therefore have to address this issue, and work hard to promote a positive orientation to economic achievement amongst ethnic minority and other working-class pupils who have little basis for pride derived from economic status or success (Verma and Bagley, 1982). It could be argued that forms of classroom behaviour such as apathy, challenging dress or speech, and explicit hostility to teachers because of their 'white middle-class' status could be alleviated by a sensible and supportive curric-ulum exploring issues of economic status and disadvantage. Only on the basis of improved economic self-esteem can 'economic and industrial understand-ing' begin to develop the confidence and positive attitudes to employment that all educationalists agree should be a key aim of the curriculum.

International Economic Awareness

EIU as taught in schools has often reflected the gap at higher education level between economics as a subject concerned almost exclusively with the content of highly developed industrial economies, and development economics, which is usually a relatively small subsidiary part of the main economics course. While economic theory is applicable to all economic situations, the overwhelming bulk of reference has been to the British economic sphere, with examples and illustrations drawn from this country's particular pattern of financial institutions, employment, opportunities, infrastructure and so on. While this is not the place to discuss the extent to which development issues should become a greater part of economics as a subject, there are strong arguments from a multicultural perspective for ensuring that EIU as part of the National Curriculum should embrace a substantial focus on economic development issues. To begin with, ethnic minority pupils are from families who have recent personal experience of the gap between living standards in developing nations and in advanced industrial economies such as the UK. Most black and Asian ethnic-minority pupils are in regular contact with relatives living in under-developed rural economies, whether this be Jamaica, Pakistan, Ghana or Bangladesh (Tierney, 1982). They are in a position to make comparisons, and again to feel personally involved, in terms of self-image and self-esteem, with the continuing images of desperate poverty that illustrate daily news bulletins and events such as Live Aid and Comic Relief. How to make sense of struggling for economic survival in such an affluent country as Britain, whilst having personal relationships with family and friends struggling for survival in desperately poor countries such as Bangladesh, are complex issues, but ones which cannot be avoided in a properly multicultural delivery of the EIU curriculum.

In a wider sense, all pupils, regardless of economic or ethnic background, must now be aware to a greater extent than ever before of the interdependence of national economies, and the direct links between global patterns of economic advantage or disadvantage on the one hand, and local and international environmental damage on the other. An international frame of reference for the discussion of economic issues should form an important dimension of the multicultural EIU curriculum. The Earth Summit Conference held in Rio de Janeiro in June 1992 reflected international concerns. The issues discussed and the economic and political positions adopted would provide excellent materials for any multicultural EIU curriculum.

Economic Identity, Cultural Difference and Stereotyping

One of the issues already noted is the close association between particular ethnic groups and specific occupational areas in the British economy. This has unfortunately led to a strong tendency to stereotype groups and to caricature, sometimes in cruelly racist ways, their economic identity. So the Chinese are 'good at running take-aways'; Pakistanis 'run corner shops and work all hours — the whole family you know'; Afro-Caribbeans are 'good at sports and music'; Asians 'all want to be dentists and lawyers'; the Irish are 'all builders and road-diggers'; and so the familiar litany goes on. The dangers are obvious and have been extensively rehearsed, for example, in the Swann report: how ethnic-minority pupils may be perceived to have 'unrealistic' expectations if they aspire to non-stereotypical occupations; and how such stereotypes tend to form part of the process of labelling ethnic-minority youngsters as having a fixed and limited set of aptitudes and ambitions (DES, 1985a). The difficulty is that most of the stereotypes are based on a grain of truth. Because of the socio-economic pressures already briefly outlined, many ethnic-minority groups have some measure of economic and survival and success in employment 'niches' and, through a complex process of racial discrimination in employment, educational underachievement and fierce determination to succeed, have developed what could almost be described as an alternative employment market. Capital is raised for small business ventures, employment opportunities are distributed, upward progress through career paths is achieved through a tendency to pool resources within families and communities. A philosophy of self-help is sharpened and deepened by negative experiences in relation to the white British majority (Brown, 1984). After several decades, a great deal of expertise and experience has been developed in these employment 'niches', further adding to the tendency of youngsters to continue in the family tradition. Furthermore, there are genuine cultural and religious attitudes to work in general, and to specific employment areas in particular, that affect occupational choice. Muslim attitudes to lending and borrowing, and different attitudes amongst ethnic groups to artistic performance, the care of the elderly, or women in employment are all examples of cultural beliefs that can and do affect employment choices and aspirations. Given that a key aim of the EIU curriculum should be to lay the ground for informed choices about economic participation, a multicultural approach must aim to examine sympathetically both the causes and effects of the stereotypes of economic identity that surround ethnic groups in Britain.

Economic Factors and Race Relations

One of the key difficulties in designing a curriculum which teaches directly about racial discrimination and efforts designed to combat racial discrimination has been deciding where to start. (Stenhouse, Verma, Wild and Nixon, 1982). Without a fairly extensive examination of the roots of modern racism, the pattern of post-war immigration and the social psychology of prejudice, lessons on the Race Relations Act, or other anti-discriminatory themes, can easily become superficial, or stir up conflict amongst pupils (and sometimes teachers!) about the validity and interpretation of key concepts. Even amongst educated adults, discussions about equal opportunities in relation to the race issue can become arguments about 'discriminating against white people' or 'bending over backwards to help an ungrateful and trouble-some minority which doesn't want to fit in'.

The multicultural and antiracist education movement has had measurable success in the past twenty years, in that race-equality issues have begun to be addressed in the school curriculum, but the area remains controversial and progress remains patchy (Verma, 1989). Teachers have raised race-relations issues within a variety of conceptual frameworks, including morality, interpersonal relationships, psychology, sociology, history and politics. Pupils have encountered the issue in a variety of subject areas including religious education, English, history, geography and personal and social education (Arora and Duncan, 1986). It can only be hoped that the National Curriculum, as it develops, allows this valuable work to continue.

However, EIU allows a new focus to be developed, from within a socio-economic frame of reference, which should be seized as a positive new opportunity provided by the National Curriculum. If we accept that racism has always had an economic rationale, in terms of the development of colonial trade during the 'Age of Empire', and if we accept that immigration to this country was motivated mainly by economic pull-and-push factors, then an important new version of multicultural and antiracist teaching is facilitated by the EIU curriculum. The interplay between personal, organizational and governmental decisions to which the NCC guidance document refers is precisely what is needed to make sense of issues of racial discrimination, in which legal requirements, organizational pressures and individual prejudices collaborate in each instance of discrimination or fair practice. Moreover, if this element of the EIU curriculum is carefully delivered in relation to the other multicultural and antiracist dimensions already discussed, a very rounded and multidimensional education can be provided which does justice to the complexity of the race issue. The challenge is to find effective methods of teaching children of differing ages and abilities the economics of race relations, in its personal, organizational, national and international aspects.

Responses

Let us take each of the four dimensions identified as relevant to a multicultural and antiracist EIU curriculum, and sketch out some ideas of how teachers might respond effectively. The difficulty is, of course, that it is impossible to go into detail about how these responses might actually be designed and delivered in the four key stages of the National Curriculum. All that will be attempted is to provide pointers for secondary-school teachers as to how to start the task of assembling materials, activities and exercises

Table 4.1: Economic and Industrial Understanding: Key Curricular Challenges

Curriculum Dimension	Curriculum Challenge
Economic Success and Self-esteem	• Ethnic communities' disadvantaged economic situation • The assumption that economic success is related directly to ability/motivation • Low expectations of ethnic-minority economic success • Low self-esteem of ethnic-minority pupils
International Economic Awareness	• Ethnic communities' personal experience of the gap between developing and developed national economies • Global patterns of economic advantage and disadvantage • International economic interdependence
Economic Identity, Cultural Difference and Stereotyping	• Stereotypes of ethnic-minority economic identity • Stereotypes of ethnic-minority ability and ambition • Low/narrow expectations of ethnic-minority people in the economy • Genuine cultural differences in attitudes to work

Economic Factors and Race Relations	• The challenge of understanding racial discrimination at the level of:
	  * individuals
	  * organizations
	  * society/government
	• The need for a multidimensional approach to race issues
	• Developing understanding of economic factors underlying race-relations issues

relevant to each topic. Available publications and other resources are not listed or referred to in detail; an excellent resource list is provided in a recent publication summarizing an LEA response to developing the EIU curriculum (Rawsay and Sivori, 1991) (See also Appendix 2).

The ideas will be organized around a series of 'key messages', each of which is put forward here as a specific response to the challenges outlined in the previous section. The question for educational practitioners teaching at all stages of the National Curriculum is: 'How can I best get across the key messages necessary to promote antiracist and multicultural perspectives in Economic and Industrial Understanding?'

Economic Success and Self-esteem

Key Messages:

- Ethnic communities have had to struggle to achieve economic success.
- It is not just talent that leads to economic success — you need opportunity too.
- Ethnic-minority people can and do achieve economic success.

- Economic success is only one of many things that makes a person valuable.

Here the curriculum focus would be on basic notions of why people work and why people do not work, on how we value ourselves and other people and what factors lead to economic success for individuals and society. An important aspect would be to explore where ethnic-minority communication came to work and what opportunities were open or locked to them in this country. Visits where possible to ethnic-minority businesses, talks from local ethnic-minority people, materials — for example those produced by the Institute of Race Relations (Institute of Race Relations, 1982; 1985) — case-studies taken from written accounts by black and Asian immigrants of their experience of employment and unemployment, and for Key Stage 4, statistics on employment amongst ethnic groups would all be relevant. Mentor schemes, where pupils are linked with black and ethnic professionals who visit and encourage them, are providing a valuable, dynamic and new way of raising the motivation and aspiration of ethnic-minority pupils. One Key Stage 1 topic successfully tried in Manchester schools is called 'People who help us' and allows younger pupils to begin to identify positive ethnic-minority participation in the local economy. One key element must be to provide strong positive images of ethnic-minority participation in the economy at all levels, whether this be through written, visual or experiential means. Another must be to challenge easy assumptions about economic reward and personal worth, so that the term 'value' is not allowed simply to become identified with job-market exchange value. An interesting topic at Key Stage 3 might be 'Hasn't he/she done well?' where pupils examine in relation to real and fictional examples how people evaluate each other's success. Here issues of cultural difference and stereotyping might well begin to surface, points which will be further discussed later.

International Economic Awareness

Key Messages:

- The era of European colonization set up a pattern of world trade and production that still largely remains today.
- There are rich and poor in all countries; due to the effects of colonialism, many black and Asian countries are relatively poor.
- While black and Asian countries may be economically poor, their people are as rich as any in talent, enterprise and culture.

The issues of development and underdevelopment are controversial and complex. However, they are so important for an understanding of economic issues in relation to racism and multiculturalism that they must form a key part of the EIU curriculum, throughout the key stages of the National Curriculum.

Here there is a growing range of highly effective classroom resources for all age groups, developed by charitable organizations, churches and specialist curriculum units such as the 'Development Education Project' in Manchester (Cooke, 1985; Fyson, 1984).

The whole area has been given great impetus by the recent high-publicity focus on issues of poverty, underdevelopment and environmental disaster. Still, sadly, a scarce and precious resource for the multicultural class-room are materials designed and produced by the people of developing countries themselves, though there have recently been some good television documentaries. Great care needs to be taken in any attempts to use children whose parents are from developing countries as reference or resource material.

It is an emotionally and psychologically sensitive area because of chil-dren's direct personal links with issues of development that may be the cause of family stress and strains, and because of the clumsily patronizing attitude behind previous charitable efforts to 'Help the Third World'. One key element of the curriculum must be a focus on positive aspects of the problem; for example, studies of successful development in poorer countries and an emphasis on the strength, determination and pride with which disadvantaged people are facing their difficulties. At root, especially at Key Stage 4, explicit efforts need to be made to challenge facile notions that industrially developed countries are more advanced, less primitive or more civilized than others, a set of assumptions that the recent ecological crisis has begun to undermine.

Economic Identity, Cultural Difference and Stereotyping

Key Messages:

- People of all different ethnic and cultural groups achieve success in all different jobs and careers.
- Ethnic-minority communities are associated with certain types of work in this country for historical reasons.
- Different cultures have different attitudes to different sorts of work and careers for men and women.

Here the curriculum focus would be on how groups of people from all ethnic backgrounds have developed an economic image, based on history and circumstance. Exploration of family histories, looking at how parents and grandparents were employed, examination of cultures that develop around occupations such as mining, fishing, heavy industry through fiction and documentary, self-examination of attitudes to work and international com-parisons of what people do in different countries and how they are paid, are all relevant. A direct focus on what stereotypes are and how they are formed and sustained, is important, and can be done in relation to a wide range of class, gender, regional and racial stereotypes. Careers services across the country and TVEI (Technical and Vocational Education Initiative) funded projects have begun to generate a range of useful materials challenging occupational stereotypes. It is important to find images which challenge ethnic stereotypes, available in increasing amount from development education sources, embassies, and agencies such as the Commission for Racial Equality and the Equal Opportunities Commission. More and more occupationally orientated bodies such as the Sports Council, the Engineering Council and the Health Education Council are producing good visual and written materials that challenge assumptions and prejudices based on racial stereotypes (Klein, 1984). This curriculum area can usefully be taught with humour, since there is an element of 'debunking' involved and comedies such as *Fawlty Towers*, comedians such as Lenny Henry and films such as *Trading Places* can all be used in the classroom to get older pupils laughing at their own prejudices and, more importantly, consciously considering and revising them.

Economic Factors and Race Relations

Key Messages:

- Migration is usually motived by economic considerations.
- Racial discrimination and harassment have been fuelled by competition for resources.
- Individuals, organizations and governments can discriminate against racial and ethnic groups.
- Individuals, organizations and governments can challenge racial discrimination in Britain.

Here there are two levels at which an effective curriculum response can work. Fundamental ideas of fairness and unfairness lie at the heart of issues of racial discrimination and, especially when teaching younger age groups, an exploration of what is meant by 'that's not fair', and how people respond to unfair treatment is often far more effective as a starting point than attempting to explore the technicalities of race relations. Drama simulations or role plays, where pupils are given opportunities to react to unfair treatment, have been used to convey the basic messages to children of primary school age. In one Manchester school, for example, a sequence of drama lessons explored a scenario where one group of children played native Americans and others the advancing United States cavalry, and were asked to negotiate over the use of their land. At all stages of education, explorations of family histories of movement (even if within a country or a region) will often raise issues of

Table 4.2: Economic and Industrial Understanding: Curriculum Responses

Dimension	Key Messages	Considerations
Economic Success and Self-esteem	• Ethnic communities have had to struggle to achieve economic success • It is not just talent that leads to economic success — you need opportunity, too • Ethnic-minority people can and do achieve economic success • Economic success is only one of many things that makes a person valuable	* Must provide strong positive images of ethnic-minority participation in the economy * Must challenge easy assumptions about economic reward and personal worth * What opportunities were open and closed to ethnic minorities when they arrived in Britain
International Economic Awareness	• The era of European colonialism set up a pattern of world trade and production that still largely remains today. • There are rich and poor in all countries; due to the effects of colonialism many black and Asian countries are relatively poor • While black and Asian countries may be economically poor, their people are as rich as any in talent, enterprise and culture	* Focus on positive aspects of the problem; e.g., examples of successful development * Challenge facile notions that industrial needs are more 'advanced' or 'civilized'
Economic Identity, Cultural Difference and Stereotyping	• People of all different cultural and ethnic groups achieve success in all different jobs and careers • Ethnic-minority communities are associated with certain types of work in this country for historical reasons • Different cultures have different attitudes to different sorts of work and careers for men and women	* Needs a direct focus on what stereotypes are and how they are formed and sustained * Must find images that challenge ethnic stereotypes * Can be successfully taught with humour
Economic Factors and Race Relations	• Migration is usually motivated by economic considerations • Racial discrimination and harassment have been fuelled by competition for resources • Individuals, organizations and governments can discriminate against racial and ethnic groups • Individuals, organizations and governments can challenge racial discrimination in Britain	* Fundamental ideas of fairness and unfairness should be explored, especially with younger pupils * Make the link between economic success and race-equality issues * Use companies with equal-opportunities policies as a resource.

how far the search for opportunities motivates us. Stories, poems, history and geography materials will often make connections between economic life and questions of just and unjust treatment. At Key Stages 3 and 4, more direct use of resources from the Commission for Racial Equality, and (if adapted) adult racism awareness training materials will begin to build understanding of organizational and governmental responses to race discrimination.

It is invaluable if a company with a local or national profile and a strong equal-opportunities policy can be used as a resource. A growing number of large companies of all types require professionals working in the personnel department who have understanding and experience of the practical issues involved. The important task for teachers is to make the link between economic success at individual, organizational and national level, and race equality (Forbes, 1990). Throughout the EIU curriculum, materials and references should reinforce the message that British workforces, customers and businesses are multicultural and multiracial, and that this has been and will continue to be of great benefit to the economy as a whole.

Conclusion

Many choices face curriculum planners as to how to organize the delivery of cross-curricular themes such as EIU. Whether the decision is to teach it through thematic projects or specific topics, through specific elements of the timetable such as personal and social education (PSE), or in a cross-subject, integrated fashion, must be left to the professional judgment of teachers in individual schools (NCC, 1990a). In general, however, the development of an antiracist and multicultural dimension should be, where possible, carried out in consultation with those who represent ethnic-minority communities. Local community relations councils, LEA advisory teams, local chambers of commerce and other professional bodies should be used to put teachers in contact with, for example, local Asian people. Not only does this immediately open doors to potential human resource for the EIU curriculum, but it allows ideas and materials for lessons to be checked for inadvertent errors of fact, bias or stereotyping.

The suggestion throughout this chapter has been that the new focus within the National Curriculum on Economic and Industrial Understanding should be seized as an exciting opportunity to develop in young people a critical awareness of how issues of race and culture interweave with issues of work and consumption. It could be that questions of stereotyping, prejudice and unfairness can be taught more effectively from within an economics perspective, since this allows some fundamental issues concerning the sources of conflict between individuals, groups and nations to be exposed. In terms of vital issues facing young people from ethnic-minority backgrounds, a well delivered EIU curriculum could be a valuable supporting and motivating factor, allowing pupils to orientate themselves with greater awareness and confidence to the choices and challenges facing them in the world of work. For all pupils, a multicultural approach will allow problems to be examined from a variety of perspectives, and can help develop a strong sense of economic life as part of cultural, political and social life.

References

ARORA, R. and DUNCAN, C. (1986) *Multicultural education: Towards Good Practice*, London, Routledge and Kegan Paul.

BROWN, C. (1984) *Black and White Britain: the Third Policy Studies Institute Report*, London, Heinemann.

COOKE, D. (1985) *Teaching Development Issues*, Manchester, Development Education Project.

DEPARTMENT OF EDUCATION AND SCIENCE (1985a) *Report of the National Committee of Enquiry into the Education of Children from Ethnic Minority Groups* (The Swann Report) Cmnd., 9543, London, HMSO.

DEPARTMENT OF EDUCATION AND SCIENCE (1985b) *Report on Economic Understanding*, London, HMSO.

DEPARTMENT OF EDUCATION AND SCIENCE (1985c) *The Curriculum 5–16: Curriculum Matters No. 2*, London, HMSO.

FORBES, A. (1990) 'The transition from school to work', in PUMFREY, P.D. and VERMA, G.K. (Eds) *Race Relations and Urban Education*, Basingstoke, The Falmer Press.

FRYER, P. (1984) *Staying Power: The History of Black People in Britain*, London, Pluto Press.

FYSON, N.L. (1984) *The Development Puzzle,*, London, Hodder and Stoughton.

HARGREAVES, D. (1982) *Challenge of the Comprehensive School: Culture, Curriculum and Community*, London, Routledge and Kegan Paul.

INSTITUTE OF RACE RELATIONS (1982a) *Roots of Racism*, London, Institute of Race Relations.

INSTITUTE OF RACE RELATIONS (1982b) *Patterns of Racism*, London, Institute of Race Relations.

INSTITUTE OF RACE RELATIONS (1985) *How Racism came to Britain*, London, Institute of Race Relations.

KLEIN, G. (1984) *Resources for Multicultural Education* (2nd ed.), London, Schools Council.

NATIONAL CURRICULUM COUNCIL (1989) *Draft Curriculum Guidance No. 4*, York, NCC.

NATIONAL CURRICULUM COUNCIL (1990a) *Curriculum Guidance No. 3*, York, NCC.

NATIONAL CURRICULUM COUNCIL (1990b) *Curriculum Guidance No. 4*, York, NCC.

RAMSAY, M. and SIVORI, A. (1991) *Economic and Industrial Understanding — a Cross Curriculum theme*, Sheffield, Careers and Occupational Information Centre.

STENHOUSE, L., VERMA, G., WILDE, R.D. and NIXON, J. (1982) *Teaching About Race Relations — Problems and Effects*, London, Routledge and Kegan Paul.

TIERNEY, J. (1982) *Race, Migration and Schooling*, Eastbourne, Holt, Rinehart and Winston.

Troyna, B. and Smith, D.I. (1983) *Racism, School and the Labour Market*, Leicester, National Youth Bureau.

Verma, G.K. and Bagley, C. (1982) *Self-Concept, Achievement and Multi-Cultural Education*, London, Macmillan.

Verma, G.K. (1989) *Education for All, A Landmark in Pluralism*, London, The Falmer Press.

Chapter 5

Careers Education and Guidance

Kanka Mallick

Context

Few would disagree that education is of crucial importance in an individual's life. It is also widely accepted that a good education can provide the necessary skills and knowledge without which an individual cannot hope to aspire to an occupation to his or her liking or perhaps to any job in the present international economic recession. In the process of transition from school to work or higher education many social and ethnic groups are vulnerable. There is sufficient evidence that unemployment in ethnic minority youth is much higher than in their white counterparts (CRE, 1980; 1985). The March 1990 *Employment Gazette* reported that an ethnic minority unemployment rate was 60 per cent above that for white (CRE, 1990). It is a salient feature in many societies that if unemployment increases, ethnic minorities suffer disproportionately.

Thus, the main debate concerning education centres around two main issues: the aspects of knowledge or skills which ought to be taught, and the appropriate ways of providing such knowledge and skills. Answers to these questions might be easier if children and adolescents came from similar socio-economic, cultural, religious and linguistic backgrounds. In a multiethnic, multicultural society such as the UK the population is composed of a number of distinguishable ethnic and cultural groups, and this inevitably affects the teaching–learning process.

All LEAs were required to provide a careers service under the provisions of the Employment and Training Act 1973. Careers teachers in secondary schools work with that LEA service. Careers service officers are often members of the Institute of Careers Officers. Careers teachers in schools are often members of either the Association of Careers Teachers or of the National Association of Careers and Guidance Teachers. The Careers Research and Advisory Centre is an important national focus for all aspects of careers education and guidance.

Careers education and guidance in secondary schools aim to facilitate the individual pupil's career — related decision-making. Most individuals have occupations; many have paid jobs; some have careers and a few have vocations. The categories are not mutually exclusive. This involves helping adolescents understand and be aware of their interests, abilities and aptitudes, including any particular strengths or weaknesses. Awareness of career options, including further and higher education, and the cost and benefits of each option is also needed. These conditions provide the basis for a more informed and rational approach towards decision-making in this field.

Careers education and guidance is one of the five 'themes' of the National Curriculum. A cross-curricular approach has been recommended in the guidance contained in the booklet, *National Curriculum and Whole Curriculum Planning* (NCC, 1989). The five themes are supposed to promote the aims defined in Section 1 of the Education Reform Act 1988 and are essential parts of the curriculum. They are interrelated. The central concern of this theme 'careers education and guidance' as outlined in the document is to prepare pupils for the choices, changes and transitions affecting their future education, training and life as adult members of society. It recommends that schools should offer:

- access to individual guidance;
- systematic careers programmes;
- direct experience of the world of work;
- access to up-to-date sources of information about educational, vocational, training and careers opportunities;
- opportunities to compile and review a record of personal achievement; and
- in key stages 3 and 4 a personal action plan (NCC, 1990).

The cross-curricular 'themes' all share features in common, such as 'the capacity to promote discussion of values and beliefs, extend knowledge and understanding, encourage practical activities and decision-making and further the interrelationship of the individual and the community' (NCC, 1990, Curriculum Guidance No. 6).

Curriculum guidance sets out a framework of school policy on careers education and guidance. It suggests that development of this policy 'should involve wide consultation with, for example, teachers, careers officers, further and higher education establishments, parents, governors and employers' (National Curriculum Guidance No. 6). Some reference is made to ethnic minority pupils, but no specific strategies are suggested as how to deal with these challenges, as discussed later in this chapter. It simply suggests ensuring that 'all pupils have access to a careers education and guidance programme will mean giving consideration, on an individual basis, to pupils with ethnic minority backgrounds and to those who are bilingual'. Such a statement with implicit objectives is based on an assumption that teachers have skills and expertise to deal with pupils from varying cultural, ethnic and linguistic backgrounds. The document further states that 'careers education and guidance should promote equal opportunities and help pupils to overcome both overt and subtle barriers which may be encountered as they progress through school and into adult working life'. The issue here is not only of provision and access but of the commitment on the part of schools to ensure that careers education and guidance adopt an increasingly plural approach, providing both integrated and parallel careers education and guidance in the values, culture and language of all ethnic groups.

The importance of careers education and guidance has been underlined by a number of recent publications. The DES/DoE report, *Working together for a better future* (HMSO,1987) required all LEAs to produce a written policy statement, including a careers-service policy, and for all schools to respond by developing their own policy statements. It further states that careers education and guidance should form part of a whole-school approach to personal and social development. HMI's report entitled *Curriculum Matters 10 — Careers Education and Guidance 5–16* subsequently provided curriculum advice to schools (HMSO, 1988). The report of the CBI Task Force *Towards a Skills Revolution*, also contained recommendations for improving the quality of careers programmes (CBI, 1989).

In the context of careers education and guidance it is necessary to make some general observations about the meanings of these concepts. The more general use of the term refers to the ways in which the school guides pupils to particular vocational or occupational destinations. This includes the process of course selection and any factors which influence post-compulsory education or employment. At a more specific level, the idea of vocational education suggests a non-academic programme, that is, preparation for the labour market. In any discussion of vocational or occupational aspirations the issues of ethnicity and equality become crucial since the school is implicated in the production of social inequalities.

One of the exciting developments in British society since the 1950s has been the development of a plural community in which people of different and perhaps conflicting cultural values and beliefs inhabit the same city, street or classroom. Given the changed characteristics of schools, one naturally assumes that the process of education would adapt to new challenges because of the varying needs and aspirations of their pupils. It is now over thirty years since ethnic minority settlement became established, but the question of what and how to teach in this emerging new society has not been resolved (Verma, 1989; Pumfrey and Verma, 1990). There is sufficient evidence in the literature to suggest that ethnic minorities have suffered from all sorts of disadvantages in terms of career advancement, education, welfare, housing and employment (Verma, 1983; Verma, Mallick and Ashworth, 1983; CRE, 1991).

The main aim of this chapter is to examine the role of careers education and guidance in meeting the challenges of cultural diversity within the educational system. As a prelude, it is necessary to consider briefly some of the challenges posed by aspects of plurality.

Challenges

Aspects of Plurality

One of the main aspects of 'culture' is that perceptions, beliefs and attitudes towards day-to-day events, circumstances and situations are generally uniform within a given cultural group. For the developing child this results in a set of normative standards which is likely to be consistent within the family groups and in the wider context of the community network. Thus, a person from a particular cultural background will most likely have a world view resulting from the way he/she has been socialized in early childhood. This implies that a child's conception of the world is determined by experiences of the immediate environment, and for most individuals families are a salient part of this environment.

One of the main principles in promoting pluralist understanding is that any one world-view is no more valid or correct that another, even if it is difficult to accept an individual on an equal footing regardless of the attitudes which he or she considers 'normal'. Such value judgments may contribute to misconceptions about the individual's worth. For example, research has shown that the Muslim parents' attitude to girls' education is markedly different from that of the prevailing attitudes in western societies. It would be as 'natural' for the Muslim to think that western parents are extremely liberal, as it is for western parents to think that Muslim parents are overprotective. Nevertheless, there is some evidence that home background of British-born Muslim girls is generally supportive of education and careers in Britain (Karim, 1986; Verma, 1986; Shaikh and Kelly, 1989). It is interesting to note that in Muslim countries, with increasing industrialization, parents are more willing than they were in the past for girls to be independent and to take up careers before marriages (Karim, 1986). It is necessary, therefore, that the educational system in western societies should be sensitive to the powerful cultural and religious traditions that to a large extent influence and inform attitudes to both education and employment. Studies have also shown that families are regarded by most ethnic minority young people as extremely influential in making decisions or seeking advice about their future careers (Cherry and Gear, 1987; Arnold, Bud and Miller, 1988). Certain social and cultural groups place particular emphasis on the family in such matters.

The process of vocational adaptation is determined by past experience, present state and future expectations of the individual in a particular social context. Therefore, it is necessary to treat any generalizations with extreme care. There has been little research, however, into the actual attitudes and experience of ethnic minorities in their transition from school to work or higher education. Little is known of the extent to which their career choices are likely to be mediated by the interaction of their immediate environment.

Some writers (Weinrich, 1979; Kelly and Weinrich, 1986) argue that a necessary conflict arises in the identity formation of young Asians in that, while their 'primary allegiances are first grounded in their own ethnic group' (Weinrich, 1979, p. 97) at home, their later exposure to the majority culture at school inevitably leads to identity conflicts. Other studies found, contrary to popular stereotypes, that the majority of young south Asians have positive, strong and supportive relationships with their parents and family (e.g., Brah and Minhas, 1985; Verma, 1986). A close relationship with parents and family, and positive orientation towards traditional values is not an absolute. Nevertheless, for the majority of young south Asians the choice of career is likely to be made within the framework of family expectations and aspirations (Stopes-Roe and Cochrane, 1984). It should be pointed out that there are subgroups of people of Asian origin whose values and beliefs differ markedly from each other. There is also evidence that a growing proportion of British-born south-Asian youngsters are coming into conflict with their parents over their career choice and marriage. The cross-curricular nature of such issues is clear. They must be identified and sensitively addressed by the school through its curriculum.

The possibility of a potential clash of values has important implications for careers education in schools. Many careers teachers and advisers in British schools have been trained within a western framework and therefore have a certain expectation of young people's place in society, the realistic level of careers choice and so on. Smolicz (1981) rightly suggests that core values vary between cultures, and that it is essential that these value systems are taken seriously by professionals. These values must be neither obliterated nor ignored by careers teachers and advisers.

Stereotyping and prejudice are other dimensions to be taken into account within the framework of careers education and guidance. Careers education has to consider existing stereotypes and prejudices which affect members from minority groups in particular during their transition from school to work or to higher education. Previous work on the transition of ethnic-minority adolescents from school to work showed that many were dissatisfied with the careers education and guidance they had received (Verma, 1986). The perceptions of prejudice which careers-education professionals have will obviously affect their own decision-making and perceptions of the aspirations of young people from cultures different from their own. Therefore, advice on how to deal with such prejudices on a personal level should form part of the cross-curricular treatment of careers education.

In a study conducted in the North of England it was found that only a small proportion of secondary-school pupils were satisfied with careers education. A majority of them (adolescents from both ethnic majority and minority) felt that it was unhelpful. In many cases careers teachers appeared to try to persuade young people to adopt unwanted or even inappropriate careers. Thus, the majority of young people from ethnic minority groups found difficulties of various kinds in their transition from school to work or higher education. It was also found that 'underemployment' among south Asians and Afro-Caribbean was much higher than among their white counterparts. On the basis of the above large-scale research it is possible to question the role and efficacy of careers education within the British educational system (Verma, 1986). Many careers teachers devote their time to persuading ethnic minority pupils from an early age to downgrade their vocational expectations. In some cases, adjustment of vocational choices is performed by only partially trained careers teachers in British schools. The challenge of the National Curriculum is to improve careers education and guidance for all pupils.

A further aspect of cultural diversity within careers education and guidance is that specific groups tend to settle in a relatively few areas of the country. Since different areas have different ethnic patterns, there would be little advantage in developing a system of careers advice based on the needs of a single ethnic group. The pluralities of London, Lancashire and the Midlands all have different social and cultural meanings within dynamic urban and employment contexts. It should also be remembered that whilst there are similarities between various ethnic and cultural groups, the process of meeting individual and collective needs and expectations may differ. No cultural and ethnic group is completely homogeneous, and therefore any attempt to treat a divergent group as a uniform entity is bound to fail. Careers education is required to adopt a strategy whereby individual response is not sidetracked while dealing with culturally diverse groups of individuals, if it is to be perceived as effective.

For the native British youth the values of home and school are likely to be consistent with those of the traditional British society at large (within this framework, social-class effects are powerful and divisive). But for the new generation of black and Asian British this congruence cannot be assumed and is likely to vary in ways which are significant for the process of careers education and guidance. It cannot be assumed that congruence is achieved entirely by adjustments on the part of ethnic minorities. Indeed no system can achieve complete congruence. Stability in systems is usually a dynamic equilibrium between expectations and actualities. The danger is when these diverge too much. Career expectations, aspirations and actualities are sensitive issues as they affect life chances in so many ways.

Responses

It must be emphasized that ethnic ad cultural issues in the careers education and guidance context are extremely complex and cannot be explained in a simplistic way. Any discussion of relationships between careers-teacher and pupil must be seen within a framework of several interrelated concepts such as ethnicity, culture, social class, religion and sex.

It can be argued that it is extremely difficult, if not impossible, to gain a thorough knowledge of the cultural values and patterns of behaviour for every ethnic group with whom the careers teacher comes into contact. It is imperative, however, that the teachers responsible for careers education and guidance and advisers be sensitive to differences in value orientations, and socialization patterns of culturally distinctive communities in a plural society such as the UK. Such understandings, perceptive and adaptive, are essential qualities if better relationships between themselves and pupils are to be developed. Careers teachers are continually undergoing personal transitions because of the challenges their work poses. They should also reflect on their own cultural characteristics from the perception of an outsider. This should enable them more effectively to share knowledge with pupils and their parents concerning important ideas and concepts, analyse these flexibly and function professionally in a more effective manner.

Attempts should be made to improve the quality and validity of careers education and advice offered in schools and careers service. The process should consider the impact of differing cultural and family backgrounds on the self-preservation of ethnic minority youngsters. Part of careers education and guidance should be to prepare ethnic minority youngsters seeking work not only to use formal channels, but also to seek out informal ones. It is necessary that careers education and advice to different groups is appropriate and must serve as an instrument of change in the individual's view of himself or herself. Teachers teaching careers education must be challenged to ascertain that development of accurate, realistic conceptions of 'self' is one of the major functions in the learning process.

Careers education should help pupils to resolve the conflicts that arise from their functioning in the private and communal world (home and community), and in the public world of the school and society. Such teaching would also help pupils to understand how their social and cultural groups influence their attitude and behaviour. They should develop an awareness of some form of cultural pluralism as the goal of careers education. They should be given an opportunity to understand the social, religious, linguistic and cultural diversity of all pupils.

Careers education and guidance needs to develop a multicultural and antiracist orientation so that it can function successfully and comfortably in a plural environment. Teachers responsible for careers education and guidance, working in such an environment, need to learn how to acknowledge, account for and, if necessary, reconstruct their own individual attitudes and practices towards, and assumptions about, those from a culture different to their own. In order to achieve these goals they need to be critical of personal responses to specific situations and interactions; of their expectations of individuals because of the assumptions they make about the nature of the culture from which such pupils come; of the ways in which the distinctive features of cultures are presented to other young people and the ways in which they are asked to treat them. In brief, the response required is to give a new emphasis to the practice of careers work in schools. No society can claim to be static and therefore institutions reflecting that society must also change. Cultural diversity in various and developing forms is becoming a permanent feature of

British society. In adapting to these social and educational changes, careers education and guidance could play a significant part in avoiding prejudicial treatment of ethnic minorities which would otherwise result in continued disadvantage and alienation of future generations.

The use of various forms of work experience as an integral part of a programme of secondary school career education and guidance has much to commend it. National guidelines exist and schools have obtained the co-operation of local companies and services to provide invaluable opportunities for youngsters uncertain of what they wish to do. The 'compact' agreements between schools and industry and commerce have provided encouragement for many pupils in socially and economically deprived areas to continue their education (Forbes, 1990). The importance of Industrial and Economic Understanding (IEU) is a closely related concern (see Chapter 4). Young enterprise business company schemes are increasingly used in schools and provide opportunities for valuable experiences in a career education programme. An excellent example of an LEA initiative in producing careers-education materials is provided by the city of Manchester. Their extensive development work has resulted in a six-part loose-leaf format containing the national perspectives, careers education and guidance in practice, involving parents and equal opportunities. The final section is entitled 'Every Teacher a Teacher of Careers' (Rogers and Wickham, 1991). The methods and materials described provide a basis from which the dimension of cultural diversity can be addressed. Appendix 2 provides further information of these topics.

The process of careers education and guidance within secondary education must attempt to prevent the giving of ill-informed, prejudicial and inappropriate advice. Responsibilities for implementing the theme of careers education and guidance as laid down by the National Curriculum Council lies with individual schools and practitioners. This has some advantages in that the process can be closely related to the local opportunity structure and to the community it serves.

Careers education in schools has not usually been given high priority in the past, and often this has resulted in staff being allocated the job with little skills or expertise. This has changed for the better over the last decade but the rise in unemployment makes careers work in schools difficult but, paradoxically, even *more* vital. Guidelines have now been developed to take account of both the pluralist nature of society and the substantial regional variations (NCC, 1990). It is to be hoped that delivery of this aspect of the National Curriculum will acknowledge the fact that ethnic minorities should be treated as individuals but with specific cultural aspirations which are not, however, deterministic in character. If individual schools and careers teachers fail to recognize this aspect of their professional work, ethnic minorities will encounter disadvantages through lack of understanding and lack of opportunity. Good careers education and guidance implies unbiased and unprejudiced teaching which treats cultural and individual needs with respect, understanding and sensitivity. Of course, such advice cannot of itself counteract the wider problems of discrimination in employment. It requires a wider set of social, educational, political and legal programmes. It is also true to say that a certain degree of acceptance of cultural diversity within the educational context has developed, but also that there are still clear limitations to this especially when questions of additional resources are raised. However, the demands of social justice require that the increasing numbers of young people from ethnic minorities growing towards maturity are given a better deal.

References

ARNOLD, J., BUD, R.J. and MILLER, K. (1988) 'Young People's Perceptions of the Uses and Usefulness of Different Sources of Careers Help', *British Journal of Guidance and Counselling*, 16, 1, pp. 83–90.

BRAH, A. and MINHAS, R. (1985) 'Structural Racism or Cultural Difference: Schooling for Asian Girls', in WEINER, G. (Ed) *Just a Bunch of Girls*, Milton Keynes, Open University Press.

CHERRY, N. and GEAR, R. (1987) 'Young People's Perceptions of their Vocational Guidance Needs: Priorities and Preoccupations', *Journal of Guidance and Counselling*, 15, 1, pp. 59–71.

COMMISSION FOR RACIAL EQUALITY (1980) *Half A Chance*, London, CRE.

COMMISSION FOR RACIAL EQUALITY (1985) *Positive Action and Equal Opportunity in Employment*, London, CRE.

COMMISSION FOR RACIAL EQUALITY (1990) *Annual General Report (1990)*, London, CRE Publication.

COMMISSION FOR RACIAL EQUALITY (1991) *Second Consultative Paper on the Race Relations Act*, London, CRE.

CONFEDERATION OF BRITISH INDUSTRY (1989) *Towards a Skills Revolution — Task Force Report*, London, CBI.

FORBES, A. (1990) 'The transition from school to work', in PUMFREY, P.D. and VERMA, G.K. (Eds) *Race Relations and Urban Education: Contexts and Promising Practices*, Basingstoke, The Falmer Press.

HER MAJESTY'S STATIONARY OFFICE (1987) *Working Together for a Better Future*, DES/DoE Report, London, HMSO.

HER MAJESTY'S STATIONARY OFFICE (1988) *Curriculum Matters 10: Careers Education and Guidance 5–16*, Department of Education, Her Majesty's Inspectorate of Schools, London, HMSO.

KARIM, R. (1986) 'Adolescent Role-stereotype of Pakistani Parents', Paper given at the National Seminar on the Pakistani Child, Islamabad, June.

KELLY, A.J.D. and WEINRICH, P. (1986) 'Situated Identities, conflicts in Identification and Own Group preference in Racial and Ethnic Identifications: Young Muslim Pakistani Women in Birmingham', UK Paper read at the International Association for Cross-cultural Psychology, 8th International Congress of Cross-cultural Psychology, Istanbul, Turkey, July 6–10.

NATIONAL CURRICULUM COUNCIL (1989) *Interim Report on Cross Curricular Issues*, York, NCC.

NATIONAL CURRICULUM COUNCIL (1989) *National Curriculum and Whole Curriculum Planning*, London, NCC.

NATIONAL CURRICULUM COUNCIL (1990) *Careers Education and Guidance*, London, NCC.

PUMFREY, P.D. and VERMA, G.K. (1990) *Race Relations and Urban Education*, London, The Falmer Press.

ROGERS, W. and WICKHAM, D. (1991) *Implementing the Whole Curriculum: Careers Education*, Manchester, City of Manchester Education Department.

SHAIKH, S. and KELLY, A. (1989) 'To mix or not to mix: Pakistani girls in British schools', *Educational Research*, 31, 1, pp.10–19.

SMOLICZ, J.J. (1981) 'Culture, Ethnicity and Education: Multiculturalism in a Plural Society', in MEGGARY, J., NISBET, S. and HOYLE, E. (Eds) *World Year Book in Education: Education of Minorities*, London, Kogan Page.

STOPES-ROE, M. and COCHRANE, R. (1984) 'The Culture Shock Absorbers', *The Guardian*, 19 December, p. 7.

VERMA, G.K. (1983) 'Consciousness, disadvantage and opportunity: the struggle for South Asian youth in British society', in BAGLEY, C. and VERMA, G.K. (Eds) *Multicultural Childhood: Education, Ethnicity and Cognitive Styles*, Aldershot, England, Gower.

VERMA, G.K. (1986) *Ethnicity and Educational Achievement in British Schools*, London, Macmillan.

VERMA, G.K. (1989) *Education for All: A Landmark in Pluralism*, London, The Falmer Press.

VERMA, G.K., MALLICK, K. and ASHWORTH, B. (1983) 'The role of attitude and experience in the transition from school to work in young South Asians in Britain', in BAGLEY, C. and VERMA, G.K. (Eds) *Multicultural Childhood: Education, Ethnicity and Cognitive Styles*, Aldershot, England, Gower.

WEINRICH, P. (1979) 'Ethnicity and adolescent identity conflicts', in KAHN, V.S. (Ed) *Minority Families in Britain*, London, Macmillan.

Chapter 6

Health Education

Julia Pilling

Context

Health education is a cross-curricular theme in the National Curriculum. It is classified as a non-statutory subject. Its elements are, however, included in the statutory National Curriculum subjects. Health education is also concerned with the statutory aims of the 1988 Education Reform Act, which states that a curriculum should be one that promotes the spiritual, moral, cultural, mental and physical development of the pupils, of the school and of society. The National Curriculum Council (NCC) published Curriculum Guidance No. 3 *The Whole Curriculum*, in 1990. This stressed the importance of health education:

> There can be nothing more important than inculcating, in the young, the values of a healthy mind in a healthy body, together with an appreciation and understanding of responsibilities of the community. (NCC, 1990, pp. 4–5)

This chapter will focus upon health education in secondary schools in relation to the needs of ethnic-minority pupils and to the multicultural education of all pupils. Health education is interrelated with the other cross-curricular themes of the National Curriculum and, like them, is not an additional subject to be added to the secondary-school curriculum. The elements of the cross-curricular themes, including health education, have implications for all aspects of school life for ethnic-minority pupils and the multicultural learning experiences of all pupils. Secondary schools are recommended to appoint a coordinator to ensure that cross-curricular themes are effectively implemented.

Curriculum Guidance No. 5, specifically on health education, was published in 1990. Emphasis was placed upon the necessity of not leaving health education in schools to chance. Health education is recognized as an essential part of every pupil's curriculum. This is to be achieved by developing a school health education policy, by developing a coherent health education programme and by recognizing the joint responsibilities of school, home and community in providing health education for pupils. In the formation of a school health education policy, consideration must be given to individual pupils' needs, including those of pupils who have an ethnic minority background. It is suggested that schools take into account the fact that learning is likely to be influenced by different cultural values, backgrounds and experience. Consideration of the needs of bilingual pupils is also included. Curriculum Guidance No. 5 again emphasizes the need for a whole-school approach to health education:

> Health education in schools does not begin and end in the classroom. The subtle message that pupils receive about health from the daily life of the school are as important as those given during lessons. (NCC, 1990, p. 9)

The relationships between staff and pupils, attitudes and standards of behaviour, the opportunity for pupils to exercise decision-making through the development of their self-confidence and self-esteem, the quality of relationships between the school and the local community and the physical environment of the school are cited as important factors in developing this whole-school approach. The messages conveyed in the taught curriculum should be consistent with behaviour practised in the daily life of the school.

The patterns of health-related behaviour established during adolescence can significantly affect unhealthy patterns of behaviour in adulthood. During adolescence the influence of peers is significant. School is where young people meet, have the opportunity to form social groups and establish health-related attitudes and behaviours which conform to the norm of the group. Research into adolescent smoking, for example, has consistently indicated that the organization and social structure of a secondary school can affect pupils' health-related behaviours in regard to smoking. Schools have an important influence on pupils' health-related behaviours, but so do families, peer groups, the community and the media. Schools are therefore advised to include parents, governors and members of the local community when planning their health education programme. Adolescence is often a time of conflict between young people and their parents despite the families' long-term influences on the health-related behaviours of their children. For families from ethnic minorities there can be tensions between the expectations and values which parents have for their children and the competing expectations and values they may encounter at school from their peers (Nagra, 1989).

The secondary school has a responsibility to provide all pupils with accurate information about health matters and to help them clarify the attitudes and values which influence health choices. Nine components of a health-education curriculum to be included in the National Curriculum are identified, with appropriate areas of study for the key stages: substance use and misuse;

sex education; family-life education; safety; health-related exercise; nutrition; personal hygiene; environmental aspects of health education and psychological aspects of health education. These components should not be taught in isolation; rather they should be linked where appropriate and planned to ensure progression within each component through the school. Individual, group and community activities should be included in all the key stages. A method of mapping health education in the whole taught curriculum to ensure that all components are taught, is a useful addition to the guidance.

In considering how this chapter could most effectively be written, the possibility of drawing up a matrix of minority ethnic groups and aspects of culture having important health education implications was considered. Many key cultural dimensions derive from differing (or non-existent) religious beliefs. Thus diet, clothing, sexual mores, smoking, alcohol (and other drugs) are highlighted, for example, in such an approach. The extensive enquiries made of minority ethnic groups revealed their reservations about such an approach because of its potentially divisive and stereotypically adverse consequences. This is not to say that an awareness by schools of the health education related issues is unimportant. The contrary is the case. Despite this, those approached favoured a whole-school approach to health education in multicultural education. These soundings have determined the stance adopted in this chapter.

Challenges

Extensive research for this chapter has revealed that development of multicultural health education takes place very much at the local level, mainly in areas with a large ethnic-minority population. Very little development across the whole secondary school system is taking place in making multicultural health education a part of every pupil's curriculum. Research into multicultural health education in secondary schools is virtually non-existent.

The publication of a health education curriculum guidance document was welcomed by health educationalists, alleviating initial fears that health education in the National Curriculum was to revert back to the medical model, taught only through science. Health educationalists are divided in their response to the content of Curriculum Guidance No. 5, some viewing it as an opportunity to make health education a whole school issue; others feeling that it has fallen short of addressing the health needs of young people in our contemporary multicultural society.

There is general concern about the actual implementation of health education within the National Curriculum in light of the non-statutory nature of the cross-curricular themes. It can be argued that the nine stated elements of health education are all included in the statutory subjects of the National Curriculum so will have to be taught by schools. The curriculum model of the National Curriculum, with its subject-specific base, with pupils' attainments in each subject assessed on a ten-point scale, has led to a curriculum focused on knowledge and understanding which is easier to define than a curriculum concerned with attitudes and values. Health education curriculum needs a base of knowledge and understanding but its aims go beyond this to enabling young people to use this information to make decisions about their own health:

> It is widely recognised that the provision and acquisition of information alone is unlikely to promote healthy, or discourage unhealthy behaviour. (NCC, 1990, p. 7)

The National Curriculum does not specify teaching methods. This means that there are features of health education in Curriculum Guidance No.5, the areas of study concerned with developing pupils' social skills through various stated teaching methods, which would not be included in the statutory National Curriculum subjects. These features could be included in the statutory aims of the Education Reform Act in promoting the spiritual, moral, cultural, mental and physical development of pupils, of the school and of society, but these can be interpreted in many different ways by a school. It is proving difficult enough to establish a system to assess how schools are meeting their statutory duties in providing the National Curriculum subjects which have specific attainment targets. What criteria could be used to establish whether schools were meeting these wider statutory aims of the Education Reform Act in relation to health education?

Schools are given freedom to include health education in the curriculum in whichever way they wish. Leaving curriculum innovation in secondary schools to the discretion of schools has proved ineffective. Much of the present health education guidance was contained in the Schools Council's/Health Education Council's *Health Education 5–13* (1977) and *Health Education 13–18* (1982). Detailed planning for health education in schools was presented but there is little evidence that schools implemented these recommendations as thoroughly as expected. HMI reports undertaken on health education show that many secondary schools lack satisfactory coordination of health education; that often the taught health education curriculum is not supported by health-related practices in the school, particularly in regard to diet; that health education is approached too narrowly, with little consideration of mental health and pupils' personal development; and that there is little evaluation to find how effective health education has been with pupils. The aims and objectives of health education encompass the development of a pluralistic society. A major achievement of the Swann report (1985) was to recognize that multicultural education is for all pupils. However, without clearly defined government policies and machinery, this too is failing to develop in many schools (Verma, 1989).

The introduction of the National Curriculum is an ideal opportunity for schools to ensure that the health education needs of its ethnic-minority pupils and its non-ethnic minority pupils are being identified and met. The implication of health education as a whole-school issue is that health education is involved with every aspect of school life and with all the people involved in the life of the school, including pupils, staff, parents and local community. To be effective health education has to take place in a positive, caring environment which values the individual. This rolls easily off the pen in writing school policies but is much more difficult to achieve in reality. School policies on health education are pointless without good practice ensuing. Ryder and Campbell (1988) draw attention to the difference between the 'really' healthy school and the 'apparently' healthy school. A strong feature of the health education curriculum guidance is to develop individual pupils' self-esteem and meet their individual health education needs. This cannot be done without evaluating how the school affects individual pupils and what their individual health needs are. Schools themselves can be unhealthy places for pupils to work in with dismal and dirty buildings, inadequate heating and ventilation, inadequate shelter at breaks and unhealthy food. Pupils can be under pressure from other pupils to smoke, drink alcohol and take illegal substances. Pupils can be physically and emotionally bullied, called names ('Non-white' pupils are particularly prone to such abuse), made fun of and isolated. There is a real opportunity for schools to find out what experiences all pupils, including those with an ethnic minority background, have in school and establish what their health-related attitudes and behaviours are. The issue of racism in secondary schools cannot be ignored in evaluation which is focused in this way. There appears to be a lack of research into the effects of the school environment on the health-related behaviours of ethnic-minority pupils.

Many school staff, teaching and non-teaching, lack knowledge of health education, particularly in regard to the health beliefs and practices of different cultures. Even a rudimentary knowledge of different cultures can lead to misleading presumptions about the actual health behaviour of individuals. Health promotion workers have found that assumptions about attitudes and behaviours cannot be made across whole populations. Many ethnic groups comprise subcultures having differences along religious, gender and age lines. Perhaps most important are the difference between cultural and religious beliefs and actual practice (Malseed, 1990). The dangers of stereotyping people is an important feature of Key Stages 3 and 4 of the health education curriculum guidance. Even in health care, where there has been more multicultural development than in health education in secondary schools, it has been found that there is disparity between the professional view of what health-related problems there are in the community and those identified by the community itself. A recent report by a working party of Lancashire social services stated that many of Lancashire's ethnic communities are afraid of using vital services because they fear discrimination. The absence of managers and the lack of representation from ethnic-minority communities have meant that these departments have lacked a multicultural perspective.

> The lack of communication has made it almost impossible to know what provision these communities consider appropriate, sensitive and responsive to their needs. (LCC, 1991)

Minority communities are vulnerable to a negative, disapproving approach if health education is planned by professionals who do not understand the daily lives of families from minority ethnic groups, their choices or understand the basis of them (Mares, Henley and Baxter, 1985). This does not disregard the fact that there are health concerns and problems which are specific to different cultural groups which need addressing.

Presently, development in multicultural education is mainly concerned with identifying and meeting the needs of ethnic minority pupils. There are university departments, LEAs, health promotion units and schools all developing good practice in multicultural health education. It cannot be assumed, however, that all schools with a high proportion of ethnic-minority pupils are delivering multicultural health education. Development is dependent upon local factors. For example, in the city of Birmingham the local authority is working hard to develop multicultural health education and yet a recent HMI survey of one area of inner-city Birmingham concluded:

> Although the great majority of pupils in most of the schools are from ethnic minority backgrounds, there is little evidence that curriculum planning has given detailed consideration to the health attitudes and needs of different ethnic and religious groups. (HMI, 1990, p. 6)

One piece of research on multiethnic health-related behaviour of secondary-school pupils found that cultural influences were an important factor in formulating the health-related behaviour of pupils (Eden, 1985). Research for this chapter found instances of a lack of understanding on the part of secondary schools, including school sports services, and of differing cultural attitudes to the body. A common problem is the practice of communal showering after PE (see Volume 1, Chapter 13). A lack of communication between ethnic minority parents and school can lead to ignorance of each other's perspectives. Not only may schools be unaware of the health needs of ethnic minority pupils, parents may not be aware of the rationale of contemporary health education. The education background of some ethnic-minority parents has been didactic rather than child-centred and parents may not understand child-centred methods of health education, particularly when an open-ended approach leads to discussion of sensitive and controversial issues.

The HMI Birmingham report indicated that the extent to which INSET has influenced the provision of health education varies between institutions and that opportunities are rarely provided for teachers who have attended courses to share their newly acquired knowledge and expertise with their colleagues. There is no national initiative to disseminate good multicultural health education practice. The Health Education Authority undertakes individual initiatives such as the sickle-cell disease project and it claims that its materials for schools are written within a multicultural context but is has no coordination role at present. There are research initiatives being undertaken into health education for ethnic minorities by various universities, institutions and charitable bodies, which can be unknown to each other and unheard of by schools. Research for this chapter found that little is known about multicultural health education in schools with few or no ethnic-minority pupils.

Curriculum Guidance No. 5 emphasizes that for health education to be a whole-school issue all the staff have a responsibility for health education in terms of having positive attitudes to health education and by their own personal example in health-related attitudes and behaviours. Consistency of approach is required from all staff in terms of staff–pupil relationships and in allowing pupils to exercise desirable health behaviours in all areas of school life. There are tremendous implications for school policies and staff development in regard to multicultural health education. This seems ironic when teachers are suffering such stress from having to cope with rapid mandatory educational change and associated administration involved without the proper time, training and resources. The stress being experienced by teachers can result in teachers themselves adopting poor health-related behaviours. The ability of teachers to give pupils time and show the patience and understanding that builds good relationships, upon which effective health education is based, is threatened. The relationship between the health of staff and the health education of pupils would be an interesting area of research.

The trend in secondary schools in the 1980s has been to develop health education within the context of social education (HMI, 1986). This was found to be a more successful approach than earlier 'shock-horror' or topic approaches. Developing discrete social education courses has strengths and weaknesses. Pupils have the opportunity to develop health-related decision-making skills which otherwise they would not have. Unfortunately the opportunities to practise healthy behaviours in school generally may be difficult. Because staff are not involved in this curriculum area, they may feel that they have no responsibility for health education and may be actually negative to, or feel threatened by, child-centred methods used in social education. Indications are that smoking education, which is the most thoroughly researched area of health education, is most effective when integrated into social education (Eisner, Morgan and Gammage, 1988; Balding, 1988). This is emphasized in Curriculum Guidance No. 5:

> However, well-intentioned attempts to shock or frighten young people rarely contribute to the development of positive attitudes and behaviours in the long term. (NCC, 1990, p. 7)

The teaching methods developed in social education, such as discussions, role plays, simulations, case-studies, questionnaires, surveys, group work and problem-solving exercises are those recommended by the NCC for a health education curriculum. These teaching methods rely upon good relationships between teacher and pupil and an open-ended approach to learning. When this style of teaching is undertaken sensitive issues are inevitably raised, some of which may impinge on cultural norms, emphasizing the need for schools to be working closely with parents and the local community (HMI, 1988).

Responses

The confusion over the statutory nature of health education needs clarification by the NCC. The overall statutory aims of the Education Reform Act need to be defined in more specific terms in regard to health education in secondary education. This will reduce the possibility of schools regarding only the National Curriculum subjects within the Education Reform Act as statutory and therefore only teaching the knowledge element of health education. Health education should be included in the monitoring processes which will be carried out to ensure that schools are meeting their statutory requirements. A mechanism for monitoring the effectiveness of health education for pupils from ethnic minorities and multicultural health education for all pupils is essential. Many intended innovations in schools in the past may never have actually occurred or may not have developed as intended (Hall and Loucks, 1978). This may be because it is not always clear to what extent change is either necessary or desirable, or on whose authority it is happening (Ryder and Campbell, 1988). In the present educational climate of secondary schools, the statutory nature of health education within the Education Reform Act needs emphasizing with some authority by the government. The mandatory school development plan represents one avenue whereby the importance of health education can be acknowledged and curricular development fostered.

The issues involved in developing a whole-school approach to health education in the secondary sector may be difficult, even painful. For instance, this can occur when staff attitudes and behaviours, established school practices and cooperation with parents and the local community are examined. The issue of racism is central to this. If health education involves giving pupils the opportunity to exercise decision-making and develop their self-confidence and self-esteem, pupils from ethnic minorities must be accorded equality of opportunity. This will not be achieved without effective policies and procedures in the secondary school structure (Singh Brah, 1988). More ethnic-minority teachers are needed in secondary schools and in senior positions to influence school policy and practice and act as role models for pupils (Nagra, 1989).

LEAs should stress the importance of a whole-school approach to health education within a multicultural context when supporting schools in constructing their development plans. All LEA officers and advisers with responsibility for secondary schools need a knowledge and an understanding of the cross-curricular themes which are interrelated and will require planning together within school development. Many LEAs already have specialist advisers in the areas, who could be used in the provision of INSET for their colleagues.

The senior management of secondary school is central to the development of effective health education for ethnic-minority pupils and multicultural health education for all. Without support from senior management, staff who are committed to health education will lack the power, the influence or the means to implement a whole-school approach. Other staff may regard their own part in health education, particularly in a multicultural context, as unnecessary or undesirable. Senior management in secondary schools need the ability to manage innovation and change in schools. Many senior teachers in school have received some form of management training but there is still a need for a more consistent and ongoing approach to management training in education. Murphy (1992) draws attention to the lack of quality training available for headteachers in contrast to senior management in industry and commerce. An evaluation of the implementation and outcome of a smoking-education innovation in secondary schools found a lack of innovation strategy management in schools. Innovation invariably failed if the teachers, who were expected to deliver the project, were not completely involved in all the decision-making processes (Peers, 1989).

Formulating a school health education policy is the first step towards a whole-school approach in secondary education. Curriculum Guidance No. 5 contains a pragmatic approach to the formulation of school policy and therefore misses an opportunity to address some of the essential issues at the heart of innovation in health education. The manner in which the school policy is drawn up is itself indicative of the values of the management system. Much of health education, particularly within a multicultural context, is about attitudes. Developing and changing staff attitudes is a long-term process. For successful health education, staff need to provide a caring, accepting and open environment for pupils. To do this they must have a similar environment in which to learn and develop themselves. Without self-esteem, pupils cannot make their own healthy decisions; teachers without self-esteem cannot effectively deliver health education. The stress from which many teachers are suffering will reduce their ability to deliver effective health education. The situation needs urgent attention from the government, LEAs and school management. Practical solutions to reducing stress on teachers and providing the sort of health care for teachers that many firms are introducing for their employees are urgently required. If a whole-school approach to health education is to be taken seriously then it has to begin in policy formation with a whole staff, including both teaching and non-teaching members. Staff need time to increase their knowledge and understanding of multicultural health education. They need time to learn and develop teaching methods with which they may not be familiar. They need time to work with each other.

In drawing up a school health education policy, consideration must be given to how the health education needs of the pupils can be identified. This is a complex issue as beliefs about health are socially determined and therefore the greater the difference between teachers' and pupils' backgrounds the more likely their ideas are to differ (Mares, Henley and Baxter, 1985). This can be particularly significant for schools with ethnic-minority pupils and a lack of ethnic-minority staff. There are professionals working with the school, such as doctors, nurses, health visitors, educational welfare officers and health-education officers who are already working in the larger community. Schools should be working in partnership with them, using such experts' knowledge and expertise to develop communication with local communities and in drawing up health education policies. Additionally, as even professional health workers can lack communication with communities, direct communication between the school, parents and the local community is essential. Secondary schools need to become part of the local community. The response by Lancashire County Council to the problems of ethnic minorities' reluctance to use social services has significance for school–community links. The social services' working group cites the need for race issues to be put on the formal agenda of the council, for greater communication with ethnic groups, for managers from ethnic groups and for appropriate representation of ethnic groups at policy and decision-making levels.

In meeting health education needs of pupils, their present health-related behaviour has to be determined. Using an instrument such as Exeter University's Health-Related Behaviour questionnaire can identify incidence and trends in such behaviours. The individual secondary school can plan its health education accordingly to meet the needs of different groups within the school. In considering the health education needs of groups, individual needs of pupils must be taken into account. It cannot be assumed that the health-related behaviours of individuals will be consistent with the norms of the cultural group to which they belong. Furthermore, in secondary schools pupils are in adolescence and it is likely that there will be a questioning of, and conflict with, parental values. Schools need to develop a system which gives teachers time to talk with individual pupils. Some schools, for example, have created small pastoral groups by using as many staff as possible as form tutors or given teachers counselling time when pupils are in assemblies. There is little point in providing this time if teachers are not skilled in listening to pupils. This again emphasizes the need for staff training and development.

Once a health education policy has been formulated it is important that it is put into practice:

> Producing a policy statement may be an important precursor to solving a problem or clarifying confusion but it is no substitute for intelligent action itself. (Wragg, 1991, p. 128)

HMI reports and Curriculum Guidance No. 5 are emphatic that health education has to be properly planned and coordinated. It is easy to map out, across the taught curriculum, content for lessons but less easy to map out methods of approach. The danger of reducing health education to a series of topics has to be avoided. There has to be coordination to ensure that health education is being taught in its broadest sense and that information about pupils such as their cultural backgrounds, attitudes and behaviours and problems is used in this planning. The whole school approach is difficult as there will be diverse needs and interests identified and having to reconcile all these different interests makes compromise inevitable (Ryder and Campbell, 1988). On a positive note, recent research has shown that it is possible to identify elements contributing to organizational health such as consistency and collaboration backed up by values such as trust, openness, clear communication, respect and support for others (Reid *et al.*, 1987). The Health Education Authority's Health-skills Project emphasizes the practicalities of a whole-school approach in its contention that health education must happen not only in the curriculum, but must also be reflected in the corridors and the staffrooms of schools, in relationships with parents and with the community of which that school is a part. Schools which are developing health education for their ethnic minority pupils, such as those in the Blackburn and Preston areas of Lancashire and inner-city areas of Birmingham, are involving parents, the local community and local religious leaders. This community development approach requires a good deal of time and commitment from teachers. It requires sensitivity to listen and to take seriously the views and often disparate values of non-professionals, a willingness to give up one's authority and status, and reconsider preconceptions and beliefs (Henderson and Thomas, 1980). It is essential that any health education carried out by schools with ethnic minority pupils is genuinely enabling to those pupils. Health education needs to be planned and carried out by teachers who understand the daily lives of families from minority ethnic groups and understand the health-related choices available to local communities. A positive, rather than a negative, approach to health education of ethnic-minority pupils is required. There are health concerns and problems which are specific to different cultural groups and these need addressing by schools in partnership which the local community.

Fortunately one LEA, (Manchester), with a significant presence of parents and pupils from a variety of minority ethnic groups, has developed a set of materials addressing cross-curricular themes (see Chapter 2). One set focuses on health education (Ramsay and Sivori, 1991). Six approaches to implementing a health education programme are described. The management and coordination of health education at Key Stages 3 and 4 is presented (pp. 44–97). Links with the other cross-curricular dimensions and the National Curriculum foundation subjects and religious education are presented in relation to:

- healthy eating;
- polution;
- drugs;
- rights and responsibilities; and
- safety.

At Key Stage 4 the development of health education through an industrial topic is described. It too is linked to the other areas of the curriculum. The central activity is a debate around an agreed main motion and a number of subsidiary motions. In the example, the main motion is 'This house applauds the benefits to the Nation provided by the pharmaceutical industry'. There are a further eight subsidiary motions bearing on the main motion and providing an extended structure. These provide pupils with opportunities to explore and debate important facets of the issue. Advice on planning the sessions and preparing pupils is given. Some valuable sources of information are listed.

Across Key Stage topics include 'HIV and AIDS education', 'Caring in a nursery school' and 'Health, safety and welfare'. There is also an example of health education for pupils with complex and severe learning difficulties, based on the topic 'Infection'.

This publication is a very rich and valuable source of information and ideas on implementing the health education curriculum. It deserves wide-spread use.

The good practice in multicultural health education which is developing in individual schools, LEAs and universities must be disseminated nationally to schools. The Health Education Authority should take more responsibility for this coordinating role. They already produce a resource list for health education for ethnic minorities. The list of organizations is useful, to a certain extent, for teachers but the list of publications tends to be for health-care workers. Health-promotion units in areas with a high proportion of ethnic minority pupils can be very supportive, although one unit contacted would only give advice to teachers in their own area. Health promotion units in areas with few or no ethnic minority pupils do not appear to be addressing the need for all pupils to have multicultural health education. This is indicative of the lack of research and development in multicultural health education for all pupils in secondary schools. The issue needs a high profile in the whole educational establishment if teachers are fully to utilize the opportunities offered within the National Curriculum. There is an urgent need for the development of health education resources to meet the needs of contemporary multicultural health education in secondary schools, particularly in light of the National Curriculum. Schools can, however, do an audit of their existing resources. It is likely that there are materials within departments which can be identified for use within the curriculum plan for health education. A useful project for Key Stage 3, for example, is 'Skills for Adolescence' which involves social-education methods and involves parents in workshops. It is important that all resources are analysed for their multicultural context as the hidden messages about race can be powerful. A GCSE biology textbook, for instance, was found to contain only pictures of races other than white in examples of Third-World countries. Pictures of scientists were all of white people. The example is not an isolated one.

The quality of life for pupils in schools has to be addressed if an effective whole-school approach is to be undertaken. The cleanliness of the school, the provision of clean toilets and washing facilities, the healthiness of classrooms, the provision of comfortable areas for pupils at break, are essential. The school has to take responsibility for the health-related behaviour of pupils in its care. Rules which are understood by pupils and consistently applied by staff are essential concerning smoking, drinking alcohol and taking illegal substances. Schools have to ensure that the foods which they are selling pupils in canteens and tuck shops are healthy. Schools have to take responsibility for the dynamic effect they have on relationships between pupils. Unless staff have sufficient training they are often unaware that personal qualities such as self-confidence, consideration for others and communication skills can actually be taught to pupils.

Once schools have established health education within the National Curriculum it is essential that its effectiveness is measured and evaluated, including its impact across different ethnic groups. Too often, because health education is planned and taught, it is assumed that it is effective. There should have been guidelines for evaluation in Curriculum Guidance No. 5. Secondary schools need to develop policies for building effective evaluation into health education as part of whole-school development. The individual pupils must have the opportunity to express their own evaluations openly and honestly if health education is going to be meaningful for them.

These responses have been collated in the light of current development in multicultural health education. It must be concluded, however, that this is an area of education that has received little attention. More research into health education in secondary education, particularly within a multicultural context, is urgently needed.

Cultural and religious differences in relation to diet, clothing, sexual mores, smoking, alcohol and other drugs are the clearly visible tips of the (metaphorical) iceberg of health education. How such differences can be acknowledged and discussed within the cross-curricular theme of health education represents the much more significant concern. If we want our pupils to make informed and rational decisions concerning their own health related behaviours, they need to be aware of the options open to them and of their respective cost to benefit ratios.

Acknowledgement

I acknowledge the support given in this work by Gulab Singh, Health Education Officer in Preston.

References

BALDING, J. (1988) 'Teenage smoking; the levels are falling at last!', *Education and Health*, 6, 3, pp. 38–43.

EDEN, P. (1985) 'A multi-ethnic health related behaviour study', *Education and Health*, 3, 4, pp. 88–91.

EISNER, J.R., MORGAN, M. and GAMMAGE, P. (1988) 'Social education is good for health', *Educational Research*, 30, pp. 20–5.

HALL, G.E. and LOUCKS, S. (1978) 'Teacher concerns as a basis for facilitating and personalising staff development', *Teachers' College Record*, 80, 1, pp. 36–53.

HENDERSON, P. and THOMAS, D.N. (1980) *Skills in Neighbourhood Work*, London, George Allen and Unwin.

HER MAJESTY'S INSPECTORATE (1986) *Health Education from 5–16*, London, HMSO.

HER MAJESTY'S INSPECTORATE (1988) *Health Education for 14–19-Year-Olds in Some Urban Areas of Essex*, London, HMSO.

HER MAJESTY'S INSPECTORATE (1989) *A Survey of Health Education in Secondary Schools in the London Borough of Hillingdon*, London, HMSO.

HER MAJESTY'S INSPECTORATE (1990) *A Survey of Health Education in One Area of Birmingham*, London, HMSO.

LANCASHIRE COUNTY COUNCIL (1991) *The Report of the Working Party on Service Delivery to Black and Other Ethnic Minority Communities*, Preston, Social Services Department.

MALSEED, J. (1990) *Alcohol in Asian and Afro-Caribbean Communities*, School of Independent Studies, Lancaster University.

MARES, P., HENLEY, A. and BAXTER, C. (1985) *Health Care in Multiracial Britain*, Cambridge, Health Education Council/National Extension College.

MITCHELL, K, (1991) 'Claim of racial bias: Ethnic fear of social services', in *Lancashire Evening Post*, 15 March, p. 13.

MURPHY, A. (1992) 'Never Mind the Quality', *The Times Educational Supplement*, 6 March, p. 20.

NAGRA, J. (1989) 'Communicating with Ethnic Minority Parents', *Pastoral Care in Education*, 7, 4, pp. 36–40.

NATIONAL CURRICULUM COUNCIL (1990) *The Whole Curriculum*, York, NCC.

NATIONAL CURRICULUM COUNCIL (1990) *Curriculum Guidance No. 5: Health Education*, York, NCC.

PEERS, I.S. (1989) 'Implementation and Outcome Evaluation of a Multi Site Educational Innovation', PhD Thesis, Manchester University School of Education.

RAMSAY, M. and SIVORI, A. (1991) *Health Education — a cross-curricular theme*, Manchester, Manchester City Council Education Department.

REID, K. *et al.* (1987) *Towards the Effective School; The Problem and Some Solutions*, Oxford, Basil Blackwell.

RYDER, J. and CAMPBELL, L. (1988) *Balancing Acts in Personal, Social and Health Education*, London, Routledge.

SCHOOLS COUNCIL/HEALTH EDUCATION COUNCIL (1977) *Health Education 5–13*, London, Nelson.

SCHOOLS COUNCIL/HEALTH EDUCATION COUNCIL (1982) *Health Education 13–18*, London, Forbes.

SINGH BRAH, H. (1988) 'A "Black Perspective" of Anti-racism in schools', *Pastoral Care in Education*, 6, 4, pp. 14–17.

TEACHERS ADVISORY COUNCIL ON ALCOHOL AND DRUG EDUCATION (TACADE) (1985) *Skills for Adolescence*, Salford, TACADE.

VERMA, G.K. (1989) *Education for All: A Landmark in Pluralism*, London. The Falmer Press.

WRAGG, T. (1991) 'Paper piles that reduce us all to pulp', in *The Times Educational Supplement*, 11 January, p. 128.

Chapter 7

Education for Citizenship

Anne Webster and Clem Adelman

Context

Citizenship education is one of the five 'themes' of the National Curriculum. A cross-curricular approach has been recommended in the guidance contained in the booklet *National Curriculum and Whole Curriculum Planning* (NCC, 1989). The framework is made explicit in *Education for Citizenship* (NCC, 1990), which comprises six sections and two appendices. The five objectives are entitled: content, activities, opportunities, experiences and whole-school policy. *Education for Citizenship* recommends five steps to cross-curricular implementation of Key Stages 1–4. Appendix 1 cites the component 'the citizen and the law' as an example of progression and continuity through the key stages, whilst Appendix 2 gives examples of how all eight components can be developed in the key stages.

Education for Citizenship credits the Speaker's Commission report on citizenship as a main source of reference. The Speaker's Commission 'was established to look at ways in which citizens can participate fully and effectively in society' (House of Commons, 1990). The Commission recognized that British society is changing and that 'Britain has been transformed into a multi-racial society'. This, together with other changes such as income, lifestyle and expectations, require that citizenship with its attendant rights and obligations be reconsidered. The Commission's purpose was to propose ways in which 'participatory arrangements can be strengthened' with a view to creating 'conditions where all who wish to can become actively involved'. Both the study and experience of citizenship 'should be part of every young person's education'.

The Commission's recommendations include a strategy for incorporating the skills, as well as the study of citizenship, across the curriculum. For instance, student-citizenship activities should be included in Records of Achievement and other assessments. Local authorities, the judiciary, civil service, the police and armed services should have 'specific training on the entitlements and duties of citizens' and should know the corresponding obligations of the institutions for which they are employed. The Commission recommends a review and codification of the law 'relating to the legal rights, duties and entitlements of the citizen' and a 'comprehensive citizen's advice service for disadvantaged groups who cannot claim their own entitlements' (House of Commons, 1990). The final recommendations were much concerned with establishing voluntary work for the citizen with appropriate recognition in the honour's system 'as long as [it] exists'.

Defining Citizenship

The Speaker's Commission had problems defining 'citizenship' and used T.H. Marshall (1980) as the starting point. The Commission accepted Marshall's account of the historical progression of citizenship from 'civil' to 'political' to 'social'. 'Citizenship' is thus perceived as a process with emphasis on rights, duties and obligations which appears to be largely equated with voluntary charitable works. Evidence of the desired outcome of citizenship education is a list of skills which include 'participating in elections', 'working collaboratively' and 'protesting, for example, by writing to a newspaper or councillor or local store' — this latter being one of the most significant political involvements of those suggested in the report. The Speaker's report follows a traditional Whig interpretation of citizenship, but in its integrity, questions whether its ideas on citizenship are fully appropriate to a multicultural society.

According to Marshall 'Citizenship requires a sense of community membership based on loyalty to a civilisation which is a common possession'. He does not define who is to be included, or excluded from active citizenship, a point of difficulty when a 'civilisation' may no longer be 'a common possession'. It is by no means clear what are 'rights' or 'duties', or indeed, which is a right or a duty. Whether this approach to 'Citizenship' was ever appropriate is open to question.

Although the Speaker's Commission recognized that 'poverty, bad housing, unemployment, religious, racial and sexual discrimination, physical and mental disability and ill-health' restricts the activity of those who suffer from such disadvantage from becoming full and active citizens, there is no recognition of shelter, work, or a reasonable level of subsistence as a social right of citizens. It was, however, in areas with such conditions, as the Commission on Urban Priority Areas observed in 1986, that there existed social disintegration (Commission on Urban Priority Areas, 1986). It should also be noted that critical incidents of social *malaise* in the 1980s, such as the Toxteth riots, revived interest in the development of citizenly activities.

Curriculum Guidance No. 8 — Education for Citizenship

As the title indicated, Curriculum Guidance No. 8 'offers guidance on ways in which education for citizenship might be strengthened in every school'.

The foreword written by the chairman of the NCC (NCC, 1990) re-commends that elements of citizenship must be taught by means of three identified avenues; National-Curriculum subjects, other provisions in the time-table 'enriched and reinforced' by the third avenue, being the wider activities of the school in the community. The emphasis is on balancing rights with duties and responsibilities in a 'democratic' society. Citizenship is inter-related with the other four 'themes': health education, economic and indus-trial understanding, careers' education and guidance and environmental education. The 'themes' all share features in common, such as 'the capacity to promote discussion of values and beliefs, to extend knowledge and under-standing, to encourage practical activities and decision-making and to strengthen the bond between the individual and the community . . . Schools must lay the foundations for positive, participatory citizenship'. This, NCC No. 8 envisages, is to be accomplished in 'two important ways', by the acquisition of knowledge and understanding of information deemed to be essential and by opportunities and incentives to participate 'in all aspects of school life'.

NCC No. 8 recognizes the efforts of some schools to provide some sort of citizenship education, and cites the survey conducted by the Speaker's Commission as evidence. But this is in no way sufficient for the NCC, which proposes that 'there must be a guarantee that they combine to form a rational entitlement'. However, Curriculum Guidance No. 8 does not set out to be a blueprint of a 'set of lesson plans' but a 'framework for curricular debate'. Within this framework there is envisaged an important role for groups outside school — parents, governors, religious and voluntary groups, indus-try, commerce and so on — in implementing and developing citizenship education. 'Required knowledge' should include 'the nature of community' and 'roles and relationships in a democratic society'. Some reference is made to cultural diversity and changing social values, but duties, responsibilities and rights, irrespective of culture, figure most prominently.

Six cross-curricular skills are identified: communication skills, numeracy skills, study skills, problem-solving skills, personal and social skills and information and technology skills. These are briefly applied to citizenship education, one of the more interesting examples being 'detecting opinion, bias and discussion in evidence, for example, materials about political issues'. Promoting 'positive attitudes' is deemed 'essential if pupils are to value democracy and its associated duties, responsibilities and rights'. This state-ment is followed by a list of what NCC No. 8 considers are desirable personal qualities and activities of the citizen as therein defined (NCC, 1990).

There is clear reference to, and recognition of, the influence of different cultural backgrounds, 'pupils should be helped to develop a personal and moral code and to explore values and beliefs'. NCC No. 8 is also explicit about the manifestation of this code in behaviour, i.e., 'concern for others, industry and effort, self-respect and self-discipline, as well as moral qualities, such as honesty and truthfulness' (NCC, 1990). Implicit in these stated objectives is an assumption of the characteristics of the well-behaved citizen, whatever the personal moral code of individual pupils might be. The emphasis is on behaviour and behavioural outcomes. Although opportunity should be given for pupils to 'compare values and beliefs by themselves and others; to identify common ground' and to 'appreciate that distinguishing between right and wrong is not always straightforward', a moral imperative has been assumed which could raise difficult questions for a multicultural school.

Section 4 headed 'Content' identifies eight 'essential components'. These are 'community', 'a pluralist society', 'being a citizen', 'the family', 'democracy in action', 'the citizen and the law', 'work, employment and leisure' and 'public services'. Britain is described as 'a multi-cultural, multi-ethnic, multi-faith and multi-lingual society' and the component, 'pluralist society', is regarded as having 'an important contribution to make to the promotion of equal opportunities'. It would seem, then, that rights, responsibilities and obligations are the key to these 'essential' components, and knowledge, understanding and justification of these rights and duties, the main content.

In the final two sections NCC No. 8 goes to great lengths to demonstrate the importance of the school in the implementation of citizenship education. 'Education for citizenship promotes the personal and social development of pupils' and encourages them 'to develop caring attitudes and the desire to participate in events'. Encouragement by the school and opportunities to make decisions such as choice in use of pupils' time ('optional curricular elements') and active participation in school councils are essential. The ways in which schools can provide activities, opportunities and experiences are illustrated in key Stages 1–4 in activities on an individual, group and whole-school level. The involvement of local voluntary or statutory organizations, especially the police, should, according to the document, be encouraged.

Challenges

Citizenship education in the National Curriculum presents a number of challenges to teachers, to schools and to pupils. There is clearly a challenge to teachers to investigate new materials, some of which may not be in line with familiar sources or methods, or possibly to produce their own. The Law in Education project evaluation (1989) however, provided evidence that 'teachers were able to adapt and develop courses to incorporate new topics and themes'. Discussion and presentation of controversial issues, such as those relating to race and ethnic differences, require careful handling, and possibly, changes of familiar teaching methods. If, for instance, the resolution of conflict by discussion towards consensus and rational understanding in a multicultural democracy is to be achieved, then current political and social issues need to be faced and tackled in the curriculum.

The problems of teaching about and conducting discussion of controversial issues have been examined from the perspectives of teacher, pupil and education administrators by the 'Humanities Curriculum' project (Stenhouse, 1970; Bailey, 1973) and subsequently by the project *Teaching About Race Relations* (Stenhouse *et al.*, 1982).

A movement away from didactic to less instructional teaching methods, with emphasis on pupil discovery, problem-solving and participation, would seem to be appropriate in the context of education for democracy. In the context of citizenship in a 'moral' democracy, it would also be necessary for the teacher to have an enabling role. That implies development of the powers of young people, in their role as citizens, to reach the kind of rational understanding that is essential for the existence of participatory citizenship, which, according to Habermas (1979), is fundamental to cultural and multicultural development.

The challenge to schools is not only to provide opportunities for citizenship education but also the desire to participate. Education for citizenship, as Vlaeminke and Burkimsher (1992), who examined 'Approaches to Citizenship in a Sample of Schools in Leicestershire and Northamptonshire' conclude that pupils can only learn about the exercise of rights and responsibilities through practical opportunities to do so. Provision of such 'access and empowerment' can be encouraged through the ethos of the school, pupil-centred approaches in the classroom, participation in the activities of an effective school council and a school policy on racial issues are outlined as examples in their study.

In the context of financial Local Management of Schools, it would not be difficult to see how some schools might prefer a bland curriculum to one that presents controversial issues for critical thinking. It is undoubtedly a challenge to citizenship education to encourage a searching approach to contemporary economic, social and political issues. These are the contexts in which the rights, duties and obligations of citizenship may be expressed. A common pupil response to the invitation to exert citizenship rights is 'Why bother? It won't make any difference'. This point of view may be taken as cynical, 'mere reflex', non-constructive and even a denial of community. It is our understanding that this is more a comment on the inequitable distribution of justice in the UK and elsewhere. For many women, justice has not been a prospect even if they were able to assert their rights, whilst children have only recently, through the Children's Act, been given statutory rights to choose, refuse and complain. For those of ethnic and religious minorities the rights, duties and obligations of UK citizens may seem acceptable or offensive. A controversial issue that should form part of school discussions is the on-going debate about the book *Satanic Verses* by Salman Rushdie. Questions arise about whether the volume is blasphemous and offensive to religious groups, although in the UK blasphemy only applies to Judaeo-Christian texts and tenets. The Rushdie case has exposed the split between the Muslim literalists and the interpreters, a split that has its equivalence in Christianity,

Judaism and Sikhism. However, the gap between citizenship and the execution of justice has become highly visible recently through, for instance, the pardon of two of those convicted after the 'Broadwater Farm' riots, and after the trials of the 'Guildford Four' and the 'Birmingham Six'. Pupils and teachers would not be able to avoid comparing these three cases with the proceedings of the 'Guinness' trials, convictions and dismissals. All the accused were citizens but the question is whether they all received the same sort of justice. One could say, however, that there has never been a more apposite moment for teaching about controversial issues and attempting to reach an understanding. For at the very least, the reconstruction of a more cohesive community is at stake.

Implementation of any curriculum for citizenship education is a challenge in itself, requiring funds, time and effort to provide both formal and informal curricula, which require active participation both in and out of school. Education for citizenship will also be a challenge to pupils. They will be required to put an active input into their studies and activities. Demands will be made on them to examine their own norms of behaviour and values especially in relation to pupils from other races and backgrounds.

Whilst much of the National Curriculum is designed to maximize technological and material development there are some cultures that place greater stress on other values. As long as the eventual goal is maximizing technological growth, equality of opportunity and local democratic control, some gaps will remain incompatible. As Feinberg (1983) warns, cohesion of society (which is the underlying aim of citizenship education, as laid down in the National curriculum) 'will depend upon such things as the compatibility of the different frameworks and the way in which members participate in the shared understanding'.

Responses

Teaching Resources

Teaching materials relating to citizenship education in the National Curriculum have been published. Some started by being law-related with aims similar to those stated in the National Curriculum. For example, the Citizenship Foundation was established in September 1989 and was a development from the 'Law in Education' project set up by the National Curriculum Council, the Law Society and the School Curriculum Development Committee. The aim of the foundation, according to the chairman of its trustees, is 'to improve general levels of citizens' understanding of their rights and responsibilities'. The editor of the journal *Citizenship*, Rowe (1990), declared an interest in developing 'positive, participatory citizenship and the legal and moral framework on which it rests'. The emphasis is on knowledge of the law to remove 'fear and ignorance of the Laws, political apathy, lack of respect for the rule of the law', which are elements 'which mitigate against the practising of citizenship' (ibid.). In the conceptual framework for the 'Law in Education' project, Rowe and Thorpe suggest that 'citizens should be able to form judgements concerning the appropriateness of the justice of current legislation and be able to relate this to their own moral code of behaviour' (Rowe and Thorpe, 1990).

This approach was essentially similar to that of *Law Matters* (Webster and Parsons, 1988), the aims of which were to introduce students to the complexities of the law, to encourage critical reflection about effectiveness and its interrelationship with social issues such as family problems and racial discrimination. The units, all of which refer to relevant issues to pupils in the secondary school, require student activity and invite experiential learning. The book was an attempt to move away from the didactic nature of many law textbooks and materials. Enough information is given to enable teachers without legal knowledge to use and develop and apply to the component of 'the citizen and the law' in the National Curriculum.

Another source of materials relevant to citizenship education is the Centre for Citizenship Studies at the University of Leicester with the co-operation of Leicester and Northants Local Authorities, which was set up in response to the Speaker's Commission on citizenship. Its approach is outlined in broadsheet 3 'Citizen Education', which is based on NCC No. 8 but shows concern for the distribution and exercise of power and the settlement of conflict. Emphasis is placed on 'critical listening' and problem-solving and on the importance of the ethos of the school and the informal as well as formal curriculum, such as an effective school council, work experience and activity in the community.

Unresolved Problems

Curriculum Guidance No. 8 reflects some of the areas of uncertainty in the Speaker's Commission report, but although there is a reference to 'the knowledge, skills and attitudes necessary for exploring, making informed decisions about and exercising responsibilities and rights in a democratic society' (NCC, 1990), there is no clear statement about what is meant by 'democratic'. As Carr (1991) points out the document's concept of 'democracy' is neither wholly 'moral democracy' nor wholly 'market democracy'. The notion of the 'moral' democracy implies that 'democracy' is a way of life according to which individuals can fulfil themselves as human beings. This concept (which accommodates the 'classical' and 'liberal' theories of J.S. Mill) involves, according to Peters (1979), concern for the common good, 'principled morality' and 'widespread participation in public life' to avoid manipulation by interest groups. Many demands are made on the citizen in this form of democracy, as Peters understands it: 'he must have a general knowledge of how the political system works, be sensitive to economic and social conditions that it has to shape and by which it is shaped'. This concept of democracy, which is participatory, encapsulates the notion of the rational, critical and active citizen.

On the other hand, Dahl (1985), for example, supports a pluralist, 'market democracy' not because of the moral principles enshrined in the concept, but because it leads to stability which, according to Dahl, leads to happiness. The aim is to maximize the production of goods for its members in order to maximize 'happiness'. Interest groups vie for influence and political power and the role of those not directly involved in government is essentially passive and supportive.

The focus in National Curriculum Council No. 8 is less on rights than on duties, responsibilities and obligations. Whilst 'active participation' through citizenship education should 'provide the motivation to join in', NCC No. 8 does not, however, say in what to join, or what information is essential to enable pupils to 'join in'. The examples given for Key Stage 4, for instance, emphasize the passive role of citizens, learning about how the system works (local government, elections, health legislation, 'the need for controls'). The activity is participation in community-service programmes. This interpretation of 'participation' lends itself to the maintenance of the status quo rather than social and cultural evolution and development through critical analysis.

Whether or not NCC No. 8 is politically neutral is problematic. As Carr (1991) points out, 'positive participative citizenship' presupposes a critical understanding of, and a desire to transcend, the limitations of its own contemporary institutional expression. NCC No. 8, by failing to address the challenge of conflict in a pluralist society, would seem unlikely to convince young people to take part in a decision-making citizenry. Where ethnic minorities are concerned, unless schools and teachers become 'agents for change and challenge as well as of cultural conservation' (Peters, 1966), the problems of citizen participation in an avowed democracy will remain just rhetoric.

The challenge, then, is to develop shared understandings, leading to cultural cohesion and development through the implementation of a curriculum for citizenship, which is based on the notion of active citizenship and effective, critical, participatory democracy.

References

Bailey, C. (1973) 'Teaching by Discussion and the Neutral Teacher', in *Proceedings of the Philosophy of Education Society of Great Britain*, 7, 38.

Carr, W. (1991) 'Education for Citizenship', *British Journal of Educational Studies*, 39, 4, pp. 373–85.

Citizenship (1991) University of Leicester, Centre for Citizenship Studies in Education, 3.

COMMISSION ON URBAN PRIORITY AREAS (1986) *Faith in the City*, London, HMSO.

DAHL, R. (1985) *A Preface to Democratic Theory*, Cambridge University Press.

FEINBERG, W. (1983) *Understanding Education*, Cambridge University Press.

HABERMAS, J. (1979) *Communication and the Evolution of Society*, Chapter 3, Translated by MCCARTHY, T., Boston, Beacon Press.

HOUSE OF COMMONS (1990) *Report of the Speakers Commission on Citizenship*, London, HMSO.

MARSHALL, T.H. (1980) *Citizenship and Social Class*, Cambridge University Press.

NATIONAL CURRICULUM COUNCIL (1989) *National Curriculum and Whole Curriculum Planning*, York, NCC.

NATIONAL CURRIMULUM COUNCIL (1990) *Education for Citizenship*, London, NCC.

PETERS, R.S. (1966) *Ethics and Education*, London, Allen and Unwin.

PETERS, R.S. (1979) 'Democratic Values and Educational Aims', *Teachers College Record*, 80, 3, pp. 463–82.

ROWE, D. (1990) 'Editorial', in *Citizenship*, 1, The Journal of the Citizenship Foundation.

ROWE, D. and THORPE, T. (1990) 'Conceptual Framework for Law in Education, 11–14 Project', London, Citizenship Foundation.

STENHOUSE, L. (1970) *The Humanities Curriculum Project: An Introduction*, London, Heinemann Educational Books.

STENHOUSE, L., VERMA, G., WILD, R. and NIXON, J. (1982) *Teaching About Race Relations*, London, Routledge and Kegan Paul.

VLAEMINKE, M. and BURKIMSTER, M. (1992) Approaches to Citizenship in a Sample of Schools in Leicestershire and Northamptonshire, Unpublished, University of Leicester, Centre for Citizenship Studies in Education.

WEBSTER, A. and PARSONS, C. (1988) *Law Matters*, London, Macmillan.

Chapter 8

Environmental Education

Chris Gayford

Context

Men and Women are not only themselves; they are also the region in which they were born, the city apartment or farm in which they learned to walk, the games they played as children, the old wives' tales they overheard, the food they ate, the schools they attended, the sports they followed, the poems they read and the God they believed in! (W. Somerset Maugham, *The Razor's Edge*)

Worlds of Difference are curriculum materials aimed at addressing the needs of teachers in relation to environmental education and religious education (Palmer and Bisset, 1985). Here the authors draw attention to the various perspectives of different religious philosophies to the environment. Striking examples are given of the attitudes that are promoted towards the natural world which range from subjugation and even exploitation with the human species as dominant to another extreme which includes harmony with nature and respect for living things as part of creation. No particular religion is singled out as being identified with one viewpoint but each is shown to have its own special perspective.

Religion is part of culture and has an important contribution to make but there are other elements which are the focus for more detailed discussion in other sections of this book. Here, in this chapter, a broad view of culture is understood, recognizing a diversity, whose origins can often be found in religion and other belief systems. These in turn relate to the environment in which these cultures are to be found. The links between cultural concerns and those of the environment have recently become increasingly apparent and are summarized in the Assisi Declaration (WWFN, 1986). That this obvious connection should have existed and been rather ignored for so long is mystifying. The curriculum is widening and the holistic approach hinted at by the National Curriculum Council and considered to be an important part of the education of all children has significant implications for environmental education. Part of the task lies in the need for environmental educators to consider the implications of the other cross-curricular elements for them and vice versa.

Before launching on a discussion of the challenges and possible first responses of those with responsibility for environmental education in our schools, we need to understand something of the changes that have occurred in recent years. These changes include fundamental developments in environmental education and related fields. Ever since the introduction of the term 'environmental education', over twenty years ago (Royal Society of Arts, 1970), this aspect of the curriculum in schools has faced problems over its nature and identity (Goodson, 1983; Gayford, 1986). Its roots were in a number of subject areas, particularly rural studies, geography and biology and these varied origins with their different methodologies and traditions have contributed to the confusion. It has taken a long time since these relatively recent beginnings for teachers in other areas of the curriculum to understand what is going on.

For many years environmental education has been marginalized in secondary schools, emerging as a separate subject in the form of 'environmental studies', which was offered by a number of examination boards (e.g., University of London Examining Board, 1988; London and East Anglian Group for GCSE Examination, 1990), or 'environmental science' (e.g., Associated Examining Board, 1990; Southern Examining Group, 1988). In all of these the subject was taken by a minority of pupils, frequently as an option from other more traditional subjects well established in the curriculum; often in rural areas with little of the cultural diversity with which the writers and readers of this book are likely to be familiar. Environmental education has also been treated as an important element of courses, usually those designed for pupils of average or below average ability (e.g., Schools Council, 1970) or as part of a general or liberal-studies course for older pupils (e.g., Association for Science Education, 1981). More recently, elements relating to the environment have been devised within what have now been identified as foundation subjects in the National Curriculum (e.g., Nuffield-Chelsea Curriculum Trust, 1988). Such courses are taken widely in schools throughout the UK.

In the period prior to the Education Reform Act of 1988, although educators were willing to recognize the importance of environmental education, there was little significant penetration of this aspect of education into the secondary curriculum. Part of the problem can be traced to a lack of identity for environmental education and the difficulty that new dimensions to the curriculum face in becoming established, if they are not closely vocationally orientated. Also, environmental education has generally been regarded as an integrated subject (Bull, 1982) and scepticism usually accompanies this type of curricular development in the UK (Goodson, 1983, Gayford, 1986). Indeed parental pressure and an explicit demand for traditional subjects in the curriculum has limited the extension of environmental education in the curriculum as a separate subject.

The National Curriculum has done a good deal, in one way, to overcome some of the problems that have faced environmental education. The identification of cross-curricular dimensions, skills and themes which relate to foundation subjects, but should not receive the same treatment, has helped to clarify thinking and planning (NCC Curriculum Guidance No. 3, 1990). The publication of the Curriculum Guidance document No. 7 (NCC, 1990), concerned with environmental education, was especially significant. However, it must be appreciated that the documents relating to the themes are for guidance only and have no statutory force. This factor alone is seen by many advocates of environmental education as being disappointing. However, it also needs to be viewed positively and as a starting point for planning and further discussion. This discussion includes ways of ensuring that themes such as environmental education and dimensions including cultural considerations are planned in a coherent way.

All of the developments relating to environmental education in the National Curriculum must be viewed against a much broader background of increasing emphasis placed upon the care and protection of the environment by the international community. Influential international reports going back to 1972 have stressed the importance of environmental conservation for human survival (e.g., *Limits to Growth*, Meadows *et al.*, 1972; *The Brandt Report*, Independent Commission on International Development Issues, 1980; *The World Conservation Strategy*, International Union for Conservation of Nature and Natural Resources, 1980 and *The Brundtland Report*; The World Commission on Environment and Development, 1987). Within these reports the need for greater environmental awareness has been identified not only among planners and decision makers but also among the general population in their day-to-day activities. The links between the environment and world development have also been firmly established and made explicit. The international community which has advocated this heightened environmental awareness and which has called for greater action is itself representative of many different cultures.

Despite the rapidly rising profile of the environment on the international political agenda, there has been a surprisingly slow appreciation of the essential role of environmental education in the process of affecting the attitudes and behaviour to the environment of those in society. Perhaps a good starting point for tracing international awareness of the importance of environmental education in the school curriculum are the threefold objectives set down by UNESCO-UNEP (United National Environment Programme) in Belgrade, 1976. These objectives can be simply stated as:

- to foster clear awareness and concern about economic, social, political and ecological interdependence in urban and rural areas;
- to provide every person with opportunities to acquire the knowledge, values, attitudes, commitment and skills needed to protect and improve the environment;

- to create new patterns of behaviour of individuals, groups and society as a whole towards the environment.

In the statements made about environmental education in Belgrade the term 'environment' was used to mean the conditions and influences that affect the life and development of the individual. Broadly, environmental education was taken to be the process which develops knowledge, understanding, attitudes and behaviours in relation to mankind and his or her socio-cultural and biophysical surroundings.

In Tbilisi, the first 'Intergovernmental Conference on Environmental Education' took place in 1977, again sponsored by UNESCO-UNEP (UNESCO-UNEP, 1978). At this conference many aspects of environmental education were drawn together. This gave a valuable platform for discussion not only on what had been agreed already but it also provided a time for formulating recommendations for future action. Special mention was made of the need for a problem-solving approach and it was emphasized that those who were producing environmental education programmes should not be exclusively concerned with disseminating information about the environment and the problems involved. There was additionally and importantly the need to help people to feel that they can participate in communities and as part of a wider society in decision-making. Further it was felt that, since environmental education should be directed to the solution of practical problems of the human environment (often these were complex and multifaceted), an interdisciplinary approach should be adopted. Without this it was felt that it was not possible satisfactorily to study interrelationships or to bring education into proper contact with the community. These aspects, it was stated, would have significant implications for the school curriculum in all parts of the world.

From what has been stated so far, it is apparent that the ultimate purpose of, and justification for, environmental education is now often considered to be education *for* the environment. Education with these objectives is as much concerned with developing knowledge and skills as with attitudes and behaviour which are consistent with conservation. Such education ultimately provides experience in problem-solving, decision-making and participation with consideration being given to ecological, political, economic, social, aesthetic and ethical aspects. Environmental education with these special aims also involves reviewing present attitudes and behaviours so that changes can be encouraged that will help to overcome present environmental problems and to circumvent new ones.

Recently there has been a much greater feeling at an international level that environmental education should be an important part of the school curriculum for pupils and students of all ages and that nations must move towards implementation rather than simply making general statements. Particular evidence for this concern in Europe is shown by the recent resolution of the Council of Ministers of the European Community (1988) in which, as a matter of priority, it is stated that environmental education should be promoted within all schools of the Community. The United Kingdom is party to this resolution and is therefore committed to ensuring that it is part of the general entitlement of all children in school. The rationale for placing such emphasis on environmental education is that, as members of society we all make decisions about how we and other people use the environment. What we do to the environment affects us in all aspects of our everyday lives. As consumers and producers in an increasingly interdependent world, the decisions we make have wide-ranging effects on other people and other living things. As children, these activities usually take place within a relatively narrow range of social contexts which include the home, family, neighbourhood and peers (NCC Curriculum Guidance No. 7). What this document does not state, but from this present discussion it is clearly evident, is that the culture surrounding the children, and with which they identify, is an essential element for consideration.

Environmental education is an important part of a wider strategy to improve the management of the environment and promote satisfactory solutions to environmental issues. As adults our activities as producers and decision makers in the workplace, local, national or international communities, become more significant. In the words of the resolution of the Council of Ministers of the European Community (1988) environmental education 'lays foundations for a fully informed and active participation of the individual in the protection of the environment and the prudent and rational use of natural resources'. All subjects of the curriculum can contribute in different ways and the development of environmental education should not be seen as an additional burden for schools and teachers, nor should it require the insertion of elements foreign to each subject. It is about improving the quality of pupils' experience of the whole curriculum, using curriculum time more effectively and the imaginative use of teaching approaches and resources.

Environmental education seeks to raise pupils' awareness of their environment by developing their knowledge and understanding of the processes by which it is shaped. It also aims to involve them in environmental issues and with the values these embody. In order to achieve these aims, pupils need to develop the skills necessary to become informed about these issues and to take appropriate action in relation to them. Environmental education is thus concerned with attitudes towards and decisions about environmental quality, informed management of resources and the ethical considerations which relate to these. Such attitudes are formed within the cultural context in which the different groups of pupils are living.

Environmental education of the kind recommended in the recent documents so far mentioned should aim to encourage and enable pupils to gain experience of, and become concerned for, the environment in a number of contexts. With these experiences they will then appreciate how human activity, past and present, causes environmental change. The environments studied are likely to include the school, the neighbourhood, contrasting environments which pupils may have visited and distant environments in Britain and the wider world. Environmental education of this kind will encourage pupils to examine and interpret their environment from many perspectives. These, as has been stated, should include the physical, biological, sociological, economic, political, technical, aesthetic, cultural, ethical and spiritual dimensions. Thus all curricular areas are able to contribute to environmental education. The danger in some respects is that environmental education may become the whole of education and its particular identity or the urgency for its promotion may then be lost.

Environmental education within the concept outlined by NCC No. 3 (1990) does have close links and areas of overlap with other cross-curricular themes and contributes to the development of a range of cross-curricular dimensions and skills. In addition, an important contribution will come from the spirit and ethos of the school, its pupils and its staff. This will include the way the school grounds and buildings are managed and the links that exist with the community. Perhaps this can be thought of as the 'culture' of the school. The successful implementation of environmental education will therefore require explicit school policies and careful coordination of work across the curriculum. Consequently, although the formal curriculum is important in environmental education, the informal and hidden curriculum is also highly significant.

The planning required to ensure that throughout the duration of their schooling all pupils have access to a coherent programme of environmental education is a matter for a clearly developed school policy. The access given to children to an environmental education should have regard to pupils' special needs, particular beliefs, gender and cultural background. The implications and opportunities that this presents in a culturally diverse society are apparent but the means of achieving it are less clear. Indeed, whilst environmental education in recent years has taken substantial strides in adopting relevant approaches to achieve the aims outlined so far, the special needs of a culturally diverse society in this context have only just started to become apparent.

Challenges

The challenges to schools in addressing environmental education in the secondary curriculum are considerable and exciting. They are summarized in Table 8.1. The implications of these challenges in the context of the cultural diversity that frequently exists in communities in Britain exemplifies the considerations that need to be taken when cross-curricular themes are introduced and related to cross-curricular dimensions. However, this is simply to make explicit aspects of curriculum planning which may not have been considered prior to the introduction of the National Curriculum but which should now be part of the agenda in all schools.

Table 8.1:   Important Curricular Challenges for Environmental Education

---

1. *Challenges related to the Nature of Environmental Education*
   - Identification of an appropriate curriculum context for environmental education
   - Breadth of scope of this theme
   - Agreement about the purposes of environmental education such as the need to encourage pupils to be responsible consumers or to value and care for the environment

2. *Planning and Management*
   - Relating environmental education to other cross-curricular areas and providing overall coordination
   - Ensuring coherence and progression
   - Identification of appropriate contributions of the foundation subjects
   - The importance of the professional development of teachers through initial training and INSET
   - Assessment should be manageable but relevant to the aims of environmental education
   - Schools should be models of effective environmental management

3. *Content*
   - Provision of a proper structure with appropriate rigour so that subject areas are not unduly affected by an 'issues-based' approach
   - Pupils should be given opportunities to value and evaluate their own environment
   - Environmental issues are often too complex or presented in an over-complex way
   - Links between environmental education and development education need to be increased

4. *Methodology*
   - Approaches are needed which reduce the possibility of indoctrination from teachers
   - Teachers and others producing environmental education resources should be aware of the issues raised in a culturally diverse society
   - The methods used should encourage attitudes of open-mindedness and respect for the beliefs and opinions of others

5. *Context*
   - Development of links between the school and community

The fact that the National Curriculum has helped to clarify an identity for environmental education and to draw further attention to the formal educational considerations of a culturally diverse society are things which can be built upon. The need for proper planning and coordination of a multifaceted curriculum is now particularly apparent. That this planning should aim to achieve a level of coherence that has eluded curriculum planners in secondary schools is perhaps one of the greatest contemporary challenges.

Delivery of the National Curriculum within the foundation subjects has a clear emphasis on developing knowledge and understanding as well as a range of skills among pupils. However, one of the major aims of environmental education is to help pupils to formulate their own attitudes in relation to the environment (NCC Curriculum Guidance No. 7, 1990). Education with respect to attitudes is highly contentious and there must always be concern about the likelihood that enthusiastic teachers may use this as an opportunity to indoctrinate pupils to their way of thinking (Gayford

1987). There is a general tendency in secondary schools to relate environmental education closely with the consideration of environmental issues and problems (Gayford, 1991). In the longer term this is likely to have an adverse effect. If subjected to constant messages of gloom, or apparently insoluble problems, invariably pupils will tire of the message and inevitable frustrations will ensue. Also, issue-based approaches lack the coherence and rigour which is important to those who are either planners, teachers or learners and are the hallmark of the traditional curriculum subjects. While it is important that children should understand the problems facing humanity in relation to the environment, an even more important challenge is to encourage pupils to explore and value their environment so that they develop an appreciation of the natural, built, social and cultural environments in their own area and elsewhere.

An aspect of the problem of recognizing an identity for environmental education has been the very breadth of its scope. On the one hand it seems to encompass the whole of education but at the same time it appears to require of individual teachers a holistic approach. In this way teachers feel ill-equipped to cope with the multiplicity of facets which relate to any aspect of the environment. Clearly the issues which relate to the environment are the concern of everyone in society but many of these issues are extremely complex. This complexity, and the fact that even experts can disagree over significant aspects of these issues, is problematic for teachers and this can easily result in superficiality, lack of balance and professional insecurity. The relationship between the formal curriculum subjects and the chauvinisms that develop around them, resulting in an unwillingness to engage in integrated or cross-disciplinary teaching, have been documented elsewhere (Goodson, 1983, Gayford, 1986). Approaches to raising the professional status of cross-curricular teaching is an essential requirement in ensuring that this part of the curriculum is satisfactorily addressed.

The foundation subjects of the curriculum, geography (1991) and to a lesser extent science (1989), have been identified as the main vehicles for the delivery of environmental education. Following the recent revisions of the science curriculum (1992), it appears that explicit contributions through this particular subject may be substantially reduced. A possible outcome of these developments may be that geography becomes almost the exclusive means of formally including environmental education in the curriculum. In terms of cross-curricular themes being central to the whole curriculum, this situation would be less than satisfactory and possible remedies should be considered.

For many years environmental concern has been associated with white, middle class values (Cotgrove, 1982). Environmental education has still some distance to go in persuading the whole range of people in society that it is not simply a matter of self-interest on the part of a relatively small section of society which is behind this pressure for environmental concern. Part of the challenge is to demonstrate to all sections of society the relevance of environmental education to everyone's needs.

Environmental education has not been identified by the government and educational planners as a priority area for those with responsibility for funding in-service training (DES, 1991) or initial training of teachers (DES, 1989). In the current climate environmental education has to compete with information technology, health education and a broad spectrum of other cross-curricular areas for limited funds and time allocation. Thus a competitive situation has developed to the disadvantage of most cross-curricular areas.

The modern curriculum can appear to be assessment 'driven' and this has been emphasized in the National-Curriculum foundation subjects. Criteria for producing successful curricula are often related to the possible efficiency of the associated assessment. Cross-curricular themes and dimensions, by their very nature, contain essential elements that are notoriously difficult to assess with any reliability. Attitudinal work in schools is not readily amenable to objective approaches to testing. Methods of recording which are reliable, valid and not excessively elaborate are necessary if environmental education is to take its place with the other cross-curricular elements in the whole curriculum with appropriate importance attached to them by pupils, teachers, parents and employers. To ensure that the schools themselves are models of environmental responsibility the managers need to be aware of the implications of the way that the school is actually run. Policies in relation to energy, use of resources, the grounds and other aspects will be important as a background to pupils' learning. Already environmental auditing of schools by pupils is a valuable way to raise pupils' awareness and perhaps also to encourage those who manage schools to adopt 'environmentally friendly' approaches.

Cultural diversity does present some particular challenges to environmental education. Pupils should value their own cultural contribution to the locality and the school but at the same time see themselves as part of a wider community. There are many contexts within the school where this dimension to environmental education can be developed and this also lends itself to the establishment of important links with the local community. Special school assemblies which celebrate the particular qualities of local ethnic groups whose children attend the school, are one method. Visits from local community leaders, emphasis perhaps on food or art in relation to the environment are also themes that are capable of considerable development and have been used as ways of integrating environment and multiethnic society in schools (Greenhough *et al.*, 1991).

There is a close relationship between development education and environmental education (WWFN, 1987). The fact that these contribute significantly to each other has been demonstrated effectively in the global environmental education programme (WWFN, 1988). However, currently there is a common perception in society that many of the major environmental problems, such as deforestation, pollution, population pressures emanate from poor countries and that the reasons for the problems often are the result of naivety or ignorance among the native populations. The opportunities for, and importance of, significant cross-cultural understanding here is considerable. Many of the major charitable organizations such as OXFAM or Christian Aid can provide materials or even speakers who are willing to come into schools and these can be included in planned programmes of activities.

Educational resources and teaching materials are becoming progressively more sophisticated and this is beginning to extend to the inclusion of cross-curricular elements in materials for foundation subjects. There is growing awareness among writers of the need to counter stereotyping but this needs to be used positively and creatively to encourage and enhance cultural understanding. An important element of environmental education is that it should enable pupils to become responsible consumers (Gayford, 1991). This is difficult enough with rapidly changing technology producing a greater range of goods and services. It also has further implications within a culturally diverse society where expectations and needs vary and teachers' awareness needs to be raised to these issues. Different cultures also have different attitudes to their involvement in decision-making. One of the aims of environmental education is to create an environmentally informed society, the members of which can then involve themselves in decision-making about their environment in the context of a democratic society. It is this latter challenge which is perhaps the most important for environmental education within a culturally diverse society. It calls for a range of educationally desirable attitudes including open-mindedness, tolerance, respect for the beliefs and opinions of others and respect for evidence and rational argument. All are prerequisites for cross-cultural understanding and environmental awareness.

Responses

Culture is a complex amalgam of ideology, politics and other factors, some of which relate to the environment, and to how it is perceived, used and explained. Cultural diversity within society and environmental education are important elements in the intricate web of considerations in developing a relevant curriculum. Such development calls for careful planning with co-ordination at the highest level within the school. A recent project currently in progress, funded by the World Wide Fund for Nature and undertaken by the Council for Environmental Education in conjunction with the University of Reading aims to provide a framework for schools to audit, plan, review and evaluate their provision in environmental education. The framework is capable of further generalization to include other cross-curricular elements.

Environmental education has many important features which justify its place in the curriculum. Concerns about the environment are shared now by many people from all walks of life and sections of society. This includes the pupils. Young people have never been better informed about the environment. Environmental education can therefore be said to be highly relevant both to the needs of society and to the pupils' present needs. As a consequence, the inclusion of environmental aspects adds relevance to the curriculum. Relevance here being used in the sense of relating what is being learned in school to the outside world and to preparation for adult life (DES, 1987) and also relevant to the needs and concerns of pupils now. Some schools have pioneered imaginative approaches to their teaching which has helped pupils to focus on their local community and communities elsewhere. Part of this approach has involved pupils in undertaking investigations outside the school to find the effects of cultural diversity in their local environment and the variety of attitudes that exist. Such work may be truly cross-curricular, calling for cooperation from art, information technology, English and drama, history, geography and other departments. Work of this kind may culminate in exhibitions, publications or even professionally produced video films which can be used in school and in the community.

Special environmental education days or even a week with a multicultural bias have been successfully attempted in schools. The enthusiasm of teachers, pupils, parents and local members of the community to join in these events has made them particularly satisfying and has helped to establish or maintain links with the community.

The concern over possible indoctrination referred to previously means that there is an obligation on teachers to be aware of methodologies appropriate for addressing controversial issues. Interactive methods designed to encourage pupils to examine their own attitudes have now been developed for use within many areas of the curriculum which call for this approach (Gayford, 1987, Greig, Pike and Selby, 1989).

The breadth and scope of environmental education together with the complexity of environmental issues call for effective interdisciplinary teaching, drawing upon each of the different foundation subjects. Whilst it is likely that geography teachers will have a great deal to offer and will often be identified as the most suitable environmental education coordinators in the school, the task becomes more demanding as other cross-curricular areas are added, such as education for a multicultural society. This calls for cohesive teamwork backed by appropriate resourcing. Consequently subject teachers all need to be involved, to identify their own contribution and to explicitly plan their outcomes. In many areas of the curriculum, including separate foundation subjects, environmental matters relating to local as well as global issues can be effectively integrated, thereby enriching the existing curriculum. Environmental education involves problem-solving and decision-making approaches. These higher-order abilities are now often advocated for all levels of education (DES, 1988). In these ways environmental education provides a valuable counterbalance to the strictly vocational and utilitarian aspects of education now widely adopted. However, the process becomes even more enriching and rewarding when these essential cross-curricular areas are effectively integrated and presented in a coherent way.

A very helpful manual on environmental education has been produced by a team involving twenty-eight members of the city of Manchester LEA and involving fourteen schools (Greenhough *et al.*, 1991). A 'web' approach is used to indicate diagrammatically some of the environmental issues that a school could include in its cross-curricular work and also shows how environmental issues link with others (p. 14). Although, the manual is designed to cover all ages and abilities of pupils, examples of cross-curricular activities at Key Stages 3 and 4 are included. The first of these concerns the topic of researching, planning and designing a new layout for the city centre, taking into account environmental factors. The second addresses the 'greenhouse effect', the possibilities for national and international action. and the implications of these. Each activity is set out in matrix format: Vertically, there is a list of the activities involved in the project; horizontally, the National Curriculum subjects, other subjects and cross-curricular themes are presented. Within the resultant matrix, under the subject headings, are listed specific Attainment Targets covered by the activities involved in the project. Both of the examples described provide a valuable means for teachers to develop cross-curricular activities. The multicultural aspect of a particular activity can be readily introduced into the matrix by adding to the list of activities ones which require pupils to consider cultural diversity. For example, in the first activity, 'What cultural groups are there in the city? How large are these groups? What are their housing, work, religious and leisure patterns?' would raise awareness of the diversity of the city's population. This could lead, for example, to a subsequent but related activity such as 'Identify the views and interests of all cultural groups within the city on how the city centre should be developed' and (adapting one of the activities listed) 'Use a computer to analyse responses to the questionnaire and/or to design and print alternative maps of the city centre'.

A detailed example of work undertaken in St. Alban's High School concerned pupils at Key Stage 3, Year 9. The topic was 'weather'. The organization of the activity is based on two planning sheets. The first is known as a 'turtle', because of the visual pattern that results. It helps those involved become aware of the cross-curricular nature of the topic. The second planning sheet is designed to help teacher and pupils analyse the topic into its component activities from which learning outcomes can be assessed. The links between the activities and the subjects and cross-curricular themes of the NC are then described in detail. The sheer curricular richness of topic work is clearly demonstrated in the manual. Again, as in the example given above, multicultural aspects could easily be made explicit by the addition of activities that required the implications of cultural diversity to be considered, explored, analysed, discussed and recorded.

Planning for a coordinated approach to environmental education will be achieved by a school policy which relates environmental education to the components of the whole curriculum, which includes consideration of the implications of ethnic diversity, and ensures progression and continuity.

Many LEAs already have a policy for environmental education and multicultural education, sometimes within the context of a broader LEA policy. Schools are likely to refer to such LEA policies when developing their own. Developing a school policy for environmental education and multicultural education is an important step because such a policy:

- provides a rationale and a framework for these areas of education;
- ideally involves all members of the school community in its formulation and commits them to it; and
- communicates the school's intentions to everyone with an interest in the school.

The following list of questions outline some of the major considerations in either developing, devising or reviewing a school policy.

- Does the school have a policy for environmental education and multicultural education? If so, who contributes to its development?
- How is it communicated to the LEA, governors, staff, pupils, parents, the wider community?
- How is the policy linked to the identification of resource and INSET needs?
- Does the school have guidelines available to all staff on these areas of education which includes explicit content as well as advice to help teachers handle controversial environmental and multicultural issues? Do they address the formal and the informal curriculum?
- How are the school's environmental and multicultural education programmes to be managed and coordinated? Does policy take into account other cross-curricular areas in the context of both environmental education and multicultural education?
- Does the school's policy include the use of the school buildings and grounds, including their use for educational purposes? For example, does the school have an energy-conservation policy or does it recycle any of its waste?
- Does the school have a programme of visits, fieldwork, community involvement or other activities that relate to environmental education and multicultural education?
- How does the school plan for progression and continuity in these areas of education across phases?
- Does the school library or resource centre reflect the school's policy and offer appropriate resources?
- Does the school encourage pupils' involvement in projects aimed at protecting and improving the environment and involving the local community?
- Does environmental education and multicultural education regularly feature on the agenda of staff and governors' meetings?

- How does the school intend to develop, monitor and evaluate its policy for environmental education and multicultural education?

These bases for devising a school policy for environmental education and multicultural education can then be used to identify INSET needs and usefully point to appropriate directions for initial teacher education using schools as models for curricular management.

The response of those with responsibility for the curriculum in schools in relation to environmental education in a culturally diverse society, with a variety of ethnic groups, is likely to be by starting with the local community (DES, 1989). Environmental education can therefore be a unifying factor within a school, drawing together people from different cultures into a situation where they can better understand and value each other's traditions. Schools in different situations have found a variety of approaches to providing pupils with the opportunities to undertake work of this kind (see the World Wide Fund for Nature *Assembly Project*, 1988, which encourages pupils to share in the different cultural traditions of children within the locality, or the example in National Curriculum Guidance No. 7, 1990, pp. 26–27, in which children exchange information with others elsewhere in the country or overseas). Local management of schools and the increased responsibility and involvement of governors provide significant opportunities for developing effective partnerships with parents and the local community.

All of the responses so far discussed will make a valuable contribution to the education of each child; however, unless suitable and manageable methods of assessing or evaluating pupil attainment and experiences are developed, they are unlikely to be given high priority. Clearly, formal assessment through written tests will not be appropriate to cover the affective aspects of the curriculum incorporated in these cross-curricular dimensions and themes. Records of Achievement and Pupil Profiles, which are in the process of development, if related back to the relevant objectives, are much more likely to be effective in demonstrating both the value placed upon it by the school and reminding pupils and parents of its importance. Schools have an important role in formulating their own methods of recording and profiling to reflect their own needs and situations.

Ultimately, perhaps, the main purpose of the cross-curricular elements of the curriculum is related to attitude development. The knowledge, understanding and skills are the means of addressing these attitudes in an educationally acceptable way. Environmental education is but only part of an even wider, whole curriculum. Teachers and teacher educators must be reflective practitioners using their own experiences and the activities they engage in with their students to explore new and more effective approaches. It seems that we have only just begun to develop in these areas and we have much to learn from each other. There is a need for appropriate research and an input into environmental education from people with culturally diverse backgrounds and experiences of working with pupils from different cultural groups. From the point of view of those who advocate environmental education and those who plan for appropriate education in a culturally diverse society, the attitudes listed among the objectives for environmental education in Curriculum Guidance No. 7 (NCC, 1990) provide a valuable and thought-provoking set of aims, 'Promoting positive attitudes to the environment is essential if pupils are to value it and understand their role in safeguarding it for the future. Encouraging the development of the particular attitudes and personal qualities will contribute to this process.'

- appreciation of and care and concern for the environment and for other living things;
- independence of thought on environmental issues;
- respect for the beliefs and opinions of others;
- respect for evidence and rational argument; and
- tolerance and open-mindedness.

References

ASSOCIATED EXAMINING BOARD (1990) *Advanced Level Syllabuses*, Guildford, AEB.

ASSOCIATION FOR SCIENCE EDUCATION (1981) *Science in Society*, London, Heinemann.

BULL, S.J. (1981) *Beachside Comprehensive School*, Cambridge, Cambridge University Press.

COTGROVE, S. (1982) *Catastrophe or Cornucopia?*, Chichester, John Wiley and Sons.

COUNCIL AND THE MINISTERS OF EDUCATION MEETING WITHIN THE COUNCIL (1988) 'Resolution on Environmental Education', *Official Journal of the European Communities*, No. C177/8.

DEPARTMENT OF EDUCATION AND SCIENCE (1987) *The National Curriculum 5–16: A Consultation Document*, London, HMSO.

DEPARTMENT OF EDUCATION AND SCIENCE (1988) *The National Curriculum Task Group on Assessment and Testing: a report*, London, HMSO.

DEPARTMENT OF EDUCATION AND SCIENCE (1989) *Initial Teacher Training: Approval of Courses, Circular No. 24/89*, London, HMSO.

DEPARTMENT OF EDUCATION AND SCIENCE (1989) *Science in the National Curriculum*, London, HMSO.

DEPARTMENT OF EDUCATION AND SCIENCE (1990) *Environmental Education from 5–16*. Curriculum Matters No. 13, HMI Series, London, HMSO.

DEPARTMENT OF EDUCATION AND SCIENCE (1991) *Geography in the National Curriculum (England)*, London, HMSO.

DEPARTMENT OF EDUCATION AND SCIENCE (1991) *Grants for Educational Support and Training for 1992–3*, London, HMSO.

GAYFORD, C.G. (1986) 'Environmental Education and the Secondary School Curriculum', *Journal of Curriculum Studies*, 18, pp. 147–57.

GAYFORD, C.G. (1987) 'Environmental Indoctrination or Environmental Education', *Environmental Education*, 27, pp. 8–9.

GAYFORD, C.G. (1991) 'Environmental Education: A Question of Emphasis in the School Curriculum', *Cambridge Journal of Education*, 21, 1, pp. 73–9.

GOODSON, I.F. (1983) *School Subjects and Curriculum Change: Case Studies in Curriculum History*, London, Croom Helm.

GREENHOUGH, P., HYDE, M., KIRBY, B. and MURRAY, P. (1991) *Environmental Education: a Cross-curricular Theme*, Manchester, Manchester LEA.

GREIG, S., PIKE, G. and SELBY D. (1989) *Greenprints*, London, Kogan Page.

INDEPENDENT COMMISSION ON INTERNATIONAL DEVELOPMENT ISSUES (1980) *North-South: A Programme for Survival*, The Brandt Report, London, Pan Books.

INTERNATIONAL UNION FOR CONSERVATION OF NATURE AND NATURAL RESOURCES (1980) *World Conservation Strategy*, Gland, Switzerland, IUCN-UNEP-WWF.

LONDON AND EAST ANGLIAN GROUP FOR GCSE EXAMINATIONS (1990) *GCSE Syllabuses 1991–92*, East Anglian Board, Colchester; London Regional Examining Board, London.

MEADOWS, D.H., MEADOWS, D.L., RANDERS, J. and BEHRENS, W.W. (1972) *Limits to Growth: A report for the Club of Rome's Project on the Predicament of Mankind*, London, Pan Books.

NATIONAL CURRICULUM COUNCIL (1990) *Curriculum Guidance No. 3: The Whole Curriculum*, York, NCC.

NATIONAL CURRICULUM COUNCIL (1990) *Curriculum Guidance No. 7: Environmental Education*, York, NCC.

NUFFIELD-CHELSEA CURRICULUM TRUST (1988) *Nuffield Co-ordinated Science*, Harlow, Longman.

PALMER, M. and BISSETT, E. (1985) *Worlds of Difference*, Glasgow, Blackie.

ROYAL SOCIETY OF ARTS (1970) *The Countryside in 1970, Third Conference*, Birmingham, Kynoch Press.

SCHOOLS COUNCIL (1970) *Geography for the Young School Leaver*, Waltham on Thames, Nelson and Sons.

SOUTHERN EXAMINING GROUP (1988) *GCSE Syllabuses 1990–91*, Guildford, Southern Examining Group.

UNESCO-UNEP INTERNATIONAL ENVIRONMENTAL WORKSHOP (1976) 'A Global Framework for Environmental Education: The Belgrade Charter', *Connect* 1, 1, p. 5.

UNESCO-UNEP (1978) *Intergovernmental Conference on Environmental Education, Tbilisi, USSR, Final Report*, Paris, UNESCO.

UNIVERSITY OF LONDON EXAMINING BOARD (1988) *GCSE Syllabuses, 1989–90*, London, ULEB.

WORLD COMMISSION ON ENVIRONMENT AND DEVELOPMENT (1987) *Our Common Future*, The Brundtland Report, Oxford, Oxford University Press.

WORLD WIDE FUND FOR NATURE (1986) *Messages on Man and Nature for Buddhism, Christianity, Hinduism, Islam and Judaism*, The Assisi Declaration, Gland, Switzerland WWF International.

WORLD WIDE FUND FOR NATURE (1987) *Global Environmental Education Programme*, Surrey, Richmond Publishing Co.

WORLD WIDE FUND FOR NATURE (1988) *Assembly Project: Resources and Ideas*, WWF in Association with Canada Life, London.

Part 3

Other Cross-curricular Dimensions

Chapter 9

Countering Racism in British Education

Horace Lashley and Peter Pumfrey

Context

Whether explicit or implicit, animosity, antagonism and acrimony between groups of any description lead to further social distancing and mutual suspicions. Highly visible (i.e., coloured) British children of parents from minority ethnic groups are typically on the receiving end of the adverse consequences of discriminatory beliefs and behaviours of the majority (white) groups (CRE, 1991). The riots in Los Angeles, San Francisco and Atlanta in May 1992 provide a salutory warning and a reminder of riots in this country in the 1980s and the continuing presence of our own cultural, ethnic, religious and socio-economic tensions reflected in the pupils attending our schools. The tragic death of Arif Roberts, a 15-year-old black pupil attending Gladesmore Comprehensive School in Tottenham illustrates the destructiveness and futility of racial hatred.

On 20 September, 1990, tension between black and Vietnamese pupils attending Gladesmore Comprehensive School in Tottenham is reported as having led to a fight between the groups during a game of football. According to the prosecuting counsel, 'It was a trivial dispute over a ball. A fight broke out between the blacks and the Vietnamese and the Vietnamese got the worst of it. They planned revenge and recruited other Vietnamese youths to come to the school and fight'. The following day, a group of Vietnamese pupils, including a 16-year-old Vietnamese from south-east London, arrived at Gladesmore School. Some of them were armed with knives.

Arif Roberts left the school by the school gates at lunch time. He was set upon by the Vietnamese. The 16-year-old Vietnamese defendant is alleged to have thrust a knife into Arif's neck and to have severed his jugular vein. Arif died as a consequence. His assailant was identified by three girls from the school and was arrested. He denies murder. His trial began in August 1992. Arif is reported as having had nothing to do with the original argument. 'He was the wrong person in the wrong place at the wrong time' according to the prosecutor.

How can such destructive interethnic antagonisms be avoided and dealt with constructively? Both interminority ethnic group tensions and minority ethnic-group discord must be addressed. Numerically, the greater number of confrontations, verbal and physical, is likely to be between ethnic minorities and the white majority group. It is towards the latter that we turn our attention.

The delivery of the National Curriculum to all pupils cannot be achieved unless the ethos of a secondary school is based on a policy of equal opportunities backed up by effective practices. Unless these conditions are consciously aimed at, the actual content of the National Curriculum becomes an irrelevance. Hence this chapter is concerned with the nature of racism in British schools and with means of countering it. Success cannot be guaranteed, but countering racism must be a central educational objective. Acknowledging and recognizing it in individuals and institutions is a necessary but not sufficient condition for success.

Since the establishment of the post-war black British community, racism has been a major characteristic of many interactions between the black community and the dominant white society. The social interaction between the groups has highlighted a significant contradiction between the economic usage of the black community and the resentment continually enacted and displayed against them by the host society. Sivanandan (1983) has pointed out that racism is about power and 'not about prejudice'. Secondly, he argued that racism never stands still, 'it changes shape, size, colours, purpose, function — with changes in the economy, the social structure, the system and, above all, the challenge, the resistance to that system'. In the fields of employment, education, housing, health and criminal justice, minority ethnic groups are still discriminated against (CRE, 1991).

In order to understand the dynamics of racism in the current relationships between the black British community and the dominant white communities, it is helpful to consider the struggles of the black community since the 1950s. Since then, some manifestations of racism have been reduced through legislative action and policy development aimed at providing equality of opportunity in an atmosphere of community antiracist struggle. The dangers of marginalizing minority ethnic-group members have long been warned against (Lashley, 1984). The struggles of the black communities resulted, particularly in the early 1980s, in some major shifts in the advocacy and implementation of effective equal opportunity and antiracist policies. This was accompanied by a heightening in the campaign against the high-street visibility and activities of racist groups and individuals (CRE, 1987a; and 1987b). McIlroy (1987) argued, 'it is clear that the present situation in Britain represents a failure of political nerve, political strategy and political action. There is a need for new policies. It is also clear that the implementation of any such policies will have to take account of the growing activism of the Blacks themselves and their increasing impatience with their continued standing as second class citizens.'

During the past thirteen years of Conservative government, the New Right movement substantially increased its influence on central government policy. This had a negative effect on the antiracist policies and practices that earlier had begun to emerge, more particularly from local government. Where it seemed that such policies were becoming effective, the institutions and structures responsible for creating them were removed or, at best, starved of resources. This was exemplified in the dismantling of the Greater London Council (GLC) and the Inner London Education Authority (ILEA). The action was defended as a demonstration of central government resolve against alleged inefficiencies and poor standards.

Education has been a prime target of the New Right. The *Salisbury Review Journal* has provided a platform for the movement's views. Gordon (1988) argued that the New Right was increasingly setting the terms of the debate around education in Britain. Sarup (1991) suggests that 'this shift has taken form since the victory of Thatcherism and that it was ideologically prepared'. In many ways the 1988 Education Reform Act (ERA) became the Trojan horse of the New Right. What do the ERA changes hold for the black British population, bearing in mind the racist ideology which underpins the political motivation of some of the ERA's proponents? It is the intention of this paper to explore this issue, with particular reference to secondary education.

Challenges

The consideration of racial issues in an educational and curriculum context has seemed essential to some people, but less so to others. The curricular responses to an increasingly visible multicultural and multiracial society during the 1970s and early 1980s were related to an increasing consciousness in schools to these changes within society. During the period we moved from the initial stages of integrative multiculturalism, where the focus was primarily on an adaptive culturalization of the school curriculum, to a more advanced stage of antiracism where the focus for change became social structures and institutions. From small beginnings, there was a mushrooming of social consciousness concerning institutional racism. This resulted in the development of antiracist policies over a wide range of local-education authorities in the statutory school years in general and more particularly in the primary sector. This development encapsulated a complex process of challenge, campaign and shifts in thinking by both minority and majority ethnic groups.

Currently there appears to be considerable evidence of a substantial loss in the gains that had been made in developing antiracist strategies and multicultural curricular responses. Troyna (1989) suggests that 'as we enter the 1990s it is clear from research into the attitudes of students and practising teachers, analysis of local education authority (LEA) policy documents and scrutiny of school handbooks and curriculum plans that monocultural education continues to have a compelling attraction for administrators, governors and practitioners in the UK.' This is not the intention of the NCC (NCC, 1990).

The 'Standards' Debate and Multicultural Education

The concerns that have been expressed about standards in education, particularly in the latter part of the 1980s and early 1990s, seem to have affected many innovative curricular developments including those that had evolved in response to aspects of multiculturalism. Palmer (1986) taking an anti-multiculturalist stance aptly cites such an example in the following: 'In February 1985, an ILEA school governor revealed that candidates for first appointments or promotion were, during interview, virtually obliged to "mouth the accepted platitudes" (about "multiculturalism" and mixed-ability teaching) as if they were the Nicene Creed'. In 1992 the effects of the Los Angeles riots may encourage a rethinking of such positions. Informed self-interest has considerable merits: it requires reciprocity.

Central government education policy developments that have taken place in the last decade advocated innovation to meet criticisms of the curriculum and of general education standards. This move has been considered in some quarters to be unfortunate. It has shifted the focus of the debate from the wider issues of performance and the causation of underperformance, to a narrower political explanation in which market ideology dominates, but masquerades as concern in the interests of all. One example of this has been the reforms around parental choice and 'opting out' of schools. It is argued that the average parent has been given greater control over the choice and type of child's education, a right to be heard 'if you think things are going wrong' and regular information (DES, 1991). In reality, this cannot work. There continue to exist choices more clearly available to middle class, articulate white parents (*TES*, 1991).

Innovations which address the issues of equality of opportunity have fallen out of favour. Such ideas have been referred to as 'loony': the product of the (political) left. Equality of opportunity is concerned with the issue of 'standards'. Despite this, a number of people have been using the appeal to 'standards' to counteract many developments which were intended to improve 'standards', particularly of members of certain minority ethnic groups. Thus, Section 11 funding has been capped and restricted to particular groups of immigrants. Commentators appear much more concerned that the traditional curriculum had been adversely tampered with, rather than with evidence on this point at the secondary school level. Additionally, for those minority group students who had not succeeded, it was easier to look for failure in a generalized causation related to curricular approaches which were derogatively labelled and deemed to be discredited.

The radical developments and curricular innovations that had taken place from the 1960s onwards were viewed as politically tied to the Labour movement and were part of a long-standing campaign for egalitarianism. The attempts to draw away from the grammar school ideal were seen by conservative education thinkers to be undermining the quality of educational outcomes. The major issue was the concept of excellence and not egalitarianism which, for them, was a non-argument. Green (1988) emphasizes this point in the following argument: 'Almost no one has a good word to say about the idea of equality of opportunity. It is as if the intellectual community has moved beyond it.'

Green further develops his argument as follows: 'But perhaps the most damaging criticism which has been levelled at the concept of equality of opportunity is that it is an ethical monster, realizable only in a grotesquely bureaucratic state pursuing intolerant political claims and driving roughshod over the particularistic integrity of the traditional family'. In education this position must be challenged. Excellence and equality of opportunity are complementary, not incompatible.

The increasing numbers of black children in British inner-city schools from the late 1950s onwards provided a major diversion from the wider challenges of educational underachievement (see Volume 1, Chapter 3, and Volume 2, Chapter 2). Both issues were seen to be related to 'immigrant' educational underachievement. It was argued that the principal educational impediment of these children in their new 'home' was that of cultural difference. A related obstacle was thought to be language, since many of the 'immigrants' were often initially non-English-speaking. This two-factor impediment led to a particular ethno-racial response. Children from Caribbean backgrounds were perceived as having a limited but workable cultural and language similarity to the white British population. In contrast, those from the Indian subcontinent were seen principally as in need of substantial English language input. It was not very long before the emerging performance patterns of the two major black 'minority' communities took on a life of their own (Taylor and Hegarty, 1985; Verma and Pumfrey, 1988; Pumfrey and Verma, 1990). The early responses to these factors assumed to affect the achievement of minority 'immigrant' children, initially took on the mantle of an ethnic-minority specific programme of cultural assimilation. The early period of this monocultural educational response was characterized by the need to assimilate minority children into the dominant culture. Lynch (1987) classified this as the 'immigrant and ESL' phase. He argued that the issues were perceived almost exclusively as an immigrant problem centred on, caused by and restricted to immigrants.

Underachievement

Over the period of the last three decades there continued to accumulate evidence of the underachievement of minority children almost to a point of the institutionalization of that experience. In this generic classification of minorities, there has developed what is almost a 'league table' of achievement of the various ethnic minority groups. Pupils from minority ethnic groups differ in terms of their *mean* scores on various educational attainments in more complex ways than is suggested by a simplistic 'league table'.

Much of the underachievement identified was located in the educational experience of Afro-Caribbean children (Verma and Pumfrey, 1988). It was argued, by some, that children of Asian background showed less under-achievement once their problems of language had been overcome. The National Association of Schoolmasters/Union of Women Teachers (NAS/UWT) (1985) divided the major ethnic groups in a way that highlighted the ethnic divide referred to previously.

Current research has indicated quite clearly that relating ethnic categories to educational success and failure had not fully indicated the complex patterns of underachievement manifest amongst the minority communities (Tanna, 1990). Recently, it has become evident that some children of particular Asian backgrounds are at the very bottom of the performance league (DES, 1985; CRE, 1990). This evidence contradicted an earlier widespread belief in a pattern of 'Asian success' and 'Afro-Caribbean failure'. The wider issues of educational underachievement were shifted from the central arena of debate and made into a problem caused, in part, by the presence of black pupils in British schools (see Chapter 12). The recent 'Dewsbury affair' highlights the effect of this 'blame transference' and points clearly to the way in which racism and some of the New Right campaigns benefit from the making of black children a 'problem' in the education system, using them as scapegoats, allegedly 'holding back the progress of white children' (Lashley, 1986; 1987).

That Britain is a multicultural multiracial society is now substantially accepted. In reaching this broad acceptance there has been a metamorphosis over time involving successive phases advocating assimilation, integration and, eventually, forms of cultural pluralism. This evolved in a framework of race relations and racial contact that has been fraught with racial prejudice, discrimination and, more recently, various forms of extreme racial intoler-ance. There are strong historical roots to this perpetrated both by a hidden and formal 'racialist agenda' (Fryer, 1988).

Despite the continued existence of racism, British society has come a long way (CRE, 1991). Developments have, in part, fulfilled the hopefulness of the words of Lester and Deakin (1967). They argued, that 'there is the paramount necessity for keeping our nerve. Too many people of all shades of opinion are now prepared to accept a determinist analysis of the situation in which the downward path to racial violence is seen to be inevitable. We would argue, on the contrary, that the situation in Britain is capable of being governed so as to achieve racial equality'. In many ways that hopeful vision bore limited fruit in circumstances when there was the political will for such measures. In the 1970s, the numbers and concentrations in specific areas of minority ethnic groups were much smaller and less visible (see Chapter 2 and

Volume 1, Chapter 3). As groups increase in size, their aspirations involve changes in existing power structures in a society. Tensions rise unless there is community cohesion and some sense of 'fairness' is accepted in how 'the system' works across ethnic groups.

In the 1970s and early 1980s a vision of equality of opportunity was perceived and antiracist developments flourished. Pearce (1986) describes it from a New Right perspective. This distorted the rationale underpinning antiracism and created a sensationalist view, distracting from the legitimacy of the movement. 'It possesses a secular version of a religious zeal, the end of which is to purge Western civilisation of evils which are seen as ingrained or "structural". It is born of both liberal and Marxist thinking and older, less rational, urges. A desire to free the oppressed is a powerful motive but not its only one — there is also hatred for the "system". The progressive temperament rejects the past and is thus enabled to accumulate the grudge holders and those whose satisfaction is to be against. It is egalitarian, of course, Utopian certainly, relativist at bottom and incipiently totalitarian'. When the 'rabid right' addresses the 'loony left', a dialogue between the deaf ensues by virtue of dangerously incompatible value systems.

Pearce's description fails to reflect any of the social realities of the period for Britain's black population. It also fails to appreciate the fact that minority groups were much more preoccupied with playing their part in the 'system' than with trying to destroy it. Despite this, the reality for them was that, after nearly three decades, they were still made to feel 'outsiders'. More particularly, their life chances and employment opportunities had not changed in any significant way during that period (CRE, 1991).

Current Race-relations Policy

Current race relation thinking and policy from central government have now reverted towards an assimilationist integrationism as the underlying principle of planning and provision. Local government agencies and authorities, which until recently had a more forward looking antiracist policy, have in many cases begun to retrench. This may lead to a system of race relations which is based on an economic theory asserting that individuals and groups find their own levels under 'market-place' forces of a capitalist society.

At some point the issues of inequality built up over the centuries in the relationships between Britain and its empire, from which the vast majority of the British black minority communities had originated, have to be addressed (see Volume 1, Chapters 9 and 11). The fact remains that a great deal of curricular material used in schools has been criticized for many years as being negative and damaging to the images of black children in British schools. This observation seems to have been of little importance to those advocating the policy in education of market-place mechanisms. The New Right is suggesting a blinkered determinism concerning the nature of standards in education. This is leading to a narrow prescriptive approach to education. It suggests that issues, such as ethnic diversity, may be seen as a diversion from the central concern of providing 'good education'. Such a view detracts from the wider equal opportunity issues that were debated through the 1970s and 1980s.

Concerns about standards in education are not confined to the Right. Many people in the black community are also worried about the effects of underachievement on the life opportunities of their children (Saba Saakana and Pearse, 1986). This concern was related as much to poor standards in basic subjects as it was to progressive curricular innovation that occurred in those schools where black children were more likely to attend because of the nature of the migration location patterns, both in terms of work and residence, which their parents experienced.

Responses

A Black-community Response: Supplementary Schools

The black community responded to the educational failure and underachievement of their offspring through the development of a supplementary school system. This operated outside of the normal school time and became popularly known as the 'Saturday school movement'. The movement was developed along a format with three approaches: (a) basic academic supplement, (b) cultural and language enrichment, and (c) the combined format of (a) and (b). The movement was crucial because it challenged existing failure regimes by meeting the needs of their children through a system of self-help (Jones, 1986). Despite the establishment of the National Curriculum, these supplementary schools continue to grow. The movement to establish separate schools for pupils of the Muslim religion is a related issue (see Chapter 2). Are such moves in the interests of racial harmony? There are no simple answers.

Local education authorities responded to the supplementary schools movement in various ways. Most felt that, in order to deal with the issues concerned, they were either to be addressed across the board or not at all. The 'ghetto' approach was looked on with suspicion. Many LEAs which were initially suspicious became more sympathetic to the movement in later years. The ILEA in particular made resources available for the appointment of teaching staff. Other authorities provided low-cost and often 'no-cost' accommodation. The main minority teachers' organizations, including the principal national ones, i.e., Association of Ethnic Minority Teachers (ATEM) and the Caribbean Teachers Association (CTA), rallied round the movement by both supplying teachers and making curricular inputs. Evidence on the academic consequences is not readily available, unfortunately.

Multicultural Education: An Answer to the Needs

Multicultural education emerged within a liberal political environment of the 1960s and 1970s. It developed as a major response to an educational and career crisis faced by many minority ethnic group adolescents. The challenges posed by the rising 'immigrant' school population of the period were new to the British school system. A feature of the response to the needs of such pupils was an isolation of that response to members of the immigrant group.

A major disadvantage resulted from this approach to multicultural education. It was seen as 'something to do with black kids'. It was largely 'within-pupil' and 'within minority ethnic groups'. As a consequence it was not seen as relevant to white children and others not geographically connected with the inner city. In some ways this meant that the black community did not always feel that multicultural education had any real currency for them, despite claims that it led to the improvement of self-image and was a response to cultural needs. It was considered in some quarters that this was not looking at the basic educational needs of the black child, but further adding to his or her disadvantage by not focusing on the central areas of the curriculum on which they would have been judged i.e., attainments. There was also a disproportionately limited number of black children in selective schools. This pointed to a narrowing of their educational experience and opportunity in the British school system. Multicultural education emerged as a response with limited scope to challenge the very system that had caused and maintained the educational debilitation experienced by its recipients. Multicultural education was seen by some as a system of educational 'undersell' to the black community (Stone, 1981; Grinter, 1990a). This did not mean that there was no serious consideration of curriculum development which addressed equality of opportunity in its widest sense. There was concern about an approach that left the Eurocentric core intact. In the process, this perpetuated the same disadvantages which were initially responsible for the inequality both in curriculum content and outcome effects.

Multicultural Education and All-white Schools

For a long time there has been a great deal of resistance from many schools, with very few or no minority ethnic group pupils, to undertake curriculum innovation on the issues of a multicultural society. Any curricular issues that drew attention away from the traditional Eurocentric curriculum were suspect. This meant that multicultural education was seen as a matter that concerned schools with a multicultural and multiracial population.

Until the publication of *Education for All*, little serious thought had been given to the need for a national policy advocating that multicultural education permeate the curriculum of *all* our schools (DES, 1985). (Fortunately, the NC does make such a curricular demand, hence this series of books.) There was also concern that the secondary school sector did not see the issue as pertinent to its curriculum and was not prepared to respond as readily as the primary sector (Lashley, 1987). By the latter half of the 1980s, some all-white schools were beginning to respond constructively and often readily (Gaine, 1987). The primary versus secondary school difference in uptake of multicultural education has been of concern for some time. This has been, in part, due to the fact that at the secondary stage the curriculum has been to a large extent determined by extrinsic agencies such as examination boards. Such agencies have been able to set the parameters that determined curriculum content, areas and standards. Very few examination boards saw multicultural education as an issue of any importance. It meant that few schools in the secondary sector, particularly those heavily involved in examinations, gave any serious attention to the needs of multicultural curriculum development (Grinter, 1990a).

Who was to be the focus of a multicultural curriculum in the secondary sector, bearing in mind that many minority ethnic group children were 'selected out' by the demands of examination courses? These very pupils were to be the recipients of multicultural education. In inner-city schools a disproportionate percentage of black pupils fell within that category. In other schools, children from lower socio-economic backgrounds fell within that category. This meant that to a substantial extent the students in the higher-ability levels of the secondary-school population were more likely to be exempt from any systematic curricular consideration of multicultural issues. Multicultural education was given to those who, in some respects, might well have least needed it. They were of a 'multicultural background' and familiar with a plurality of cultures. Often they were pupils whose dominant needs might have been to improve their academic situation and attainments in order to compete in society on a much more equal footing and gain greater access to higher levels of education and better career opportunities.

Socially disadvantaged white pupils were forced to address the needs of other cultures. To many, this seemed to be a double imposition. First, these pupils were already experiencing socio-cultural oppression and exploitation at the hands of the existing dominant ruling class and culture. Second, they were being asked to focus on cultures that were alien to them and towards which they may have had high levels of prejudice (Verma, 1986; Pumfrey and Verma, 1990). It was not surprising that in some cases there was an exacerbation of the differences that existed between those culturally deprived white groups and minority black groups.

In the case of black pupils, they felt equally frustrated because they were expected to learn more about their parents' 'back-home' cultures, often from people who had a very sketchy cultural knowledge, in circumstances where this knowledge was not seen as relevant by many pupils. Pupils' dissatisfaction arose, in part, because they were having to adjust to and synthesize differing cultures into a new one. In the case of 'poor whites', they were having to learn about others with whom they felt that they were in competition and for whom they felt no need to concern themselves. Social Darwinism is a powerful force! Pecking orders are powerful phenomena.

The very nature of the physical, social and cultural interactions that took place between the dominant and minority groups resulted in the formation of new 'street-level' cultures. These were noticeable, particularly in some areas of popular culture and communication such as music and dress. One example was the 'two-tone' movement which had its origin in the Midlands. Such syntheses typically resulted from young people being 'friends', and 'peers', and in many cases being in situations where cooperative activity resulted in greater understanding and accommodation being developed between them. Many schools in the borough of Haringay were (and are) in this position of cultural flux since a significant number of children in areas of the borough were from a range of 'immigrant' cultures. These included Cypriots, Afro-Caribbeans, Asian and many other minority groups. Multiculturalism was an experience they all shared by the very nature of their home backgrounds and their interactions with peers. Multicultural education in some cases therefore seemed to be overstating the obvious. It was not the development of strategies for *all* pupils to address a new cultural challenge. These comments are not intended to undervalue multicultural education as an important facet of the curriculum. They question its curricular validity to those who may, by the very nature of their living circumstances, be exposed to such experience. So too did some educators.

> In the short term, an antiracist curriculum will neither alter the unequal distribution of power in British society nor banish discrimination, but it can encourage the next generation to question the ideas and concept that sustain racism, sexism and elitism. It can help make students more critically aware by showing them the inadequacies of a nationalist, ethnocentric view of the world restricted to students' existing perceptions, and how and why stereotypes of 'race', 'class' and 'culture' and 'gender' have developed'. (Grinter, 1990a)

Reflecting on one's experiences is essential, if learning is to take place for all ethnic groups.

Following this critique Grinter outlines a strategy whereby an antiracist National Curriculum can be implemented. His helpful proposals are based on five blocks of questions addressed to teachers (Grinter, 1990b). Examples of how these questions can be used in a wide range of curricular fields are presented. The questions are reproduced in Table 9.1. Has your school considered them in relation to the whole curriculum? If not, why not? If it has, in what ways have the answers affected policy and practice?

Table 9.1: Antiracist Education

A. **Implementing Antiracist Strategies**
   Questions:
   Have we:

- examined our own thinking on a given subject for ethnocentric assumptions?
- examined the values and assumptions that underlie our treatment of particular topics and revealed these to our students?
- explored the possible local, national and global links in the topic?
- introduced world perspectives for comparative purposes?
- stressed commonalities, universal needs and interdependence in examining differences between societies?
- given the contributions, achievements and values of non-European societies in a field their due recognition?
- related the study to all human beings in terms of resources and its impact on socio-cultural welfare on the world scale?
- raised, through the examples used, questions of justice and rights?
- 'problemized accepted notions'? (Brandt, 1986)

B. **Relating Learning to Students' Experiences**
   Questions:
   Do we:

- encourage our students to express and examine their existing views on the topic?
- examine material used in the study of the subject with our students, asking questions to reveal any racist, cultural, gender or class stereotyping and bias:
  - in the text through selection of information, omissions or phraseology that devalues people?
  - in illustrations through choice of items, omissions or placing people in roles that confirm stereotypes?
  - in our course structure through emphases or omissions?
- explain how and why these stereotypes have come about?
- explore with our students the possible implications and effects of these stereotypes?
Above all, have we consulted with black people about the impact of racial stereotyping, and compared their perceptions with those of all other groups who suffer from negative stereotyping?

C. **Methodologies to Combat Racism**
   Questions:
   Do we:

- involve students in the learning experience in terms of defining problems and asking appropriate questions to investigate situations?
- encourage students to think for themselves through open-ended questioning, hypothesizing, experimentation and problem-solving activities?
- train students in the necessary skills to work in these ways?
- encourage students to discover the perspectives of a variety of groups and societies on developments?
- make sufficient use of experiential activities like role play, drama, discussion and simulations?
- train students in the skills of cooperative learning?

D. **Relating Learning to Students' Experiences**
   Questions:
   Do we:

- begin the study from a context familiar to our students?
- use the life experiences of our students, their parents and the local community as valid learning resources?
- relate the study to a context familiar to our students, either by analogy or present day applications?
- add to students' experiences by introducing considerations that will encourage them to reassess their views?
- raise issues that students can recognize from their own life experiences?
- relate studies to experiences in terms of race, culture, class and gender?

Table 9.1 (Cont'd.)

E. Interdisciplinary Approaches and Thematic Work
  Questions:
  Have we:

- explored possible links between disciplines that would benefit antiracist purposes?
- considered a thematic approach to a topic that could raise further issues and allow the use of other disciplines to explore them further?
- explored ways in which topics could be extended to develop antiracist perspectives?
- brought in a comparative dimension to provide a critical approach to European or more local perceptions?

The successive and overlapping phases of accommodation within a multicultural society have been described as (a) immigrant education; (b) multicultural education and (c) racism awareness. Each phase had its respective strengths and weaknesses. In practice, all three are operative in varying degrees in different areas and schools. If schools consider their own policies and practices in the field of cultural diversity, a basis for identifying and implementing more adequate programmes arises.

A valuable survey of race-relations training approaches and an analysis of its objectives and rationale are available (Avari and Joseph, 1990). Their ten-years experience in the field lead them to produce a range of courses. A 'menu' comprising five key elements, and themes within each of these, based on their work is given in Table 9.2. The practical guidance they provide on running and evaluating race relations courses is invaluable.

Areas of cultural and leisure interest often provide platforms on which young people of diverse backgrounds of culture and class are able to develop friendships and understanding, and to exchange cultural ideas and behaviours. The dynamics of black–white culture 'synthesis' in Britain can be seen in aspects of music, dress styles and other mutual concerns of youth (Hewitt, 1986) (See Volume 1). Lynch (1987) explored this phenomenon in relation to schools, teachers and curriculum materials as a source for the development of prejudice-reduction strategies. However, reducing prejudice and conflict is no easy or short-term matter (Pennington, 1988). 'Changing attitudes, beliefs and behaviour by increasing contact between different groups of people is successful to a degree but not over-whelmingly so'. There appears to be a 'street-level' meeting place at which young people in racially and ethnically mixed situations are engaged in an important but informal multicultural education. This can bring about its own forms of further cultural interaction and produce some reduction in prejudice. Such interactions provide two ingredients necessary for prejudice reduction: contact between ethnic-group members and common goals. The goals of the system must have genuine appeal to both groups, drawing on equitable involvement, contributions and participation by both groups (Shaw, 1990).

Table 9.2: Key Elements in Antiracist Education

Unit Title	Possible Themes
A. Historical and global perspective	• Bias in history • Black presence in Britain over the last five hundred years • Science and Mathematics outside Europe • Unequal exchange = unequal development: the political economy of poverty • The race factor in international relations • Malthus and the population lobby: Differing perspectives on large families
B. The visible presence	• Migrations within the British Empire • Socio-economic profiles and settlements of migrant communities • A demographic analysis of the migrant communities • Assimilation and cultural diversity: Can they coexist? • Challenges facing ethnic-minority women in Britain
C. Race, realities and encounters in contemporary Britain	• Ethnocentrism, racialism, racism: terms and definitions • Racism, fascism and the politics of race in a democratic society • Racial discrimination in employment • Racial discrimination in health and housing • Media and race relations • Youth, neighbourhood and policing
D. Social dynamics of black-community life	• Family and social structures within minority communities • Rites of passage across cultures • Gender issues • Generation issues • Opportunities in recreation and diversity in leisure forms
E. Challenges and rewards of a multicultural society	• Non-Christian faiths • Black Christian churches • Ethnic art • Ethnic cuisine • Ethnic contributions to British sport • Black literature in English

Source: Avari and Joseph, 1990

Acculturation and Education

Acculturation of the 'multicultural' child in the British school system takes place at several levels. First, there is the level of the hidden curriculum. Here the values and mores of the school, society, and the education system activate their own self-maintenance mechanisms, independent of the outlined curriculum. The social-value systems that make for a socio-economic status quo tend to be perpetuated. Changes tend to be evolutionary, rather than revolutionary. Second, there is the overt National Curriculum based on the curriculum materials, resources and public texts that will determine what is to be learnt and considered as required and accepted knowledge (NCC, 1990). There is a third level. This is the stage in which the students begin to operate at an independent level, developing their own cultural syntheses. These may be in direct competition to both the overt and hidden curriculum. One example of this is the phenomenon of white usage of Creole in many inner-city areas. This has been noted by teachers and youth workers. Hewitt (1986) raises an important question: 'Given the symbolic significance of Creole to many young Blacks, how has it been possible for some young Whites to negotiate for themselves the right to employ it with their black friends?' This points to a departure from an accepted current norm into a new area in which young people negotiate and determine, through their own interactions, new areas of agreement that are seen as pertinent to their own social and cultural lives.

Youth culture itself is beginning to produce common effects across ethnic boundaries. These collaborations are much more evident in areas where there is a more identifiable multicultural population. (They could hardly take place where no visible minority groups exist.) This particular development takes place despite schools and not because of schools. Very often they also occur in defiance of the overt curriculum and not because of it.

Such exchanges are sometimes seen as creating a threat to the accepted cultural establishment. Right-wing organizations feel this to be developing into the 'enemy within' syndrome. The Tebbit cultural test is an example of this fear. It derives from Norman Tebbit's comment on loyalty being based on the 'cricket test' i.e., 'immigrants showed a lack of loyalty if they failed to cheer-on the English cricket team'. Bhikhu Parekh's response was that Tebbit 'was also guilty of equating citizenship with loyalty and of defining loyalty in irrelevant and crude sporting terms' (Parekh, 1990).

The widespread use of racial abuse and racial name-calling in secondary schools has been clearly described by Kelly (1990). Her data are based on 902 first and fourth-year secondary-school pupils in a large urban LEA. The evidence describes and demonstrates the offensive, alienating and pervasive nature of this phenomenon. Is the incidence of racial language and racial abuse in your school systematically considered? All too easily this everyday index of racial discrimination is overlooked or ignored.

Community Empowerment and Multiculturalism

Recently, a community-work student on work experience on a predominently multiracial Lewisham housing estate claimed that race was not a major issue on the estate. He suggested that this situation had been achieved by the provision of adequate opportunity for the vast majority of residents to meet and share their problems through a variety of community development-led programmes. This enabled adults and young people, both black and white, to interact productively in circumstances where they were empowered to aim at common goals within a shared community structure. This experience was unique at a time when other estates in the same borough were witnessing the resurgence of fascist activity and the creation of disharmony among residents. Does this provide lessons for teachers on how schools are organized?

The success of the project was associated with the nature of the social interaction between members of a variety of ethnic groups. Cooperative endeavours that provide for mutual problem-solving help to reduce the degree of prejudice in interethnic situations (Avari and Joseph, 1990). The community project on which the student was placed was organized around common, pressing social interests. To what extent can we provide a similar environment in multicultural schools which would attempt to address issues pertinent to the vast majority of young people in that flux of cultural diversity and adolescence? To what extent do we attempt to ensure that the curriculum, hidden as well as overt, is relevant to the psycho-social life experience of young people in and out of school? The range of 'responses' described in Volumes 1 and 2 of the present series open up many possibilities for secondary schools to use cultural diversity to help deliver the National Curriculum. Grinter's questions (Table 9.1) should be asked by all schools and his illustrative responses considered.

One of the major issues for young people in the last decade or so has been unemployment. This has disproportionately affected black young people during the period. It has become more important for schools to make employability a principal objective and outcome of the curriculum to be, as well as employment. Young people require an education that will help them cope constructively with the challenges of changes associated with the socio-economics of a post-industrial world. These challenges are likely to be exacerbated as we move through the 1990s with the socio-political changes in the world order that are emerging, as well as those that can be anticipated as a consequence of such profound socio-political changes (see Chapters 1, 2, 3 and 13).

The 1988 Education Reform Act (ERA) has in many ways 'damped down' opportunities for the development of the curriculum innovations suggested by the Swann Report (DES, 1985). The implementation of the core curriculum recommended by the ERA has been seen by many involved in multicultural and antiracist education to be a slowing down of constructive developments. In some cases, a loss of ground has occurred. In other respects, the National Curriculum has provided an opportunity to create further developments in the area by a conscious consideration of cultural diversity and its curricular implications in *all* schools.

Some major factors maintain the ethno-racial disparities that exist in British society. Of particular note is the position in which black minorities find themselves. First, there is the issue of underachievement. This continues to plague these groups, and not in a way that is only ethnic-specific as has been claimed (See Chapter 12). Secondly, there continues to be a disproportionately high unemployment amongst black young people and ethnic minorities. This can be followed by a list of others disadvantages which, to some extent, mark the creation of an underclass (CRE, 1991). Schools cannot resolve all such problems, but they can make constructive contributions to delivering the ERA 'entitlement' curriculum.

A recent survey provided some pointers about contemporary racism in Britain (Cohen, 1991). Three ethnic groups consisting of Whites, Afro-Caribbeans and Asians were interviewed. The general conclusion was that racism remains a fact of life in Britain today. 57 per cent of Whites, 53 per cent of Afro-Caribbeans and 50 per cent of Asians concluded that Britain is 'fairly racist'. An average of 33 per cent for the three groups suggested that Britain is a 'little less racist' now than nineteen years ago. These results indicate the complexity of the issues with which we deal in secondary schools. There is broad agreement that Britain is still significantly racist. On the positive side, the current level of racism seems to be less than it was ten years ago. This contrasts with the earlier assertions that current circumstances are less conducive now to antiracist education than they were some years ago. The political climate that exists at present is one of diffidence in dealing with the issue of racism. To some extent it suggests that racism is merely the construction of left-wing ideologists. In addition, there is the view that racism is not a serious problem, despite the information that surfaces to suggest otherwise. The consequences of this view is that there are no pressing reasons to improve race-relations laws and the race-relations industry that has emerged. This attitude has filtered through to the education services. It has been argued that multicultural and antiracist education are forms of indoctrination and result in the introduction of politics into the curriculum. 'Back off' is currently the implied message.

In this particular climate, multicultural education is likely to be weakened and fail to address the issues of oppression and inequality that exist in our society. It is also seen as a threat to education standards and quality. In addition, antiracist education is often equated with a Marxist conspiracy to destroy the system. These simplistic views are highly suspect. It is essential to deal with the structured inequalities in the educational and social systems. Only then will all British citizens, black as well as white, girls or boys, working-class or middle-class, fulfill their potential. Both multicultural and antiracist education for all are essential. In this book there are a variety of examples of cross-curricular curriculum developments that can be undertaken to achieve this goal.

The secondary-school phase is crucial in the development of social attitudes in young people. As they move from childhood to adulthood they increasingly question the status quo in a much more coherent and vigorous way than earlier. The 'rationalization' of racist attitudes begins to take on divisive meanings, if it is left unchallenged. The so-called common-sense statements such as 'they are taking all our jobs', 'they are taking all our women', or 'they are everywhere' acquire more significant meaning to secondary school pupils facing the perennial identity challenges of adolescence and impending work or joblessness.

Despite our knowledge of patterns of adolescent development, many schools continue to be reluctant to introduce multicultural and antiracist curriculum reform at this stage. The ERA does provide such an opportunity, but yet again the issue is clouded by arguments about educational standards, preoccupation with particular types of examinations and the effect of LMS. These objections distort the real reasons for procrastination. 'One of the tasks facing those who would combat the new educational right is not just to present the truth against distortion, but to show that antiracist education is extricably linked to good education' (Gordon, 1989). But what is 'the truth'? Assertion is not evidence. The secondary school curriculum must be much more concerned with the development of multicultural and antiracist education. It is equally concerned with social education and social attitudes, and with ensuring that the knowledge base of the curriculum is not distorted by having only a eurocentricized content. All professionals, parents and pupils should read and discuss the book entitled *The Fire Next Time* written by the black American author James Baldwin. Artists' insights can be invaluable. The lessons of the 1981 inner-city riots in London, Manchester, Liverpool and Bristol, in which both black and white youth played prominent parts, must not be forgotten.

Social justice is a major priority at the secondary phase of education. It is of importance to all persons concerned with the transition of young people to responsible adulthood. 'Those concerned with social justice in education whether parents, teachers, pupils or other educationists need to maintain their critique of current education policy at the same time as continuing to campaign to put gender, "race", and other equal opportunities' issues high on the educational agenda of the 1990s' (Burton and Weiner, 1990). The National Curriculum Council is in complete agreement (NCC, 1990). Implementing the National Curriculum in British education requires both resolve and resources if the multicultural aspects of school and society are to be addressed. Has the teaching profession sufficient of either?

References

AVARI, B. and JOSEPH, G.G. (1990) 'Race Relations Training: The State of the Art', in PUMFREY, P.D. and VERMA, G.K. (Eds) *Race Relations and Urban Education*, Basingstoke, The Falmer Press.

BRANDT, G. (1987) *The Realisation of Antiracist Teaching*, Lewes, The Falmer Press.

BURTON, L. and WEINER, G. (1990) 'Social Justice and the National Curriculum', *Research Papers in Education*, 5, 3, October.

COHEN, N. (1991) 'Racism: Someone else is to Blame', *The Independent on Sunday*, 7 July.

COMMISSION FOR RACIAL EQUALITY (1987a) *Learning in Terror*, London, CRE.

COMMISSION FOR RACIAL EQUALITY (1987b) *Racial Attacks: A Survey in Eight Areas in Britain*, London, CRE.

COMMISSION FOR RACIAL EQUALITY (1990) *Bangladeshi latecomers in Tower Hamlets Schools*, London, CRE Research Section.

COMMISSION FOR RACIAL EQUALITY (1991) *Second Review of the Race Relations Act 1976*, London, CRE.

DEPARTMENT OF EDUCATION AND SCIENCE (1985) *Education for All:* The Report of the Committee of Inquiry into the Education of Children from Ethnic Minority Groups, London, HMSO.

DEPARTMENT OF EDUCATION AND SCIENCE (1991) *The Parents Charter: You and Your Child's Education*, London, DES.

FRYER, P. (1988) *Black People in the British Empire*, London, Pluto Press.

GAINE, C. (1987) *No Problem Here: A Practical Approach to Education and Race in White Schools*, London, Hutchinson.

GORDON, P. (1988) 'The New Right, Race and Education — or how the Black Paper became a White Paper', *Race and Class*, 29, 14.

GORDON, P. (1989) 'The New Educational Right', *Multicultural Teaching*, 8, 1, Autumn.

GREEN, S.T.D. (1988) 'Is Equality of Opportunity a False Ideal for Society?', *British Journal of Sociology*, 39, 1, pp. 1–27.

GRINTER, R. (1990a) 'Developing an Antiracist National Curriculum: Constraints and New Directions', in PUMFREY, P.D. and VERMA, G.K. (Eds) *Race Relations and Urban Education*, Basingstoke, The Falmer Press.

GRINTER, R. (1990b) 'Developing an Antiracist National Curriculum: Implementing Antiracist Strategies', in PUMFREY, P.D. and VERMA, G.K. (Eds) *Race Relations and Urban Education*, Basingstoke, The Falmer Press.

HEWITT, R. (1986) *White Talk, Black Talk*, Cambridge, Cambridge University Press.

JONES, E. (1986) *We are our Own Educational System*, London, Maria Press.

KELLY, E. (1990) 'Use and Abuse of Racial Language in Secondary Schools', in PUMFREY, P.D. and VERMA, G.K. (Eds) *Race Relations and Urban Education*, Basingstoke, The Falmer Press.

LASHLEY, H. (1984) 'Black Youth and Education: A Process of Marginalization', in McLEOD, K. (Ed) *Multicultural Education: A Partnership, Canadian Council for Multicultural Education (CCME)*.

LASHLEY, H. (1986) 'The Implications of the Dewsbury Affair', *Education*, 170, 17, 23 October.

LASHLEY, H. (1987) 'Prospects and Problems of Afro-Caribbean in the British Education System', in BROOK, C. (Ed) *The Caribbean in Europe*, London, Frank Cass.

LESTER, A. and DEAKIN, N. (1967) *Policies for Racial Equality*, London, Fabian Society.

LYNCH, J. (1986) *Multicultural Education: Principles and Practice*, London, Routledge and Kegan Paul.

LYNCH, J. (1987) *Prejudice Reduction and the Schools*, London, Cassell.

MAXWELL, M. (1969) 'Violence in the Toilets', *Race Today*, September.

McILROY, J. (1987) 'The Politics of Racism in Britain', in JONES, B. (Ed) *Political Issues in Britain Today*, Manchester, Manchester University Press.

NATIONAL CURRICULUM COUNCIL (1990) *The Whole Curriculum: Curriculum Guidance No. 3,* York, NCC.

NATIONAL ASSOCIATION OF SCHOOLMASTERS/UNIION OF WOMEN TEACHERS (NAS/UWT) (1985) *Issues in Education: Multi-Ethnic Education,* NAS/UWT, Birmingham.

PALMER, F. (1986) *Antiracism: An Assault on Education and Value,* Nottingham, Sherwood Press.

PARAKH, B. (1990) *Sunday Correspondent,* 23 April.

PEARCE, S. (1986) 'Swann and the Spirit of the Age', in PALMER, F. (Ed) *Antiracism: An Assault on Education and Value,* Sherwood Press.

PENNINGTON, D.C. (1986) *Essential Social Psychology,* London, Arnold.

PUMFREY, P.D. and VERMA, G.K. (1990) *Race Relations and Urban Education,* Basingstoke, The Falmer Press.

RICHARDSON, R. (1989) 'Manifesto for Inequality — some features of the new era', *Multicultural Teaching Journal,* 8, 1, pp. 19–20.

SABA SAAKANA, A. and PEARSE, A. (1986) 'Towards the Decolonization of the British Education System', *Frontline Journal,* Karnak House.

SARUP, M. (1991) *Education and the Ideologies of Racism,* London, Trentham Books.

SHAW, J. (1990) 'A strategy for Improving Race Relations in Urban Education', in PUMFREY, P.D. and VERMA, G.K. (Eds) *Race Relations and Urban Education,* Basingstoke, The Falmer Press.

STONE, M. (1981) *The Education of the Black Child in Britain: The Myth of Multiracial Education,* London, Fontana Paperback.

SIVANANDAN, A. (1983) 'Challenging Racism: Strategies for the 80's', *Race and Class,* 25, 2.

TANNA, K. (1990) 'Excellence, equality and educational reform: the myth of South Asian Achievement levels', *New Community,* 16, 3, pp. 349–368.

TAYLOR, M.J. and HEGARTY, S. (1985) *The Best of Both Worlds? A Review of Research into the Education of Pupils of South Asian Origins,* Windsor, NFER-Nelson.

Times Educational Supplement (1991) 'Opt out may lead to colour bar', *TES,* 22 March.

TROYNA, B. (1989) 'A New Planet? Tackling Racial Inequality in All-white Schools and Colleges', in VERMA, G.K. (Ed) *Education For All,* London, The Falmer Press.

VERMA, G.K. (1986) *Ethnicity and Achievement in British Schools,* London, Macmillan.

VERMA, G.K. (1989) *Education for All: A Landmark in Pluralism,* Basingstoke, The Falmer Press.

VERMA, G.K. and PUMFREY, P.D. (1988) *Educational Attainments: Issues and Outcomes in Multicultural Education,* Basingstoke, The Falmer Press.

Chapter 10

Personal and Social Education: A Black Perspective

Ken McIntyre

Context

An Introduction to Pastoral-Care Systems

The notion that the role of teachers should encompass both 'teaching' and 'caring' responsibilities for pupils has a long and complex history (Daws, 1973; Clemett and Pearce, 1986). Its roots lie deep within the schooling of the eighteenth and nineteenth century when class teachers taught a variety of subjects to their pupils and so became involved in their personal and social development as part-and-parcel of promoting the academic progress and personal development of their pupils.

The nature of that interaction changed considerably over the decades so that by the 1950s, when the London County Council began its programme of large purpose-built comprehensive schools, it was recognized that new organizations would be required, not just for the delivery of subject teaching, but also for providing an active system of support and guidance for pupils.

That trend continued and with the rapid growth in comprehensive schools in the early 1960s, an important boost to the organization of care and guidance within schools saw the rapid proliferation of new structures within secondary schools. A number of authors cynically regarded the development of those structures as merely based on expedience and saw two factors, diversity and size, as the main influences in its development (Marland, 1974; Lang, 1984).

By the early 1980s, that aspect of school life had begun to move from its original focus on individuals and emphasized the need for group activity and interaction. That development was described as 'the third phase' by Bulman and Jenkins (1988), and gave rise to the concept of the 'pastoral curriculum' (Marland, 1989). Thus, for the first time, the concept of personal and social education as a distinct feature of pastoral care influenced the development of 'technique' (Best and Ribbins, 1983).

A number of publications resulted which attempted to promote that aspect of the school's curriculum. Amongst them were schemes by Button *et al.*, (1974); Baldwin and Wells (1979); Hamblin (1978) and more recently, Foster (1988). These publications, in particular those by Baldwin and Foster, contained units of work which could be 'developmentally' applied and used with pupils throughout their secondary school life, which corresponded roughly to levels 4 to 6 of the National Curriculum. This was probably the first recognition of personal and social education as a feature of school curriculum.

More recently, the trend has been for schools to produce their own in-house schemes which are arguably more in tune with the demands and needs of their own pupil population and perceptions of their staff. It was thought more likely that those schemes, rather than the more celebrated publications, would take into account the multicultural and multiracial dimensions of school life which became more salient during the 1970s and 1980s in British schools (Duncan, 1988). There has been no widescale evaluation of the effectiveness of this practice.

However, since its emphasis in the late 1960s, the general practice of pastoral care has been a relatively neglected aspect of school life (Marland, 1985). A number of observations can be adduced in support of that view. They would include: the lack of widespread evaluative research in the field (Marland, 1974; Clemett and Pearce, 1986; McIntyre 1990); its subservient role when compared with the academic curriculum (Ribbins and Best, 1985; McIntyre, 1990); its function as a mechanism of control (Williamson, 1980; Raymond, 1985); the lack of training of staff (Best and Maher, 1984; Raymond, 1985) and the poor status of pastoral care staff (Raymond, 1985; Clemett and Pearce, 1986).

Moreover, if those issues were of general concern to researchers in the field of pastoral care, then there was an even more specific concern with regards to its application and relevance for meeting the needs of black (Afro-Caribbean) Pupils in secondary schools. It was Marland who drew attention to the absence of literature in that field of study:

> The relationship between Pastoral Care and the educational needs of Ethnic Minority children and of the whole population of pupils with regards to their perspective of a multi-ethnic society, is a major and urgent focus for educational research. (Marland, 1985, p. 89)

Marland's observations underlined the serious neglect of these issues both in terms of the literature on pastoral care and of general evaluations based on content, aims and outcomes of such programmes. Moreover, he was critical in turn of the lack of consideration within widescale studies, surveys and evaluations of the educational experiences of black Pupils in British schools. In that respect, he did not consider the Swann Report (DES, 1985) 'illuminating', and argued that the report showed a poor understanding of the broad features of pastoral care by restricting its discussion to only that of school rules regarding school uniform, separate showers etc. as the main issue rather than including such issues as its conceptualization and organization (Marland 1985, p. 88; DES, 1985, pp. 203 and 513).

Since then, other writers in the field have sought to articulate the multicultural dimension to pastoral care. A review of some of the articles published in this field of study confirmed this view (Goodhew, 1987). Others argued that multicultural education and pastoral care seemed to develop independently from one another and were bold in their statement that 'Pastoral Care was part of the structure which disenfranchises Black Pupils' (Garnett and Lang, 1986). A study found that black Pupils in a sample of schools from the Midlands did not perceive pastoral care 'as relevant to them' (Woods, 1984).

More recent articles have begun to add to our knowledge and perceptions in this very important field by considering the relationship and implications of developments in the field of multicultural education for pastoral-care development (Garnett and Lang, 1986; Pelleschi, 1986; Scadding, 1988; Singh, 1988; McIntyre, 1990).

However, the recent implementation of the Education Reform Act 1988 has raised a number of issues as to the ways in which pastoral care and personal and social education will be defined and practised generally in secondary schools in future. Whether these developments can be considered as a 'new opportunity' for shaping and delivering pastoral care as part of the implementation of the National Curriculum will need careful analysis (Marland, 1989). This cautious optimism will need to be evaluated with reference to the demands of that Act (as we know them) and their implications in the specific instance of black pupils.

Section 1 of the Act defined one of its most important themes which was that of a 'National Curriculum'. The Act states its position thus:

> The Curriculum for a maintained school satisfies the requirements of this section if it is a balanced and broadly based curriculum which
> a) promotes the spiritual, moral, cultural, mental and physical development of pupils at the school and of society; and
> b) prepares such pupils for the opportunities, responsibilities and experiences of adult life. (DES, Education Reform Act 1988, Section 1, par. 2)

Those aims were viewed as broadly encapsulating a more 'pastorally oriented' perspective than had been the case with previous education Acts (Marland, 1989). It seemed to find some support within the debates on the Act at a time when the summary by the DES seemed to indicate the importance of personal and social education and pastoral care:

Adult Life' embraces all aspects of adult experiences — home life, employment, citizenship and social responsibility . . . (DES, 1987, p. 2)

The emphasis given by the DES harped back to some earlier observations which indicated the need to introduce a wider syllabus of personal and social education to the curriculum of all pupils (HMI, 1979). That group recounted a similar view in its support for the statement of the DES by offering an overview of those topics that personal and social education should encompass within its definition:

Personal and Social Education is concerned with the qualities and attitudes, knowledge and understanding, and abilities and skills in relation to oneself and others, social responsibilities and morality. It helps pupils to be considerate and enterprising in the present, while it prepares them for an informed and active involvement in family, social, economic and social life. It plays an important part in bringing relevance, breath and balance to the curriculum. (HMI, 1989, p. 1)

However, what is also apparent from this is that its emphasis has excluded the broader dimensions of pastoral care which take into account the motivation and support of pupils amongst its other aims. This seems an unfortunate trend since, if pastoral care is to be effective, it would need to be recognized and accepted as having a much broader and pervasive role in schools:

Pastoral Care should be about motivating pupils to achieve their aspirations through supporting their emotional and academic development. In this way its tasks should be preventative, supportive, and developmental in their function. (McIntyre, 1990, p. 376)

Personal and social education can only be one aspect of this, albeit, a very important part. However, this broad view has not been reflected in recent educational trends and changes in the philosophy of education. A recent article seemed to lend weight to this observed neglect and marginalization of the broader features of pastoral care (Marland, 1989). Its recount of a letter from Sir Keith Joseph the then Secretary of State for Education, gave his insight of this debate as, 'I am inclined to believe that the term "Pastoral Care", in itself, can be unhelpfully vague.' That narrow focus of pastoral care, in the context of the Education Reform Act and its implementation, probably laid emphasis that those needs might be met more easily within existing subjects areas.

The Education Reform Act thus located personal and social education within the category of cross-curricular dimensions meaning that its many issues could form the basis of teaching material in those subjects which were deemed to be part of the 'core-curriculum' and others within the category of 'foundation subjects'. Further support for that arrangement came from other important sources who considered personal and social education as 'the most important of the cross-circular dimensions' and further stressed that area should be the responsibility of all teachers (Elton Committee, 1989; HMI, 1989; NCC, 1989). The view that it should be thus, also received support from the then Home Secretary, Douglas Hurd, who stated in his Tamworth speech in 1988:

> Personal and Social Education does not necessarily need to be treated as a subject in its own right. It should pervade the curriculum. (Marland, 1989, p. 5)

There is a clear advantage to having personal and social education as the responsibility of all teachers in the school and fully integrated within and across subject specialisms. However, a number of potential obstacles and disadvantages are immediately evident in such an organizational change which will affect black pupils and all others if the tasks are to be carried out effectively.

The first concerns the status of personal and social education as a cross-curricular dimension without a clearly defined syllabus as compared with subjects which are part of the National Curriculum core and foundation subjects. The fear that the lack of emphasis and, in particular, the lack of direct attainment targets in this aspect of the curriculum, will mean that only where there is overlap between the design of the syllabus and the requirements within the core-curriculum, will there be careful planning and structuring. Thus, where an issue appears relatively low priority or not defined as an objective within the National Curriculum, chances are that even if there was some moral, social, political or even multicultural appeal, there will not be the careful and skilful input required in its teaching, if it is taught at all.

Recent research has also indicated that issues of 'racism' as an important feature in the experiences of black pupils should be part of the syllabus for all pupils (Macdonald, 1989; McIntyre, 1990). Given traditional reticence on the part of many schools, it is difficult to envisage how this need will be met in the context of no specified syllabus (Verma, *et al.*, 1986). The option of such open-endedness will inevitably mean that some schools will neglect areas which they do not consider important or relevant to them.

A second obstacle raises the question of the role of tutors within these new arrangements, which is seen as crucial (NCC, 1989; DES, 1989). Within such a structure, the tutor is envisaged as the person who would have not just specialist knowledge of the child and overall responsibility for his or her welfare and progress, but also, the person who would be in the best position to deliver a 'core' part of the personal and social syllabus.

For tutors, there is the additional problem of lack of time. Many researchers have found that the majority of tutor-time has centred around issues of discipline and administration (Hilsum and Strong, 1978; Lang, 1984). This, as an issue, has been noted by the National Curriculum Council who warned that guidance was 'not just provision for when things go wrong' (NCC, 1989, p. 6). However, given that relatively little emphasis and status has been given to personal and social education, it is difficult to see where there is extra time for delivering the wider issues of welfare and guidance to all pupils, integration and coordination of cross-curricular inputs plus responsibility within their own subject specialism. There is no evidence of extra time having been set aside within the guidelines of the new Act as has been suggested for other subjects.

Moreover, the research available tended to indicate that most teachers felt that they had been inadequately prepared for the task of being a tutor (Best and Maher, 1984; Raymond, 1982). If it is the case that tutors will have important responsibilities within this new framework, then the issue of training in the techniques of pastoral care and also in working with children from various cultural and racial backgrounds will require further resources, i.e., staff time and INSET.

From the preceding issues and comments, the proposals for personal and social education will present many organizational challenges if the aims of the Education Reform Act 1988 are to be realized. For black pupils, there remains the issue of the content of such programmes and whether they would include issues of direct relevance to them and those general to all pupils living in a multicultural society. These topics include the identification and erad- ication of racism. Indeed, if the CRE (1990) is correct, much of the emphasis of the present Act is in favour of a return to 'assimilationist thinking' and its main thrust will be the elimination of diversity in favour of promoting the adoption of traditional white British values that characterized an earlier phase of education in this country (Troyna, 1982). That means it is question- able whether any emphasis will be given to the special problems which black pupils might face within the school setting, or as a consequence of having left school as a result of cultural and racial differences. Some of those issues will be considered next.

Challenges

Many issues regarding the overall pastoral and educational needs of black pupils within the school setting have been well documented in the literature (DES, 1985). A recent study, evaluating pastoral care, concluded that black pupils, though sharing many similar pastoral needs as their white peers, nevertheless, have needs that are significantly different (McIntyre, 1990). These will pose an additional challenge to schools in their planning of pastoral care systems and for personal and social education in particular.

The planning of personal and social education must take into account a number of the issues research has shown to be characteristic of the experiences of black pupils within British schools.

The most consistent conclusion of such research and reports over the last thirty years has been that of underachievement by black pupils in examination results (DES, 1981; DES, 1985). Such major reports have shown black pupils to be performing at mean levels lower than that of their white peers. Of course these conclusions have been criticized for being imprecise and crude in their treatment of black, Afro-Caribbean pupils as a homogenous, monolithic cultural group and for not taking sufficient account of the dimensions of class or gender (Figueroa, 1974; McIntyre, 1990), or even the differential effects of schools on the attainments of black pupils (Tomlinson, 1989). Other issues are also fundamental to any new developments.

Developing healthy self-esteem amongst black pupils is a central challenge within schools (Bagley, Mallick and Verma, 1979; Verma *et al.*, 1986). The countering of poor teacher expectations and stereotyping of black pupils are other features (Tomlinson, 1984; Tomlinson and Smith, 1989). The eradication of discriminatory practices in careers guidance will be fundamental in assisting these pupils in vocational guidance (DES, 1981; Ali *et al.*, 1987; Department of Employment, 1990). The development of the confidence of black pupils in their relationships with pastoral staff will determine the extent to which these pupils will trust the advice and teaching offered in schools (McIntyre, 1990).

The list is not exhaustive but represents some of the crucial challenges that must be addressed if the broad aims of personal and social education and, for that matter, pastoral care, are to be implemented as envisaged by the 1988 Education Act. Therefore, developments in this area will need to take into account the following summary of points in the earliest stages of planning:

1   Britain is now a multicultural society and a philosophy and policy based on pluralism must be developed as part of the work with black and white pupils in order to eliminate racism and other negative attitudes (Verma *et al.*, 1986).
2   This requires direct work on the elimination of cultural impoverishment which is a feature bearing heavily upon most pupils exposed to a monocultural, anglocentric and parochial environment (Duncan, 1988).
3   It would also mean that specific work on attitude modification aimed at improving the interaction between pupils and that of staff and pupils would need to be undertaken. That would probably require a reappraisal of antiracist and assertiveness training and the development of new programmes based on the positive elements within them.
4   The content of personal and social education programmes would need to be devised so that issues of racism, discrimination, and

disadvantage in its general form, do figure in discussions amongst pupils in schools.

5 The training and knowledge base of all staff, especially those with responsibility for specialist input, would require specific consideration as part of INSET.

6 Teachers, especially those with pastoral responsibilities, would need to be aware of the distinctive needs of black pupils, for example, in their motivation, the effects of racism, in their preparation for work, and other significant cultural or ethnic variations which might pose additional problems for pupils and teachers in their interactions and adjustments within school.

7 Personal and social education programmes should seek to involve parents and other members of the black community in their delivery, and to act as positive role models for the pupils.

8 The government will need to identify a source of funding for such developments, as part of the promotion of the cultural development of pupils, as outlined in Section 1, par. 2 of the Education Reform Act 1988.

Responses

Figure 10.1: A Model for the Development of Pastoral Care

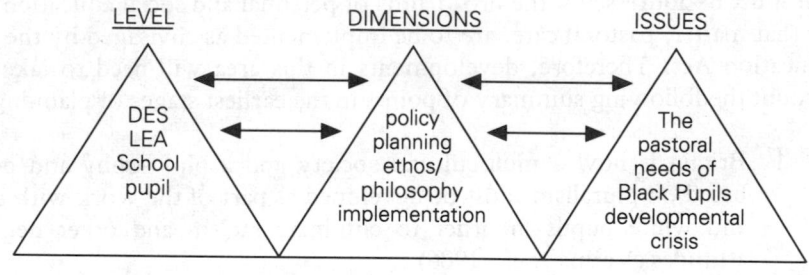

Source: McIntyre, 1990, p. 376

The model above was devised as a way of shaping the development of whole school pastoral provisions, part of which would include the development of personal and social programmes. It embraces a 'top-to-bottom' approach to the issues of policy, planning and implementation across many dimensions. It is an interactive model which provides one approach to developing a caring and effective school which will meet the needs of all pupils (McIntyre, 1990).

The Education Reform Act and its emphasis on personal and social education as being a cross-curricular dimension has provided the most appropriate context for its delivery. That is, as the primary concern of all staff and all subject areas. However, the difficulty is that given the emphasis on the importance of the core-curriculum and foundation subjects, the chances are that issues which lend themselves to such a programme of personal and social education run a realistic possibility of being ignored, marginalized, or inadequately or amateurishly delivered. In the specific instance of black pupils, some of the above proposals might be further marginalized in the thinking and planning of such programmes since they will inevitably make more demands on the expertise, knowledge base and orientation of staff at a time when they will be almost totally concerned with the demands of attainment targets and testing. There is a danger that personal and social education will be 'sunk' by SATs in subjects.

The argument is essentially that personal and social education has a crucial part to play in assisting those aims and issues of motivation and academic endeavours central to the delivery of the National Curriculum, and cannot be ignored as irrelevant to its aims. What is needed now is a stronger commitment from central government to the promotion of pluralist principles and the eradication of racial and cultural disadvantages amongst all pupils backed by adequate resourcing for this area of work.

References

ALI, N., COOK, J. and RYAN, A. (1987) 'Processing Black Clients: A Careers Service Perspective', in CROSS, M. and SMITH, D. *Black Youth Future:- Ethnic Minorities and the Y.T. Schemes*, Leicester, NYB.

BALDWIN, J. and WELLS, H. (1979–81) *Active Tutorial Work, Books 1 to 5*, Oxford, Basil Blackwell.

BAGLEY, C., MALLICK, K. and VERMA, G.K. (1979) 'Pupil Self-esteem: A Study of Black and White Teenagers in British Schools', in VERMA, G.K. and BAGLEY, C. *Race, Education and Identity*, London, Macmillan.

BEST, R.E., JARVIS, C.B. and RIBBINS, P.M. (1980) *Perspectives in Pastoral Care*, London, Heinemann.

BEST, R. and MAHER, P. (1984) *Training and support for Pastoral Care*, London, NAPC.

BEST, R. and RIBBINS, P. (1983) 'Re-Thinking the Pastoral–Academic Split', *Pastoral Care in Education*, 1, 1, Oxford, Basil Blackwell, pp. 112–16.

BULMAN, L. and JENKINS, D. (1988) *The Pastoral Curriculum*, Oxford, Basil Blackwell.

BUTTON, L. (1974) *Developmental Groupwork with Adolescents*, London, Hodder and Stoughton.

CLEMETT, A.J. (1982) 'Evaluation and Pastoral Care: The need and the response: Towards a framework for Evaluating and Developing Pastoral Care', Unpublished M.Ed., Dissertation, University of Warwick.

CLEMETT, A.J. and PEARCE, J.S. (1986) *The Evaluation of Pastoral Care*, Oxford, Basil Blackwell.

COMMISSION FOR RACIAL EQUALITY (1990) *Annual General Report*, CRE Publication.

DAWS, P. (1973) 'Pastoral Care, Guidance and Counselling in English Secondary Schools in Eggleston', *Paedogogia Europea*, 8, pp. 34–42.

DEPARTMENT OF EDUCATION AND SCIENCE (1981) *West Indian Children in Our Schools. Interim Report of Enquiry into Education of Children from Ethnic Minority Groups*, (The Rampton Report) London, HMSO.

DEPARTMENT OF EDUCATION AND SCIENCE (1985) *Education For All: Report Of The Committee Of Inquiry Into The Education of Children From Ethnic Minority Groups (The Serann Report)*, London, HMSO.

DEPARTMENT OF EDUCATION AND SCIENCE (1987) *Education Reform Bill Notes On Clauses (Commons)*, London, DES.

DEPARTMENT OF EDUCATION AND SCIENCE (1988) *The Education Reform Act*, London, HMSO.

DEPARTMENT OF EDUCATION AND SCIENCE (1989) *Discipline in Schools: Report of the Committee of Enquiry*, London, HMSO.

DEPARTMENT OF EMPLOYMENT (1990) 'Ethnic Minorities and the Careers Service: an investigation into processes of assessment and placement', *Department of Employment Research Paper Series No. 73.*

DUNCAN, C. (1988) *Pastoral Care: An Anti-Racist/Multicultural Perspective*, Oxford, Basil Blackwell.

FIGUEROA, P. (1974) 'West Indian School Leavers in London: A Sociological Study in Ten Schools in a London Borough 1966–1967', Unpublished PhD Thesis, London School of Economics.

FOSTER, J. (1988) *Lifelines*, London, Collins Educational.

GARNETT, B. and LANG, P. (1986) 'Pastoral Care and Multiracial Education', in *Pastoral Care In Education*, 4, 3, pp. 158–164, Oxford, Basil Blackwell.

GOODHEW, E. (1987) 'Personal and Social Education and Race', in *Pastoral Care In Education*, 5, 3, pp. 16–24, Oxford, Basil Blackwell.

HAMBLIN, D.H. (1978) *The Teacher and Pastoral Care*, Oxford, Basil Blackwell.

HILSUM, S. and STRONG, C.R. (1978) *The Secondary Teachers Day*, Slough, NFER.

HER MAJESTY'S INSPECTORATE (1979) *Secondary Survey*, HMSO.

HER MAJESTY'S INSPECTORATE (1989) *Personal and Social Education from 5 to 16*, London, HMSO.

LANG, P. (1984) 'Pastoral Care: Some Reflections on Possible Influences', *Pastoral Care in Education*, 2, 2, Oxford, Basil Blackwell, pp. 136–146.

MACDONALD, I. *et al.* (1989) *The Burnage Inquiry: Murder In The Playground*, London, Longsight Press.

MARLAND, M. (1974) *Pastoral Care*, London, Heinemann Educational Books.

MARLAND, M. (1985) 'Parents, Schooling and The Welfare of Pupils', in RIBBINS, P. *Schooling and Welfare*, The Falmer Press.

MARLAND, M. (1989) 'Shaping and Delivering Pastoral Care: the New Opportunities', *Journal of Pastoral Care*, December, London, pp. 14–21.

MCINTYRE, K. (1990) The Pastoral Needs Of Black Pupils: An Evaluation of Current Trends and Practices, Unpublished PhD thesis, University of Manchester.

NATIONAL CURRICULUM COUNCIL (1989) *Interim Report On Cross Curricular Issues*, York, NCC.

PELLESCHI, A. (1986) 'Screening Pupils in a Multicultural School', in *Pastoral Care In Education*, 4, 3, Oxford, Basil Blackwell, pp. 148–58.

RAYMOND, J. (1982) 'How Form Tutors Perceive Their Role', *Links*, 7, 3, pp. 25–30.

RAYMOND, J. (1985) *Implementing Pastoral Care in Schools*, Dover and New Hampshire, USA, Croom Helm.

RIBBINS, P. and BEST, R. (1985) 'Conventional Wisdom Vs Research and Evaluation', in LANG, B. and MARLAND, M. *New Directions in Pastoral Care*, Oxford, Basil Blackwell.

SCADDING, H. (1988) 'Anti-Racism in Schools'. A Discussion of the Difficulties a Pastoral Care Team may face in promoting Anti-racist policies and practices', in *Pastoral Care In Education*, 6, 1, pp. 16–22.

SINGH, B., HARBHAJAN, (1988) 'The Black Perspective of Anti-Racism in Schools', in *Pastoral Care In Education*, 6, 4, pp. 14–16, Oxford, Basil Blackwell.

TOMLINSON, S. (1984) *Home and School in Multicultural Britain*, London, Batsford Academic.

TOMLINSON, S. and SMITH, D.J. (1989) *The School Effect: A Study of Multicultural Comprehensives*, London, Policy Studies Institute.

TROYNA, B. (1982) 'The Ideological and Policy Response to Black Pupils In British Schools', in HARTNETT, A. (Ed) *The Social Sciences in Educational Studies*, Heinemann.

VERMA, G.K., MALLICK, K. and MODGIL, C. (1986) *Multicultural Education: The Interminable Debate*, London, Croom Helm.

WILLIAMSON, D. (1980) 'Pastoral Care Or Pastoralisation?', in BEST, R. *et al.* (Eds) *Perspectives On Pastoral Care*, London, Heinemann.

WOODS, E. (1984) 'The Practice of Pastoral Care In An Urban Comprehensive School', in *Pastoral Care In Education*, 12, 3, Oxford, Basil Blackwell, pp. 17–21.

Chapter 11

Gender Issues in Education for Citizenship

Elinor Kelly

Context

One of the objectives of a National Curriculum is to set out a common educational entitlement to all pupils that challenges many accepted gender stereotypes. That is why 'schools need to take account of and challenge the attitudes present in society which consider that subjects such as mathematics, science and technology are less relevant for girls than boys' (NCC, 1990). A commitment to equal opportunities for all pupils, coupled with the acknowledgment that preparation for life in a multicultural society is relevant to all pupils, is expected to permeate the curriculum.

'Equal opportunities is about helping all children fulfill their potential. Teachers are rightly concerned when their pupils underachieve and are aware that educational outcomes may be affected by factors outside the school's control such as a pupil's sex, or social, cultural or linguistic background' (ibid.). In principle, equality of opportunity for both males and females is a cornerstone of the educational system in the UK. In practice, equality is more honoured in the breach than in its observance. In part, this is because of differing views concerning the nature of equality and its implications for policy and practice.

In an ethnically diverse population, the differing ethical, moral, religious and value systems underpinning gender issues in education for citizenship, are extremely sensitive. For example, religious views concerning the roles, education and responsibilities of males and females differ between ethnic and religious groups. To question the traditional gender roles characteristic of any culture is to challenge its status quo. The suffragettes challenged a male dominated system and suffered considerably in their quest for an electoral equality that is now an accepted fact of life in the UK. The feminist movement continues its endeavours to raise awareness of, and change, what are perceived as continuing, systematic gender inequities.

This chapter addresses the key cross-curricular dimension of gender. It is concerned with identifying and redressing practices that can reinforce gender stereotyping, irrespective of a pupil's cultural, ethnic or religious group.

In particular, the issues of bullying and harassment in school are highlighted as the context for discussion of domestic violence and harassment in adult life. The issues have been chosen for several reasons. They are high on the agenda of pupils who have good reason to fear what they may experience at the hands of other pupils and staff. They connect school experience with key issues of power and injustice in adult life. They demonstrate graphically the need for the voices of victims to be heard if any form of effective action is to be developed. They cut across social class and ethnic boundaries.

In this discussion the focus is very much on female victims and on the ways in which they are trapped by male hegemony. In school, it is argued, girls' individual and collective experiences are submerged beneath the noise and clamour of male demands and the consequent neglect of their concerns. In adult life, the dominance of men is overwhelming. In the home, women are hemmed in by economic dependence and they have little redress other than escape. At work, there are few women, even those in senior positions, who have not been subjected to forms of harassment which ruin the quality of their working lives and over which, again, they have little redress.

One has only to point to the experience of women teachers for the connection between pupil and adult experience to be made. How can a school develop an effective whole-school behaviour policy if some of its own teachers are being bullied or harassed?

Challenges

The way in which the issues are posed is intended to challenge crude notions of 'respect for other cultures' which imply that minority ethnic groups should be treated as if they were social monoliths. There is no ethnic group, majority or minority, which is internally homogeneous. There is no ethnic group, majority or minority, which has a viable claim to being more 'liberated' than another. Male hegemony and women's subordination are being contested in all ethnic groups, as girls and women seek the means by which they can gain more power and free themselves from bullying and harassment.

The data selected for the discussion have been drawn from newspaper articles and other material which teachers can find easily and which can be used as the basis for classroom work connecting experiences in school with questions of rights and justice in adult life. The material on school experience should be drawn from the pupils themselves.

Bullying and Harassment in School

In the past three years there has been a sea change in attitudes about behaviour in school, precipitated in part by revelations about bullying. The most recent and tragic case was that of Katherine Bamber who killed herself rather than face another day of torment. Her parents have decided to make Katherine's death the catalyst for a national campaign, spearheaded by the television broadcaster, Esther Rantzen. In this way, they are urging forward a process which first gained prominence in 1989. This was the year in which the first serious studies of bullying were published in Britain. Besag compared bullying with child abuse.

> Bullying in schools is one of the dark, hidden areas of social inter-action, along with child physical and sexual abuse and adolescent violence in the home, which has thrived on a bed of secrecy and which has been neglected by professional investigation. (Besag, 1989, pp. 10–12)

Lane stated that there are 'thousands of islands of personal grief' because the pupils concerned have been failed (Tattum and Lane, 1989, p. 10) and Atwood (1990) has published a powerful novel which evokes the depth of misery experienced by victim and bully.

Nobody should underestimate the damage which is done, not just to the victims but also to the bullies.

> Bullying causes deep pain because it comprises an intensely 'personal' mistreatment of individuals by means of secret, calculated and pro-longed forms of abuse; the victim/s are isolated and instructed in helplessness; the bullies learn and practise distorted interpersonal skills; bullies and victims are locked into relations of dominance and subordination, intimidation and threat; the observers collude in the submission of the victims and the gratification of the bullies. (Kelly, 1991, p. 18)

When Childline opened their 'bullying line' and their 'boarding school-line' a year later in 1990, they were inundated with calls, especially from girls. They concluded that when pupils are encouraged to talk in their own terms, free of adult definitions of what may or may not be bullying, they reveal a scale of fear and threat about the effects of bullying which is 'only the tip of the iceberg' (La Fontaine, 1991). Bullying is not a matter of rare misfortune. One study after another has revealed that at least 10–30 per cent of pupils in school have been affected by bullying (Besag, 1989; Munthe and Roland 1989: Tattum and Lane, 1989). Teachers who were first dis-believing of these findings have surveyed their pupils and found that these figures may even be an underestimate.

In her analysis of the Childline data, La Fontaine discussed the fact that 65–71 per cent of calls were from girls and commented that while girls may be more likely than boys to take advantage of an opportunity to talk to someone in confidence about a problem, they may have been under-represented in previous studies because

> some research defines bullying in such a way as to exclude from consideration much of the behaviour from which girls suffer. Thus, when children are allowed to define bullying, girls have something to talk about. For example, girls seem to be more involved in psychological bullying: excluding victims from a group of friends or picking on them for no apparent reason. Were one to use many of the definitions current in research, much of this behaviour would not be included as bullying. (La Fontaine, 1991, p. 10)

There is danger that girl-bullying will continue to be submerged in spite of the publicity given to cases such as that of Katherine Bamber, because girls come last in the hierarchy of power in schools, as the Elton Committee learnt to their considerable embarrassment. After commissioning their own research and receiving evidence from sixty-eight local education authorities, fifty-nine teacher-training establishments, eighty-eight regional and national organizations and 394 other submissions, the report comprised 292 pages of which only twenty-one actually discussed pupils. There were three paragraphs which discussed 'forms of behaviours which only or mainly affect pupils' (p. 102) and gender issues were not raised at all. The committee received some evidence relating to bullying and racial harassment, but not at all about sexual harassment. They were moved to comment

> Misbehaviour is usually defined as behaviour which causes concern to teachers. But there are also some serious forms of bad behaviour which only or mainly affect pupils. Bullying and racial harassment are cases in point. Bullying includes both physical and psychological intimidation. Recent studies of bullying in schools suggest that the problem is widespread and tends to be ignored by teachers. Research suggests that bullying not only causes considerable suffering to individual pupils but also has a damaging effect in school atmosphere.
>
> We consider that sexual harassment is also an aspect of bullying, and are concerned that this was given very little attention in the evidence put before us. It is hard to see how a school can win the confidence of its pupils if it fails to deal with behaviour which so seriously damages the quality of their lives. (Report of the Committee of Inquiry, 1989, p. 103)

In the 1950s feminists campaigned for coeducation because single-sex schools had failed to develop the full potential of girls — too many girls were leaving school without any qualifications, and the few who completed a full school career were leaving with qualifications in feminine subjects. Girls were not qualifying in the science and technological subjects which were strategic in job and career terms. In the late 1970s, educationalists realized that coeducation had not achieved what was hoped (Byrne, 1978). Instead of being channelled by schools into the full range of the curriculum, disproportionate numbers were still leaving without any qualifications and far too few were gaining qualifications in science and technology — subjects which by now had even greater significance in job and career markets.

In their search for explanation of this enduring inequality, researchers studied the employment profiles of school staff and found that secondary schools are male-dominated institutions in which senior managerial staff are overwhelmingly men, with the women confined to junior grades and to a smaller range of subjects. In other words, girls had few models to follow if they were seeking jobs in science or engineering or if they wanted to succeed and get to the top in a profession. Curriculum materials were found to be genderized — domestic science and English were feminine; science and technology masculine (Weiner, 1985).

More recently research studies have shown that 'One of the most consistently emerging barriers to girls' equality of opportunity in mixed schools is the behaviour of boys, their greater degree of teacher attention and their tendency to dominate lessons' (Deem, 1984, p. 28). Boys dominate spatially, physically and verbally and they demand and receive more attention. For the boys, teacher attentiveness may have contradictory effects, because they are both rewarded and punished. But for girls, it amounts to consistent neglect (Lees, 1986).

This neglect had educational as well as social consequences. In subjects, such as Maths, which are often dependent on one-to-one assistance, girls retreat, give up asking questions and trying to catch the attention of the teachers. Smith records the experience of a girl in one school which experimented with single-sex sets for the first two years.

> When I was in the all girl set, the atmosphere in the classroom was a lot friendlier. The girls were not afraid of going up to the front of the class when they didn't understand . . . With the boys there, it is difficult to admit you need help . . . I went into a mixed set in the Third Year and hated it. I became a lot quieter and whispered to my friend when I didn't understand. The boys seemed to understand so well — I withdrew from answering — my marks fell . . . Boys sit in groups together — they shout the teachers over — they keep the teacher with them for ages — my friend and I get fed up of waiting for help . . . and we try to carry on with the next problem . . . I have given up trying to understand on many occasions this year. (Smith, 1984, p. 91)

Away from the supervision of teachers, for instance in corridors and stairways, the boys' behaviour becomes more extreme. Girls tell of learning to avoid groups of boys because of the risk of 'sexually appraising looks, many types of threatening gestures, boys holding their noses when girls passed in corridors and pretending to talk about them in a very obvious way' (Mahony, 1985, p. 36). Girls who could compare a coeducational school with their previous experience of a girl's school described their shock and consternation when they realized that such behaviour on the part of the boys was not confined to an extremist few, but was 'normal'. Within a short time they changed their behaviour. In order to avoid such encounters they chose certain routes, waited for others to walk with them, acknowledging that they could no longer walk freely.

Physical education is another arena in which sexualizing is rife. School policies and programmes mirror the male domination in national and international sports organizations which give smaller financial rewards, fewer headlines and column inches to female tennis, hockey, cricket and athletics, and ridicule new female sports such as synchronized swimming. In school sports facilities the boys take priority, and the girls are confined to the margins. The most prestigious sports are the ones which, like football, celebrate masculinity and make 'wimps' out of the delicate boys who do not take part. Reducing the sexualizing in sports could open up a whole range of options which would allow boys and girls to participate together or alongside each other — cricket, tennis, water polo, gymnastics are all options which could win prestige if the participation of girls was taken seriously.

This emphasis on the superiority of the masculine sports is reflected in hierarchies of domination in the playground. It is quite usual for playgrounds to be dominated by physically active boys whose football games take up all the central space, confining girls and 'untypical' boys to the margins. This domination is not often questioned. Instead the ways in which girls respond, by clustering in small groups round the periphery, is interpreted as confirmation of their feminine ways. The purpose of the playground and the recreational time spent there by pupils needs to be questioned. As Blatchford has put it, 'it is very important to look and act on forms of inequality and abuse in the playground. I doubt that abuse based on ethnic origin or gender will diminish without deliberate attempts to stop it' (Blatchford, 1989, p. 2). He estimates that in the case of the infant school he studied, as much as 28 per cent of the school day was spent in playtime and lunch and much of this in the playground. Moreover, this significant chunk of the day was supervised by untrained ancillary staff who have no part in staff meetings or policy discussions.

In the absence of positive alternative approaches what develops is a form of harassment in which girls are kept in their place by boys. Some teachers actively collude in the harassment, encouraging masculine domination. Others ignore what is going on or, when the girls complain, they trivialize the incidents as being minor and exceptional. Very few teachers acknowledge that the everyday incidents, however commonplace and seemingly trivial, have cumulative and collective effects — the girls are harassed into retreat (Herbert, 1989).

Girls are not likely to use the term harassment to describe their experiences, and inappropriate application of a definition may obscure rather than clarify. Nonetheless it is useful to summarize what is now recognized by this term. The definition is not created in order to develop a terminological straightjacket, but in order to distinguish this form of behaviour from others which affect girls, and boys, in different ways and which require different responses.

> It is now possible to outline a working definition of harassment as comprising three main elements — 'impersonal', unreciprocated and unwelcome physical contact, comment, suggestion, joke, attention; the mistreatment is offensive to the person/s concerned and causes the victim/s to feel threatened, humiliated, patronized, embarrassed; it dehumanizes, makes objects of the victims; the harassers base their mistreatment on notions of 'normality' — a normality which is hierarchical and which justifies mistreatment of those who are different and therefore not equal. In deciding whether harassment has been experienced, it is the view of the victim/s which should take primacy because they present more reliable indicators that do the harassers. (Kelly, 1991, p. 18)

The implications of such a definition are wide-ranging because it suggests that individual, occasional responses to incidents will not be effective (NUT, 1987). The need is for schools to move beyond a fire-fighting approach to whole-school policies, such as those developed by Ross and Ryan (1990) and the Scottish Council for Research in Education (1992).

It is not just the behaviour which needs to be tackled, but the underlying ethos which allows, even encourages, some pupils to dominate. Girls are not the only victims of harassment, but the frequency with which they have to conform to a male ethos in mixed-sex secondary schools is a graphic illustration of processes which impinge on them and on other pupils who are picked out as targets by those who have gained ascendancy.

Domestic Violence and Sexual Harassment

Some of the most disturbing findings in studies of bullying and harassment relate to the enduring effects of what is learnt in childhood: bullies continue their quest for dominance; harassers seek out new targets; their victims remain fearful. There is a clear implication that if youthful experience is carried into adult life, the consequences are even more serious and dangerous because positions of enduring ascendancy can be achieved, closeted in the privacy of the home, or as part of routine at work.

> Why was Thomas Scotland so unhinged and obsessed with controlling his family that he forbade his wife to show affection to the children, threw meals across the room if he didn't like them, threw his children's toys into the fire and sexually abused his daughter? One

probable answer is that he had no proper role model to show him what a father — or a man — should be. (*Daily Telegraph*, 25 March 1992)

Women in all social classes and ethnic groups face the greatest risk of serious or fatal injury at the hands of the men who are their domestic partners or lovers. One in four women is subject to mental or physical abuse by men. Women are four times as likely as men to be murdered by the person closest to them. Yet the courts are inconsistent and often unjust — Joseph McGrail received a two-year suspended sentence after being found guilty of manslaughter, because he claimed he had not intended to kill his wife. Rajinder Bisla, who said he was provoked by his nagging wife, was also found guilty of manslaughter and was given an eighteen-month suspended sentence (*Independent*, 24 March 1992).

Women endure abuse and violence for many years before their reserves of tolerance, protectiveness and hope are exhausted. When at last they turn on their abusers, they run great risk — if they do not choose their moment carefully, they can be overpowered by the greater strength and brutality of the man; if they do succeed, their actions may be considered 'premeditated'.

Kiranjit is serving a life sentence for murdering her abusing husband: one day, after he had beaten her up and put a hot iron on her cheek, she poured petrol over him and set him alight. But because she waited till he was asleep, the jury considered that he had time to calm down. (*Independent*, 15 March 1992)

Sara Thornton took a kitchen knife from the drawer [and] stabbed her husband Malcolm in the stomach and killed him. She called an ambulance and police, was arrested and charged with murder. She was convicted and jailed for life . . . She appealed, seeking to have the charge reduced to manslaughter on grounds of provocation since Malcolm . . . had been violent and abusive to her and her daughter. (*Guardian*, 23 March 1992)

What, campaigners ask, determines why Sara Thornton and Kiranjit Ahluwalia should be imprisoned, when men, such as McGrail and Bisla are freed? This issue has mobilized women across social classes, ethnic and party-political lines. For instance, the Conservative Asian peer, Baroness Flather, has given strong support to the 'Southall Black Sisters', a feminist campaigning group formed in 1979 by five Asian and Afro-Caribbean women, and which now has a prominent leading role in the campaign for the release of women imprisoned for killing the men who had been torturing them. She explains her support in this way:

They are doing valuable work. I am not very keen on people who only yell and demonstrate. OK, everyone has seen you with your

placard but then what? You have to do things. Southall Black Sisters
do things.

Asian women are tremendously dynamic because they start from so
little. In Asian society, from the moment he is born, the boy is the
little king, he is given everything. It must give you so much confidence. Whereas the women, they must create everything from
nothing. (*Guardian*, 15 April 1992)

Should schools stay aloof from a controversy which is featured so
prominently and frequently in the media and which raises so many questions
about the justice system and its protection of women? Should schools ignore
the fact that young people, boys as well as girls, face a conspiracy of silence
about the distorted relationships which are featured in these cases and which
they fear for themselves?

If the question of domestic violence is too challenging, then what about
all the women who are being mistreated not by their domestic partners, but
by men who see them as an easy target in the workplace? Do schools have
any guidance to offer their pupils on this issue? Sexual harassment is usually
associated with a male boss and female secretary, where the boss, because of
his masculinity and status is able to use sexualized language and familiar
gestures as a way of extracting favours from the woman employee. But this
is a very restricted perspective because schools are work arenas where women
and men come to earn their living, not just as teachers, but also as cleaners,
cooks and caretakers. It is therefore both a microcosm of the wider society's
structures and hierarchies, and an arena in which girls and boys are learning
about behaviour by precept and example.

In December 1986, the Birmingham branch of three teacher unions
undertook a survey of women teachers' experience of sexual harassment. 65
per cent of the secondary-school teachers had experienced sexual harassment
at school. They found the innuendo and *double entendre* of staffroom con-
versation unacceptable or tiresome, but, for the most part, avoided it
or tolerated it, not wanting to seem a 'prude'. Examples were given of
unwanted physical contact — such as a male senior teacher putting his arms
around junior women teachers.

The principal problem which we have identified is that, apart from
extreme cases, people are unwilling or unable to accept a female
understanding of what constitutes sexual harassment. It is seen as
the idiosyncratic behaviour of particular men which women, as
individuals, just have to cope with. The less fuss one makes, the
better . . . Because of this difference in definition, experience and
awareness, sexual harassment is trivialized and its relevance is not
seen in terms of people's well-being and ability to perform well.
(Addison and Al-Khalifa, 1988)

The issue of sexual harassment is now being taken seriously. The Department of Employment has published booklets and leaflets for employers and employees with the backing of the Confederation of British Industry (CBI) and the Trades Union Congress (TUC). The European Commission has published a code of practice to combat sexual harassment at work, endorsed by the European Council ministers. The National Union of Teachers has issued guidelines which make clear that sexual harassment should be viewed as undermining any attempt to achieve equality on the ground that it is wrong to treat any teacher, female or male, as a sexual object.

Responses

In their chapter on education for citizenship (chapter 7), Webster and Adelman emphasize the challenge to schools in initiating discussion on controversial issues and in choosing the best pedagogic methods for engaging pupils in a learning process. They favour pupils learning about rights and responsibilities through participation in, for instance, an effective school council, and a school policy on racial issues. The opportunity to devise such methods does exist, in spite of all the demands for conformity, according to an officer of the National Curriculum Council, speaking at a recent conference.

> Although the attainment targets and programmes of study are statutory, the ways in which they are taught are not. Teachers are responsible for determining teaching materials and teaching methods, and to some extent the content, through the examples used. (Donaghue, 1991)

In this concluding section it is suggested that discussions of the issues of bullying and harassment provide an effective vehicle for pupil-centred, participative learning in which pupils' own experiences should feature prominently. It is also suggested that such an approach should ensure that the victims are heard.

In the course of work in Manchester schools, pupils have repeatedly told the author of this chapter that they would welcome the opportunity to discuss taboo topics such as racism and sexism with their teachers, on condition that the teachers will take them seriously. Brah suggests that too many well intentioned people, including teachers, are held back from opening controversial issues by the 'ethnicist' trap which posits 'ethnic difference' as the primary modality around which social life is constituted and experienced. Cultural needs are defined largely as independent of other social experiences centred around class, gender, racism or sexuality. This means that a group identified as culturally different is assumed to be internally homogeneous, when this is patently not the case (Brah, 1992, p. 129).

Troyna and Hatcher in their important study of pupils in mainly white schools point out that for both black and white children, 'race' and racism are specifically features of the cultures of children. There is wide variation in the experiences of children and:

> The attitudes and beliefs of white children range from those who make use of racist frameworks of interpretation to those who are committed to well-developed notions of racial equality. Many children display inconsistent and contradictory repertoires of attitudes, containing both elements of racially egalitarian ideologies and elements of racist ideologies. (Troyna and Hatcher, 1992, p. 197)

They argue that children's cultures should be analysed in terms of the interplay of processes of domination and equality, which reveal themselves through the complexities of their social interactions, and the children's interpretations of such interactions. Lee suggests that one of the first items on the pedagogic agenda must be the question of trust. She realized how deeply pupils feel about their exclusion from all forms of policy-making when she discovered that respect had become the dirtiest word in their vocabulary. It had become synonymous with

> [A] form of tyranny to them because they had been used to it as a one-way transaction; it was a way that adults exercised authority over them. As young people they were required to pay respect, but they were never given it ... They were used to respect being demanded of them ... regardless of their feelings and never as part of a two-way transaction. It was not surprising therefore, that the words and phrases they gave me for 'respect' were: ordering, listening to, being told what to do and keeping your mouth shut. (Lee, 1986, p. 54)

While trapped into feeling they are always at the receiving end, pupils will be left where they are now, encouraged to collude in secrecy, hiding the humiliating and painful experience of the victims, protecting harassers and bullies from exposure and believing that it is dangerous to tell. In some instances, this intimidation can reach pathological levels, affecting the whole of a school, as analysed by the Macdonald Inquiry report (1989).

As part of a three phase project initiated in 1990 to identify the nature and incidence of bullying in infant, junior and secondary schools and to develop means of countering bullying, one LEA has recently published details of their 'Bullying in Schools Initiative' (Wolverhampton Education Department Safer Cities Project, 1991). A representative cross-section of nineteen schools in the borough took part in the first phase of the project. The data presented are analysed by sex and, in some cases, by ethnic group. The secondary school sample comprised five mixed sex schools from which responses from 475 girls and 503 boys were analysed. The behaviours construed by pupils as comprising bullying were identified. The respective percentages of boys and girls in each age group indicating that particular aspects of being bullied had happened to them *more than once* during the last week present an important empirical definition of pupils' perceptions concerning the nature and incidence of bullying. For girls overall, the four highest ranked events were 'called me names' (23 per cent). 'teased me' (11 per cent), 'tried to trip me up' (8 per cent) and tried to get me into trouble' (8 per cent). For boys overall, the four highest ranked events were 'called me names' (28 per cent), 'tried to hit me' (17 per cent), 'tried to trip me up' (14 per cent) and 'teased me' and 'tried to trip me up (jointly 10 per cent).

'As with pupils' definitions of bullying, there appears to be a tendency for girls to be more the victims of verbally based bullying, rather than physical bullying' (ibid., p. 4). Moreover Asian and Afro-Caribbean pupils experienced considerably more comments about their skin colour than white pupils.

Phase two, from May 1991 to July 1992, involved piloting a variety of interventions designed to reduce bullying in schools. From September 1992 to July 1993, a wider implementation of the strategies will take place. The efficacy of these strategies will then be evaluated against the baseline figures found in Phase one.

This work is of interest on four major counts. First, it clearly describes a strategy that can be used in any school or LEA to identify the nature and incidence of bullying; using it, both sex and ethnic group similarities and differences can be identified. Second, it provides suggestions for reducing bullying. Third, baselines for evaluating the efficacy of interventions are obtained. Finally, the publication contains a valuable list of recent references concerning bullying in schools and a list of ten important resource packs designed to reduce bullying.

It must be clear by now that a school cannot eliminate sexual harassment without reforming its ethos; and it cannot eliminate bullying without winning the trust of its pupils. It is difficult to see how schools can make progress on the behaviourial constraints on girls and the boys who are sexualized until and unless they acknowledge that it is the pupils who are the participant observers and who know what is going on. Changing ethos and winning trust implies a whole-school approach to behaviour which extends beyond the usual confines of the classroom and core-curriculum subjects and which develops positive policies in which pupils can cooperate.

Work done in Norway and in a few schools in Britain confirms that the most effective strategies are based on mutual respect (Munthe and Roland. 1989; Casdagli *et al.*, 1990). If teachers are listening, then they will not only be trained by their pupils into what is going on in their formerly secret world, but will be able to intervene with good effect. The rate of bullying drops when a school starts to supervise the playground and other pupil spaces more closely. However, it drops even more markedly when the teachers engage in an approach which draws pupils into discussion and decisions about behaviour, what is acceptable and why, what is unacceptable and why. 'Whole-school' policies have become something of a catchphrase, but if they are based on generating mutual respect and confidence between pupils and their teachers then harassment and bullying can be exposed for what they are — cruel and unnecessary processes which damage everyone involved.

Not only the victims but also the bullies are in need of guidance and assistance if they are to turn away from the abnormality of their behaviour and find alternative ways of dealing with the complexities of their interpersonal relations. But neither will recover from the bullying until and unless adults become much wiser in their handling of the processes and hierarchies which are perpetuated by schools. Richardson has summarized the two principles which should guide schools as they seek liberation from oppressive systems:

> The one tradition is learner-centred education, and the development and fulfilment of individuals. This tradition is humanistic and optim-istic, and has a basic trust in the capacity and will of human beings to create healthy and empowering systems and structures . . . The second tradition is concerned with building equality and with resisting the trend for education merely to reflect and replicate inequalities in wider society of race, gender and class; it is broadly pessimistic in its assumption that inequalities are the norm wherever and whenever they are not consciously and strenuously resisted. (Richardson, 1990, pp. 6–7)

One of the most important lessons for any young person to learn is the ability to resolve disputes amicably. Those who can deflect aggressive situations are valued by their peers and have learnt skills which will stand them in good stead in adult life. Whole-school behaviour policies should not only *dis*courage harassment and bullying, but also *en*courage the learning of interpersonal and social skills in dealing with injustice and inequality. They should provide a framework and reference point for pupils to engage in discussion about rights, responsibilities and participation as apprentice citizens. Learning how to deal with bullying and harassment could lay the foundation for a safer and happier future in which sex inequalities are dealt with in a multiethnic context.

References

ADDISON, B. and AL-KHALIFA, E. (1988) ' "It's All Good Clean Fun" — Sexual Harass-ment: A Case Study', in *Educational Management and Administration*, 16, pp. 173–85.

ATWOOD, M. (1990) *Cat's Eye*, London, Virago Press.

BESAG, V. (1989) *Bullies and Victims in Schools: A Guide to Understanding and Manage-ment*, Milton Keynes, Open University Press.

BLATCHFORD, P. (1989) 'Playtime in the Primary School: Problems and Improvements', *Dorothy Gardner Memorial Lectures*, Institute of Education, University of London.

BRAH, A. (1992) 'Difference, Diversity and Differentiation', in DONALD, J. and RATTANSI, A. (Eds) *'Race', Culture and Difference*, London, Open University Press, pp. 126–45.

BYRNE, E. (1978) *Women and Education*, London, Tavistock Publications.

CASDAGLI, P., GOBEY, F. and GRIFFITH, C. (1990) *Only Playing Miss: The Playscript and a Workshop Approach to the Problem of Bullying*, Stoke-on-Trent, Trentham Books.

COMMISSION FOR RACIAL EQUALITY (1988) *Learning in Terror, a Survey of Racial Harassment in Schools and Colleges in England, Scotland and Wales, 1985–1987*, London CRE.

Daily Telegraph (1992) 25 March.

DEEM, R. (1984) *Co-Education Reconsidered*, Milton Keynes, Open University Press.

DONAGHUE, J. (1991) 'A Perspective from the NCC', *Multicultural Teaching*, 10, 1, Autumn, p. 12.

Guardian (1992) 23 March, 15 April.

HERBERT, C. (1989) *Talking of Silence: The Sexual Harassment of School Girls*, Lewes, The Falmer Press.

Independent (1992) 15, 24 March.

KELLY, E.A. (1991) 'Bullying and Racial and Sexual Harassment in Schools', *Multicultural Teaching*, 10, 1, Autumn.

LA FONTAINE, J. (1991) *Bullying: The Child's View*, London, Calouste Gulbenkian Foundation.

LEE, C. (1986) *Sex, Schooling and Mystification*, London, Unwin Hyman.

LEES, S. (1986) *Losing Out: Sexuality and Adolescent Girls*, London, Hutchinson Education.

MACDONALD, I. (1989) *Murder in the Playground: The Report of the Macdonald Inquiry into Racism and Racial Violence in Manchester Schools*, London, Longsight Press.

MAHONY, P. (1985) *Schools for the Boys? Co-education Reassessed*, London, Hutchinson Education.

NATIONAL CURRICULUM COUNCIL (1990) *The Whole Curriculum: Curriculum Guidance No. 3*, York, NCC.

NATIONAL UNION OF TEACHERS (1987) *Dealing with Sexual Harassment: Guidelines for Teachers*, London, NUT.

MUNTHE, E. and ROLAND, E. (1989) *Bullying: An International Perspective*, London, David Fulton Publishers in association with the Professional Development Foundation.

REPORT OF THE COMMITTEE OF INQUIRY (1989) *Discipline in Schools. (Chair: Lord Elton)* Department of Education and Science and the Welsh Office, London, HMSO.

RICHARDSON, R. (1990) *Daring to be a Teacher: Essays in Holistic Education*, Stoke-on-Trent, Trentham Books.

ROSS, C. and RYAN, A. (1990) 'Can You Stay in Today Miss?', *Improving the School Playground: Ideas and Issues Developed form Work with Islington Schools*, Stoke-on-Trent, Trentham Books.

SCOTTISH COUNCIL FOR RESEARCH IN EDUCATION (1992) *Action Against Bullying*, Edinburgh, SCRE.

SMITH, S. (1984) 'Single-Sex Setting', in DEEM, R. (Ed) *Co-education Reconsidered*, Milton Keynes, Open University Press.

Elinor Kelly

TATTUM, D.P. and LANE, D.A. (1989) *Bullying in Schools*, Stoke-on-Trent, Trentham Books.
TROYNA, B. and HATCHER, R. (1992) *Racism in Children's Lives*, London, Routledge.
WEINER, G. (1985) *Just a Bunch of Girls: Feminist Approaches to Schooling*, Milton Keynes, Open University Press.
WOLVERHAMPTON EDUCATION DEPARTMENT/SAFER CITIES PROJECT BULLYING IN SCHOOLS INITIATIVE (1991) *Safer Schools, Safer Cities*, Wolverhampton, Wolverhampton Education Department.

Chapter 12

Children with Special Educational Needs

Peter Mittler

Context

Can the Education Reform Act in general and the National Curriculum in particular benefit all children or will some children benefit disproportionately more than others? Are there groups of children who are particularly at risk of being overlooked or marginalized by these reforms?

This chapter will be concerned with a large and heterogenous group of children, mostly from the most socially and economically disadvantaged groups in society who are particularly at risk of underachievement. Within this wider group, estimated to be as high as 40 per cent of school-age children, at least one half are regarded as having special educational needs. Most of these children can be helped within the resources of ordinary schools but a small proportion will require additional provision and resources either in ordinary or special schools or classes.

Social class and socio-economic differences in our society reflect the wider cultural diversity which constitutes the theme of this book. The extent to which these differences affect educational attainments and outcomes whether positively or negatively is relatively little discussed. Since low attainment is strongly associated with poverty and social disadvantage, to what extent can or will the current changes in education benefit these children? Can these reforms narrow the large gap in educational attainment between children from different social backgrounds? Is there a danger that children from the poorer sectors of our society who have always been particularly vulnerable to educational underachievement will be even further disadvantaged? Or are there real possibilities of harnessing the reforms to make for more equal access and a better quality of education?

The implications of the Education Reform Act for children from ethnic minorities have not been as publicly debated as those for children with special educational needs, though they share many common concerns. Indeed, a comparison of the Warnock report on special educational needs and the Swann report on the education of children from ethnic minorities reflects striking parallels (Department of Education and Science, 1978, 1985; Mittler, 1989). Both are concerned with ways in which schools as organizations as well as individual teachers can cause or complicate underachievement — by underestimation of children, by failing to engage the confidence and collaboration of parents and by the imposition of a curriculum which takes insufficient account of the social and cultural diversity of the background from which children come. Both reports call for a reappraisal and restructuring of the curriculum to ensure that it reaches all children in the school, regardless of social background, ethnicity or the nature or degree of learning difficulties, however caused.

Because single factor explanations, whether in terms of ethnicity, social class or special needs, are clearly misleading, more refined analytic methods are required to unravel the complex interactions and interrelationships involved. The Swann report summarizes a large volume of evidence on the educational attainments of children from ethnic minorities. Since then, more refined studies using multilevel modelling techniques have sought to differentiate more clearly between the complex set of variables which affect the performance of pupils in schools (Drew and Gray, 1991). Thus, the Swann report emphasized that differences in the educational performance of children from different ethnic-minority groupings could be largely, though not entirely, accounted for by differences in social class and parental expectations but failed to discuss the operation or possible modification of these social class effects.

It also remains to be seen whether the National Curriculum, even though acknowledging the importance of multicultural education as an essential cross-curricular element, will be seen to be relevant to the interests of all children from ethnic minorities; there are real concerns about the nature of religious education to be provided, the insistence on acts of Christian worship and the anglocentric or Eurocentric bias of the history curriculum, inserted as a result of direct ministerial interventions. It is also a matter of great concern that the National Curriculum Council chose not to publish the report of a working party on access of pupils from ethnic minorities to the National Curriculum and that the Department of Education and Science has withdrawn support from at least two relevant research projects.

The ethnic minority and special needs constituencies have much in common, not least their vulnerability to marginalization and exclusion, though they have chosen to pursue their goals independently rather than within a single equal-opportunities framework.

Challenges

Poverty and Disadvantage

Even on a conservative estimate, ten million people were experiencing poverty in the 1970s and 1980s, four million of them with young children in the family (Pilling, 1990; National Children's Homes, 1990). Associated with poverty are grossly unsatisfactory housing, unemployment and chronic physical or mental ill health, as well as low educational achievement. What, then, is the evidence for the link between socio-economic disadvantage and low educational attainments?

Nearly twenty years ago, the 'National Child Development Study' (NCDS) which has followed the progress of all children born in the United Kingdom in a single week in March 1958 showed that children with objective indicators of social disadvantage were more than seven times as likely to be sent to special schools than children from the population at large (Davie, Butler and Goldstein, 1972; Wedge and Prosser, 1973). At that time, social disadvantage was defined by the presence of all three indicators of low income qualifying for supplementary benefit, overcrowding (more than 1.5 persons per room) and being either in a single-parent family or in one with more than five children.

The NCDS and other studies clearly showed that social class differences in educational attainment were already marked by the age of 7 and that these differences increased rather than decreased as the children went through school and were still marked at 16 (Fogelman, 1983). Thus, children from families where the father was in a non-manual occupation were on average three years higher in their reading and maths attainments at the age of 11 compared with children from social class 5. At 16, three quarters had reading and maths scores that were below average and a high proportion were reported as showing behaviour problems (Essen and Wedge, 1982).

Similar data are reported from other studies of staying on rates and of examination performance at 16 and also of access to higher education (Office of Population Censuses and Surveys, 1987). A series of studies of access to selective education and later of results of the School Certificate and General Certificate of Education show that, despite the raising of the school-leaving age, the introduction of comprehensive education and a substantial increase in the percentage of all pupils obtaining GCE O levels, the size of the gap between middle-class and working-class children has not changed significantly between children born at the end of the nineteenth century and those born in the 1960s (Heath, 1989). Although 'standards have risen', as measured by the proportion of pupils with O levels, the relative advantage of middle-class over working-class children has remained static over a long period. Only 2 per cent of university graduates come from homes where the father's occupation is described as semi-skilled or unskilled, compared with 17 per cent from all families and 29 per cent from professional families.

The NCDS is only one of several national longitudinal studies which have exhaustively documented socio-economic differences in educational attainments and access (Douglas, 1964, 1968; Wiseman, 1964). Gross inequalities have also been reported in the field of health and in access to health care, particularly in the Black report (Townsend and Whitehead, 1988). These reports made many positive recommendations for ways in which inequalities in health care could be addressed and perhaps remedied but these recommendations were immediately rejected as totally unrealistic by the government.

Studies of the educational attainments of children from ethnic minorities tend to indicate poorer attainments among Afro-Caribbean pupils compared with Asian and total population samples. But these results are not found in all studies and on all parameters and there are suggestions that differences can be considered as a reflection of educational inequality in access to opportunities. Furthermore, these studies have employed a variety of methodologies and interpretations which are open to criticism (Figueroa, 1988).

It is important to emphasize that these studies merely document general trends and risk factors which mask a great deal of variation and to which there are many individual exceptions. In research terms, the standard deviations within each social class are fairly large (Fogelman, 1983) and the amount of variance explained by a single variable such as social class remains relatively small. Thus, the majority of socially disadvantaged children in the NCDS study did *not* present significant educational or behavioural difficulties. Indeed, one in seven of this group scored above the median for non-disadvantaged children on educational attainment tests. Conversely, children from middle-class families frequently do less well than expected.

A particularly interesting study by Pilling (1990), drawing again on NCDS data but including interviews with the cohort members themselves at the age of 23, is concerned with those young people who did comparatively well, despite the severely disadvantaging circumstances of their childhood and adolescence, in contrast with a comparison group from the same background. Escape from disadvantage was strongly associated with parental support and interest in education and achievement, favourable life experiences and opportunities and temperamental qualities, particular persistence, resilience and high achievement motivation. Males were more likely than females to escape disadvantage.

Can Schools Make a Difference?

Social-class differences in educational outcomes are well established and documented. Whether they are inevitable and whether schooling can reduce their impact is clearly an issue of the first importance. At one time, socio-economic factors were regarded as an endemic and inevitable feature of the educational system of this country. The low attainments of children from poorer backgrounds were simply attributed to home circumstances.

There is a considerable volume of research which suggests that schools can make a substantial impact on narrowing the gap between children from different social backgrounds though there are suggestions that the evidence on this point is not as conclusive as some would claim (Reynolds, 1991). A series of school effectiveness studies both from the United States (Boyd, 1991; Edmonds, 1989) and from this country have suggested that the way in which schools are managed and led and in which the curriculum is planned and delivered in individual classrooms can have a significant effect on all children but particularly on children from the poorest sections of society. Amongst the most notable of the British studies is *Fifteen Thousand Hours* (Rutter, Maugham, Mortimore and Ouston, 1979) and its later junior-school counterpart *Schools Matter* (Mortimore, Sammons, Ecob, and Stoll, 1988) and a recent study of six inner-city multiracial comprehensive schools by Smith and Tomlinson (1989). The last of these is one of several studies which show that some schools are particularly successful in helping children from ethnic minorities to increase their rate of progress relative to low initial performance at 11.

One of the agreed characteristics of effective schools is that they are staffed by people with high expectations for all pupils, regardless of family or cultural background. Other characteristics include intellectually challenging teaching, two-way communication between teacher and pupils, the matching of tasks to pupils, a work-centred environment, the use of praise and parental involvement. Effective schools are those that value and seek to harness the child's family and cultural background and never attribute all a child's difficulties to home background or the lifestyle of the family. A staff-room comment along the lines of 'What do you expect of a child from a home like that?' would be regarded as unacceptable as any racist or sexist remark.

Despite the research evidence that schools can narrow the achievement gap and despite a renewed interest in school-management styles, many teachers still believe there is little that can be done by schools to offset the educational disadvantages of poverty. Nor is such pessimism confined to teachers. Even the report of the widely praised Task Group on Assessment and Testing (TGAT) (DES, 1987) after briefly summarizing the evidence for the effect of socio-economic factors on educational attainments, concluded that 'it is difficult to see how such factors can be taken into account in reports of the performance of individual schools'. Instead, they recommended that the local education authority should set the results of individual schools in context by indication 'the nature of socio-economic and other influences which are known to affect schools . . . and the known effects of such influences on performance' (pars. 133–5). It is not easy to do this without using language and assumptions which devalue the local population and which may be racist in tone. Furthermore, would schools in prosperous areas be criticized for failing to achieve even better results?

It is also unfortunate that the TGAT report failed to take account of information from school-effectiveness research, which stressed the importance of assessment through measures of *progress* over a period of time, as did the ILEA junior-school study, rather than by the simple snapshot which is now regarded as standard national practice. Two children from similar backgrounds and with identical test scores at the age of 7 can have totally different outcomes at 11, 14 or 16, depending on the school which they attend. Under current government policy, parents and the local community are asked to judge a school on the basis of assessments which take no account of starting levels and cannot therefore record degree or rate of progress made by individuals or by groups of children. The published information on which parents and the community are asked to judge schools is therefore incomplete and misleading and may fail to do justice either to their strengths or their weaknesses.

Responses

Reducing Disadvantage

Inequalities in education largely, though perhaps not wholly, reflect inequalities in the structure and workings of society and its institutions. As long as a substantial section of our society continues to live in poverty, to be unemployed and badly housed and to be disproportionately vulnerable to poor health, there must be limits to what can be achieved by education alone, however much it is reformed and restructured. But what are these limits and are individual teachers and society as a whole in danger of underestimating what can be achieved? The paradox remains that removal of all intergroup differences in attainments that were a consequences of social deprivation of *all* sorts, would still leave differences attributable to individual characteristic. But that situation is far off.

There is a long-standing debate about the extent to which education can 'compensate for society'. But can even a pessimistic perspective on this question justify a passive acceptance that schooling cannot affect inequalities in educational outcomes for children from disadvantaged families? Policy makers and legislators as well as heads and governors need to consider what can be done with the means at their disposal, however limited these may be. At the very least, they have a responsibility to ensure that reforms which are intended for all do not differentially disadvantage some sections of the population and give additional advantages to others.

Being a member of one of the majority of minority ethnic groups comprising the population of the UK means that the individual is likely to face both institutional and individual racism. If, in addition, an individual has special educational needs, further problems often arise from the combination of these two factors. 'Race and Disability: Dual Oppression' was the title of an address given on 14 May 1992, by Bernie Grant, MP for Tottenham as his contribution to the launch of a research report into this field.

The race and disability research project carried out in the London Borough of Waltham Forest sheds light on a relatively poorly studied area (Nasa Begum, 1992). The objectives of this study included identifying the needs of, and issues affecting, Asian people with disabilities and their carers; reviewing existing service provisions with a view to highlighting ethnic groups' concerns; and identifying the obstacles to employment faced by black and ethnic-minority people with disabilities. The methodology used was based on survey and interviews. Both quantitative and qualitative data were elicited.

Two questionnaires were designed, one for Asian people with disabilities and the other for Asian carers. The latter group was able to provide information concerning 'the needs and wishes of people with severe learning difficulties, and those who were under the age of 16' (p. 3). Copies of the questionnaires can be obtained from the Race Relations Unit, Town Hall, Forest Road, Walthamstow, London, E17 9JD. The areas covered by the enquiry included: accommodation and living circumstances; education; day-time activities; leisure and social life; transport; attitudes towards disability; information requirements; and financial circumstances.

The sample studied was of Asian citizens with physical, sensory and learning disabilities and their carers. A leaflet in both Urdu and English was distributed throughout the various community agencies. 172 volunteers came forward to take part in the study. There were ninety-six carers and seventy-six disabled persons involved. The subjects ranged from under 5 years to over 55 years. The youngest was aged about 4 weeks; the oldest was 87 years of age. Thirty-two carers were involved with children under 5 years, thirty-five with children aged from 5 to 15 years and nineteen with young people aged from 16–24. Sixteen disabled adolescents comprised the youngest group of disabled individuals responding directly.

The richness of the interview data presented demonstrates vividly the effects of the double handicap of disability and minority ethnic-group membership. The section of the report on 'racism and racial harassment' underlines this point. The reproduction of a response to an advertisement in the council's newspaper concerning the research exemplifies the racist attitudes against which multicultural education battles (p. 32). The verbatim reports taken from the interviews with both the carers and the handicapped make telling points. There is a danger that a failure to address racism and racial harassment results in some disabled persons internalizing racism and failing to value their own racial identity. The point is made in the following quotation:

> Day by day my awareness of race came second to my awareness of disability, because it seemed the most practical way to deal with my life. The attitude of my teachers could be summed up as 'Disabled, first and foremost' . . . All of my teachers and tutors were white. Some of them did not want to risk offending anyone, or they did not think of race as the most important issue in special schools . . . But, my classmates and I were just as likely to swap 'Love Thy Neighbour' type jokes as anyone else, and to think of it as nothing more than a good laugh (ibid., p. 40)

The report concludes that 'for many Asian people with disabilities and carers, their lives are strongly influenced by the everyday reality of racism and racial harassment. Whilst to a large extent the experiences highlighted in the research are not dissimilar to the situation and problems described by Black and ethnic minority people generally, it has to be recognised that racism and racial harassment compound the difficulties faced by Black and ethnic minority disabled people and their carers' (p. 39).

The materials contained in this report could, to advantage, be used within the 'Education for Citizenship' cross-curricular theme within a school as part of multicultural antiracist education.

A video produced by disabled people and entitled 'Different Lives, Same Rights' has also been produced. Extracts from it were shown as part of the day's programme. A training manual accompanying the video has also been produced. Although not specifically concerned with secondary-school pupils, the material has potential in connection with the cross-curricular themes included within the secondary-school curriculum. It can be obtained from:

The Race Relations Unit,
Education Department,
Town Hall,
Forest Road,
London Borough of Waltham Forest,
London, E17 45Y

As is argued in this chapter, social class is a central, cultural concept having equal-opportunities implications for pupils with special educational needs, irrespective of any ethnic-group allegiances. Separately, and even more so in combination, social class, or socio-economic background, or parental occupational status, ethnic group identities and disabilities are professionally and politically highly sensitive areas. In part, this is because social class, ethnicity and disability are dimensions on which there are important inter and intraindividual differences. Their resource implications depend on whether society collectively views these differences sympathetically or otherwise. In a democratic society, the practical manifestations for individuals and groups of the abstract concepts of equality of opportunity and of justice are central to social cohesion. They are highlighted for schools and society when considered in relation to access to the 'entitlement' curriculum for pupils of all social and cultural backgrounds and disabilities.

Demands for resources in society in general, and in education in particular, always outstrip those available to schools through the public purse. The electorate's paradoxical demands for excellent public services and low taxes, does not help. Determining priorities is a task which, under the financial rights and responsibilities devolving to state schools through Local Management of Schools (LMS) and Local Management of Special Schools (LMSS), presents ethical and moral issues concerning the ethos of each school, and beyond. How can cooperation, competition and caring coexist? The Waltham Forest materials, and similar ones available through AIMER, raise equal-opportunity issues central to citizens of all ages, social and cultural groups and abilities, in our society (see Chapter 1). 'Education for Citizenship', one of the cross-curricular themes, must include such matters.

Preschool Projects
Educational reform must be an integral element of a comprehensive strategy to reduce the crippling effects of poverty, poor housing, unemployment and ill health. The 'war on poverty' launched by President Kennedy, though only partially successful, clearly included a major educational thrust, particularly at the preschool level (Begab, Haywood and Garber, 1981).

The Headstart movement of the late 1960s represented a massive attempt to compensate for social disadvantage by means of stimulation and enrichment programmes delivered both in day centres and in the children's homes, working largely through the parents. Although few of the programmes resulted in clear, immediate gains in scores on various tests, long-term follow-up studies over a twenty year period reflected substantial benefits compared with control groups from similar backgrounds who did not experience such programmes (Lazar and Darlington, 1982). Fewer children experiencing Headstart were referred to special education and more remained at school beyond the statutory period. They also had better employment records, lower divorce rates and fewer offences against the law. The British version of Headstart — the 'Educational Priority Areas' programme — was also characterized by a strong attempt to involve parents in the educational and personal development of their children and was able to report positive results (Halsey, 1972).

Working with Parents
The concept of partnership with parents has perhaps not had the same impact in ordinary schools as in special schools, though the case for a reappraisal for teacher–parent relationships was most forcefully made by the Plowden committee (DES, 1967) and later by the Court Committee on Child Health Services who stated

> We have found no better way to raise a child than to reinforce the ability of his parents, whether natural or substitute, to do so. (DHSS, 1976)

These conclusions seem obvious, almost trite, until one remembers that it was not so long ago that parents were kept at a firm and respectful distance from the activities of the classroom. Moreover, many secondary schools still have only tenuous links with parents, through annual parent evenings or through summoning parents when there is a problem with their child. The reappraisal of home–school links is as urgent as ever. If successful, it could make a major contribution to narrowing the educational attainments and life chances of children from economically poorer backgrounds.

Since these Headstart programmes, there have been a number of projects which have sought to develop effective working partnership with parents. The most extensive of these has been the 'shared-reading' initiatives which have developed in many primary schools (Topping and Wolfendale, 1985). These and other forms of home–school links have richly demonstrated that children make better progress in learning when parents and teachers collaborate. Similarly, work reported by Widlake (1986) from the Coventry Community Education Centre documents in some detail that families from the poorest and most disadvantaged sections of the population could work in full partnership with teachers, once they became convinced that teachers were willing to treat them as equals and to meet them on their own terms.

The 'Lower Achieving Pupils' Programme 1982–1988

The Lower Achieving Pupils Programme (LAPP) was launched by the Department of Education and Science in 1982, aimed specifically at fourth and fifth-year low-achieving pupils in secondary schools — i.e., the 40 per cent of pupils identified by the then Secretary of State, Sir Keith Joseph, as not benefiting from school and who were likely to leave without any formal qualifications. The project involved thirteen LEAs, who were given considerable freedom to develop their own approaches in devising activities and experiences which would enhance the motivation and achievements of these pupils and provide a better transition to adult and working life.

An initial evaluation of the projects by HMI (1989) concluded that positive results could be reported in terms of personal and social education for the pupils and in enhancing the status of work with these pupils in the schools. On the negative side, many of the programmes effectively separated the pupils from their peers. Levels of pupils' school attendance were also disappointing. A much fuller evaluation by NFER, including a detailed follow-up of longer term developments, provides an excellent study of the varying approaches used by schools to develop an integrated approach to meeting the needs of these pupils (Stradling and Saunders, 1991). In-service training materials are also included.

Who Are Children with Special Educational Needs?

Many people still think of special education as concerned largely with handicapped children who tend to come from all sections of society. While this is largely true of children with sensory and physical impairments and applies to some degree to children with severe learning difficulties (mental handicap), the reality for the generality of children with special educational needs is very different. Nearly all the children in schools for pupils with moderate learning difficulties (who constitute about half of all children in special schools) are drawn from the poorer and poorest sections of our society. Most have

Table 12.1: *Placement of Ethnic Groups in Special Schools and EBD Units*

	% in population up to 19 years of age (England and Wales)	Proportion in schools and units for EBD pupils
Afro-Caribbean	2.4	4.8
Indian	6.7	0.5
Pakistani	2.9	1.4
Bangladeshi	0.1	0.03
Remainder	1.7	1.3
TOTAL	14.0 (N=12,673,300)	8.0 (N=8,566)
White European	86.0	92.0

Notes: 1. EBD units are units for pupils manifesting emotional and behavioural difficulties.
2. The above figures do not include the estimated 7,000 pupils attending local school-based units.

Source: (Cooper *et al.*, 1991)

previously attended ordinary schools but have been excluded from them on the grounds of unsatisfactory progress, often in association with difficult or disruptive behaviour.

The process of referral, assessment and decision-making for such children has been documented in some detail by Tomlinson (1981), with particular reference to the high proportion of Afro-Caribbean children referred and selected for special schools for children with moderate learning difficulties. Concern has been expressed for many years about the disproportionate number of children from Afro-Caribbean backgrounds who are sent to special schools, usually schools for children with moderate learning difficulties and emotional and behavioural difficulties (Coard, 1971; Tomlinson, 1981). It is difficult to obtain information on whether this is still the case, as the government does not collect statistics on ethnic grouping or on types of special school or categories of special need.

There are indications that disproportionate ethnic-related placements in specialist facilities still exist. One recent survey studied the distribution of pupils attending special schools and units for pupils with emotional and behavioural difficulties (Cooper, Upton and Smith, 1991). Questionnaires were sent to all 355 special schools and units in England and Wales concerned with the education of such pupils. A response rate of about two-thirds provided information concerning 8,556 pupils. These were categorized according to ethnic group. The result are summarized in Table 12.1.

Boys were much more likely than girls to be attending the facilities surveyed. The data concerning some 1,900 teachers showed that the vast majority were white-European and that women teachers were under-represented. The various imbalances identified are a cause for concern. One irony is that although this form of special education represents a much greater per-capita investment in the education of pupils compared with the resources available in the mainstream, it is a provision viewed with suspicion.

Some of the wider issues concerned with the sociology of special education raised by Tomlinson (1982) are even more relevant today in the more competitive climate created by the 1988 Education Act. She sees special schools for children with moderate learning difficulties, as well as those for children with emotional and behavioural difficulties, as a safety valve created by the educational system and by professionals with vested interests in the maintenance of the status quo. Their underlying purpose is to remove from mainstream schools those children who are thought to be unable to contribute to an increasingly technological and market-orientated society. An alternative viewpoint would emphasize that despite the social and other disadvantages of segregated special schooling, such schools provide a form of positive discrimination by virtue of their very small classes and the training and experience of their staff.

Children from social classes 4 and 5 are greatly overrepresented among the 18 per cent or so of all children with special educational needs found in ordinary schools and among the 40 per cent identified by Sir Keith Joseph, as leaving schools without any recognized qualification or failing to benefit from what schools have to offer. The difficulties experienced by these children are part of the spectrum of underachievement and low attainment associated with socio-economic differences in our society.

The continuum of special educational needs thus includes not only the whole range of children with disabilities and those in special schools but a varying number of children in ordinary schools who are experiencing learning difficulties of all kinds and for whatever reason. The challenge for the future is to develop a whole-school approach which aims to ensure that each area of the curriculum and each aspect of the work of the school is planned and delivered in such a way as to guarantee access and participation to every single child in that school, irrespective of social or cultural background or learning difficulty.

Schools vary immensely in the degree and quality of access they provide to the whole curriculum for all pupils or in the obstacles placed in the way of access to an individual subject or activity. Individual teachers vary in the extent to which they differentiate a subject or a single classroom session to ensure that all pupils understand the nature of the task in front of them, that the language used by the teacher is also accessible and that books and worksheets reflect realistic levels of literacy and comprehension for a given group of pupils (Fish, 1989; Norwich, 1990).

The Warnock Report and the 1981 Education Act

The Warnock report recommended that for purposes of planning and provision, one child in five at some time and one child in six at any time should be assumed to have special educational needs. Such children will need one or more of the following:

- provision of special means of access to the curriculum through special equipment, facilities or resources, modifications of the physical environment or specialist teaching techniques;
- the provision of a special or modified curriculum; and
- particular attention to the social structure and emotional climate in which education takes place. (DES, 1978, par. 3.19)

In the 1981 Education Act, special educational needs are defined in terms of:

- significantly greater learning difficulties than the majority of children of the age group;
- having a disability which either prevents or hinders a child from making use of the use of educational facilities generally available in schools. (DES, 1981)

The number of children who can be encompassed within the extraordinarily loose and tautologous definition has become so large and so disparate that it is difficult to conceptualize common elements and needs. Indeed, it has been argued that the term has now outlived its usefulness and could be quietly laid to rest (Pumfrey and Mittler, 1989).

Nevertheless, the conceptual framework within which special needs are now seen has certain strengths. In particular, the origins of special educational needs are no longer seen as lying solely in the child or even in the child's family. It is increasingly accepted that schools can cause, complicate and, conversely, also prevent special educational needs. Special educational needs are therefore relative and interactive. A pupil can have special educational needs in one school but not in another, if the first school can meet the child's needs and the second will need to modify its curriculum or require extra resources.

The 1988 Education Reform Act: Background and Challenges
Can the 1988 Education Reform Act affect these gross inequalities which have been an endemic feature of the British education system for decades? The political and economic objectives of the Education Reform Act are to raise educational standards, to secure better education for all and to ensure that future generations are equipped with the knowledge, skills and understanding to further their own personal development as well as to make a better contribution to society by securing the economic success of the country against its 'competitors'. The Act and all the accompanying regulations, circulars and guidance documents are unambiguous in their affirmation that the National Curriculum is an entitlement for all pupils. Its main purposes are to:

- promote the spiritual, moral, cultural, mental and physical development of pupils at the school and of society [why is social development omitted?]
- prepare such pupils for the opportunities, responsibilities and experiences of adult life. (DES, 1989)

It is also authoritatively stated that 'the principle that each pupil should have a broad and balanced curriculum which is also relevant to his or her particular needs is now established in law' (DES, 1989).

These aims bear a close resemblance to the goals of education as set out by the Warnock committee:

> The goals of education . . . are first to enlarge a child's knowledge, experience and imaginative understanding and thus his awareness of moral values and capacity for enjoyment; and secondly to enable him to enter the world of work after formal education is over as an active participant in society and as a responsible contributor to it, capable of achieving as much independence as possible. (DES, 1978, par. 1.4)

All commentators are agreed that the 1988 Education Reform Act is the most far-reaching and radical piece of education legislation since the 1944 Act. Perhaps the 1870 Education Act is a more appropriate starting point, since it is this Act which marks the beginning of the process of making education as a right available to all children. That process was completed 100 years later when children with severe learning difficulties who had previously been officially regarded as ineducable became the responsibility of the Department of Education and Science and the local education authorities in England and Wales.

In parallel with the opening of schools to all children, we can trace the history of increasing access to the whole curriculum, defined in the broadest sense as 'all the learning experiences provided by a school'. Such a history would be concerned with the opening of free, publicly funded education to all sections of society, and with the process of ensuring access to the curriculum for all pupils, e.g., girls, children from ethnic and linguistic minorities, as well as pupils experiencing difficulties in learning in the widest sense.

There is disturbing evidence that all is not well with the quality of provision not only for children with special educational needs but for a larger group of low-attaining pupils. This concern is reflected in a series of some twenty national reports from Her Majesty's Inspectors of Education. An HMI summary of these specialist reports conclude that 'the sector is not well prepared to meet the challenges of the new legislation' (HMI, 1990). Furthermore, the former HM Senior Chief Inspector for Education, in his annual review of the whole education service, regularly singled out this group of children as the least well served by the education system and as 'suffering disproportionately from whatever chronic or acute problems affect the education service' (HMI, 1991a).

Threats to the quality of provision arise from a variety of sources, of which the most immediate is probably Local Management of Schools (LMS), involving the delegation of funding and decision-making direct to schools (see Chapter 15). At the same time, the role and influence of local education authorities are being greatly weakened. Headteachers and governing bodies will in future have a much greater say in determining and financing their own priorities. With the exception of pupils with statements, for whom funding will to some extent continue to be provided through the LEA, the cost of providing appropriate education and support for pupils with special educational needs will fall largely on the schools themselves. The extent to which schools and governing bodies respond to this challenge will reflect the degree of priority accorded to children with special educational needs.

In balancing the needs of children with special educational needs against other priorities, schools will be considering the need to publish results of children's educational attainments on Standard Assessment Tasks. They will be aware that the financial health and therefore the survival of the school depends on pupil numbers and that the government is encouraging parents to take account of assessment results in exercising their choice of schools. However, governing bodies still have a statutory responsibility under the 1981 Act to identify and make appropriate provision for pupils with special educational needs. This applies equally to grant-maintained schools. One must also hope that parents will judge schools on wider criteria than those of National Curriculum assessments alone.

What, then, are the general and specific challenges posed by the 1988 Act, with particular reference to children with special educational needs of secondary age?

1. Exclusion from mainstream schools

There is a real risk that children with special educational needs will be less welcome in mainstream schools and that the competitive and market-orientated ethos of secondary schools is likely to result in pressures for their exclusion. There is already evidence from national organizations of a substantial increase in requests for multiprofessional assessment and for statements under the 1981 Act. Children with behaviour as well as learning difficulties seem particularly vulnerable to exclusion. Afro-Carribean pupils appear more vulnerable than others.

2. Threats to support and advisory services

Pressures to exclude arise from the growing gap between the educational attainments of children with SENs and those of their peers. Teachers as well pupils therefore need support to ensure that the curriculum is accessible and if necessary modified by, for example, breaking it down into smaller steps. In the absence of such support, there will be increased pressure to remove children from ordinary to special schools.

Although learning-support departments are now established in most secondary schools, these vary greatly in effectiveness and in the support which they themselves receive from their colleagues and from the headteacher and governors. In some schools, learning-support departments are headed by an experienced and appropriately trained teacher who is a member of the senior-management team and who has status equivalent to that of the head of a subject department. In the best schools, the learning-support teachers work with their subject colleagues in ensuring that the curriculum is accessible to all pupils in the school and that individual lessons take account of the needs of all members of the class. Some also provide in-class support in the light of the individual needs of pupils for at least some of the time. This is part of a 'whole-school' approach which aims at the minimum of withdrawal from mainstream activities (Stradling and Saunders, 1991). Nevertheless, many teachers feel that the needs of certain children still call for individual teaching outside the ordinary class, at least for limited periods of time.

In addition to in-school support, the role of the LEA's learning-support advisory services is crucial. These services are staffed by advisory teachers, often with specialist experience and training in specific areas of support — e.g., to pupils with specific learning or language difficulties, sensory or physical impairments or emotional and behavioural difficulties. They also carry out a wide range of INSET work. A recent HMI report (1991b) provides a useful analysis of their growing roles and responsibilities.

The provision of appropriate support to both pupils and teachers is the key to the successful meeting of special educational needs in ordinary schools. But the future of this service is now in serious doubt as a direct consequence of LMS. It seems likely that schools will in future have to pay for any advisory and support services which they receive; such services can be purchased from independent and private sources, as well as from the LEA.

3. Threats to integration

The education of children with special educational needs in ordinary schools is the central challenge of special education and of education itself. Although progress has been slow and uneven, there are enough examples of good practice to indicate that good quality mainstream education can be made available to many children with special educational needs. Once again, high-quality support to both pupil and school, parental involvement and the setting of clear objectives are key elements of a successful integration policy (Center, Ward and Ferguson, 1991).

Threats to integration are bidirectional. Children now in ordinary schools are more likely to be referred to special schools as a result of lowered thresholds of tolerance and fewer resources and also because the National Curriculum is thought to be too demanding for them, particularly if they also have associated behaviour difficulties. Here again, Afro-Carribeans appear to be at more risk than others. Conversely, it may be harder to secure an ordinary-school place for children now in special schools. The same difficulties face children around the age of 5 for whom a first school placement is being sought.

4. Threats to link schemes

During the last decade some 75 per cent of special schools developed strong working links with neighbouring primary and secondary schools and to some extent with colleges of further education (Jowett, Hegarty and Moses, 1988). These links are now under threat, at least temporarily, partly because of the intense pressures imposed on schools by the demands of the new legislation, partly because there are doubts about how such schemes will be funded under local management of schools.

Now that all special schools are following the National Curriculum, it is essential for them to receive support from specialist teachers in mainstream primary and secondary schools, particularly in subject areas with which they are relatively unfamiliar, e.g., technology, modern languages, history and geography. In return, special-school teachers often have valuable experience in aspects of assessment and record keeping, task analysis and working with parents.

Conclusions: Prospects

This chapter has sought to highlight a number of deep-seated structural and historical features of British society and its institutions which could frustrate the stated intentions of the Education Reform Act to achieve curriculum reform for all pupils, regardless of age, gender, ethnicity and ability. Significantly, socio-economic status is rarely considered within an equal-opportunities framework, despite the overwhelming evidence of social-class differences in educational achievements and outcomes in British society. But the Education Reform Act will be judged in the long term not only in relation to the raising of educational standards in general but whether it has contributed to a narrowing of the achievement gap between different socio-economic groups and resulted in improved educational opportunities for children from socially disadvantaged and impoverished families, amongst whom children with special educational needs are overrepresented.

Although a review of the evidence and of current trends does not justify an optimistic response to these questions, several aspects of the Education Reform Act could lead to improvements in the quality of educational provision.

With some significant exceptions, the curriculum reports themselves have been well received. Although experience and common sense suggested from the outset that there would not be enough time to teach ten subjects, as well as religious education, the cross-curricular elements and extra-curricular activities, there are signs of greater flexibility and sensible modifications of the curriculum without recourse to formal procedures and, hopefully, without loss of entitlement to the 'broad, balanced and relevant curriculum' promulgated in the Act. Few schools seem to be using their powers to exempt pupils from parts or all of the National Curriculum.

The implementation of the National Curriculum has accelerated a process of curriculum reappraisal which was already under way in many schools, LEAs and professional associations. The National Curriculum has generated a high level of professional activity, particularly in the field of special needs provision. Working parties have been set up in many parts of the country to work out ways in which children with special educational needs can be helped to gain access to the broad, balanced and relevant curriculum to which they are entitled in law. Some of these working parties have published curriculum guides to support the more general documents issued by the Department of Education and Science and the National Curriculum Council (1989) (Fagg, Aherne, Skelton and Thornber, 1990; Mittler, 1992).

For the first time, teachers have a common language to describe Programmes of Study and levels of attainment reached by individual children (see Volume 1, Chapter 3). This could be a positive benefit not only in negotiating integration for children with special educational needs but for all children moving between schools and between stages of education. In many areas, special-school teachers are attending National Curriculum and other training courses alongside mainstream colleagues, to their mutual benefit. These and other developments are beginning to break down the segregation between teachers as well as those between children.

The quality of provision for pupils with special educational needs is now at a critical stage. The government has provided a statutory framework for educational reform which did not originally consider the needs of these pupils, except in terms of exclusions and exemptions. Since then, official pronouncements consistently emphasize the theme of 'curriculum for all' but without providing very much by way of detailed guidance or earmarked resources to enable the rhetoric of entitlement for all to be translated into reality.

Recently some helpful official publications have appeared. Two address the situation of pupils with severe learning difficulties (NCC, 1992 a, 1992b). The first is produced in the *INSET Resources* series and covers auditing, planning, record-keeping, English, mathematics, science, exploring inter-subject links and also the cross-curricular elements on which this volume concentrates. The second provides a set of matching *INSET* materials. In connection with teaching science to pupils with special educational needs, the NCC has published *Curriculum Guidance No 10* (NCC, 1991). It covers planning for differentiation, presents activities and describes case studies at KS 1, 2, 3 and 4. It is a start, albeit a small one. The resources and training issues remain the major stumbling blocks to the delivery of the NC to pupils with special educational needs.

The key to progress undoubtedly lies in the development of coherent policies for all pupils in which there are clear indications of ways in which pupils with special educational needs will be identified and supported within a whole-school and whole-authority approach and not as an afterthought. The Department for Education seems unwilling to take any major initiatives to provide leadership, guidance or finance to improve the quality of special needs provision and to help schools and LEAs to address the weaknesses identified in HMI reports. The ball is now in the court of some 30,000 schools and colleges and what is left of the local education authorities. It is to be hoped that the Audit Commission's report on the working of the 1981 Education Act (Audit Commission, 1992) and the government's reaction to it will be positive.

References

AUDIT COMMISSION (1992) *Getting in on the Act. Provision for Pupils with Special Educational Needs: the National Picture*, London, HMSO.

BEGAB, M., HAYWOOD, C. and GARBER, H. (1981) *Psychosocial Aspects of Retarded Performance*, (2 vols) Baltimore, Md., University Park Press.

BOYD, W. (1991) 'What makes ghetto schools succeed or fail?', *Teachers College Record*, 92, pp. 331–62.

CENTER, Y., WARD, J. and FERGUSON, C. (1991) 'Towards an index to evaluate the integration of children with disabilities into regular classes', *Educational Psychology*, 11, pp. 77–96.

COARD, B. (1971) *How the West Indian Child is Made Educationally Subnormal by the British Educational System*, London, New Beacon Books.

COOPER P., UPTON, G. and SMITH, C. (1991) 'Ethnic minority and gender distribution among staff and pupils in facilities for pupils with emotional and behavioural difficulties in England and Wales', *British Journal of Sociology of Education*, 12, 1, pp. 77–94.

COSIN, B., FLUDE, M. and HALES, M. (1989) *School, Work and Equality*, Milton Keynes, Open University Press.

DAVIE, R., BUTLER, N. and GOLDSTEIN, H. (1972) *From Birth to Seven*, London, Longmans and National Children's Bureau.

DEPARTMENT OF EDUCATION AND SCIENCE (1967) *Children and their Primary Schools* (The Plowden Report), London, HMSO.

DEPARTMENT OF EDUCATION AND SCIENCE (1978) *Special Educational Needs* (The Warnock Report), London, HMSO.

DEPARTMENT OF EDUCATION AND SCIENCE (1985) *Education for All* (The Swann Report), London, HMSO.

DEPARTMENT OF EDUCATION AND SCIENCE (1987) *Report of the Task Group on Assessment and Testing*, London, HMSO.

DEPARTMENT OF EDUCATION AND SCIENCE (1989) *National Curriculum: From Policy to Practice*, London, HMSO.

DEPARTMENT OF EDUCATION AND SCIENCE (1992) *Children with Special Needs: A Guide for Parents*, London, HMSO.

DEPARTMENT OF HEALTH AND SOCIAL SECURITY (1976) *Fit for the Future*, Report of the Court Committee on Child Health Services, London, HMSO.

DOUGLAS, J.W.B. (1964) *The Home and the School*, London, McGibbon and Kee.

DOUGLAS, J.W.B. (1968) *All our Future*, London, Peter Davis.

DREW, D. and GRAY, J. (1991) 'The black–white gap in examination results: a statistical critique of a decade's research', *New Community*, 17, pp. 159–72.

EDMONDS, J. (1989) 'Effective schools for the urban poor', in COSIN, B., FLUDE, M. and HALES, M. (Eds) *School, Works and Equality*, Milton Keynes, Open University Press.

ESSEN, J. and WEDGE, P. (1982) *Continuities in Childhood Disadvantage*, London, Heinemann.

FAGG, S., AHERNE, P., SKELTON, S. and THORNBER, A. (1990) *Entitlement for All in Practice: A Broad, Balanced and Relevant Curriculum for Pupils with Severe and Complex Learning Difficulties*, London, Fulton.

FIGUEROA, P. (1988) 'Pupils of Caribbean backgrounds, educational inequality and achievement', University of Southampton (mimeo).

FISH, J. (1989) *What is Special Education?* Milton Keynes, Open University Press.

FOGELMAN, K. (1983) *Growing up in Great Britain*, London, Macmillan for National Children's Bureau.

GOACHER, J., EVANS, J., WELTON, J. and WEDELL, K. (1988) *Policy and Provision for Special Educational Needs*, London, Cassell.

HALSEY, A.H. (1972) *Educational Disadvantage*, London, HMSO.

HEATH, A. (1989) 'Class in the classroom', in COSIN, B., FLUDE, M. and HALES, M. op. cit.

HEGARTY, S. (1987) *Meeting Special Educational Needs in Ordinary Schools*, London, Cassell.

HER MAJESTY'S INSPECTORATE (1989) *The Lower Attaining Pupils Programme 1982–1988*, London, Department of Education and Science.

HER MAJESTY'S INSPECTORATE (1990) *Special Needs Issues*, London, Department of Education and Science.

HER MAJESTY'S INSPECTORATE (1991a) *Standards in Education 1988–1990*, Report of the Senior Chief Inspector, London, Department of Education and Science.

HER MAJESTY'S INSPECTORATE (1991b) *The Work of Learning Support and Advisory Teachers*, London, Department of Education and Science.

JOWETT, S., HEGARTY, S. and MOSES, D. (1988) *Joining Forces: A Study of Links between Special and Ordinary Schools*, Windsor, NFER-Nelson.

LAZAR, I. and DARLINGTON, R. (1982) 'Lasting effects of early education', *Monogrs. Soc. for Research in Child Development*, 47, 2, 3.

MCPHERSON, A. and WILLMS, D. (1989) 'Comprehensive schooling is better and fairer', in COSIN, B., FLUDE, M. and HALES, M. op. cit.

MITTLER, P. (1989) 'Warnock and Swann: similarities and differences', in VERMA, G. (Ed) *Education for All: A Landmark in Pluralism*, London, The Falmer Press.

MITTLER, P. (1992) Educating children with severe learning difficulties: challenging vulnerability, in TIZARD, B. and VARMA, V. (Eds) *Vulnerability and Resilience*, London, Jessica Kingsley.

MORTIMORE, P., SAMMONS, P., ECOB, R. and STOLL, L. (1988) *Schools Matter: The Junior Years*, Salisbury, Open Books.

NATIONAL CURRICULUM COUNCIL (1989) *A Curriculum for All, Curriculum Guidance 2*, York, NCC.

NATIONAL CURRICULUM COUNCIL (1991) *Teaching Science to Pupils with Special Educational Needs*, Curriculum Guidance No. 10, York, NCC.

NATIONAL CURRICULUM COUNCIL (1992a) *The National Curriculum and Pupils with Severe Learning Difficulties*, Curriculum Guidance No. 9, York, NCC.

NATIONAL CURRICULUM COUNCIL (1992b) *The National Curriculum and Pupils with Severe Learning Difficulties*, NCC INSET Resources, York, NCC.

NATIONAL CHILDREN'S HOMES (1990) *Children in Danger: the NCH Factfile*, London, NCH.

NASA BEGUM (1992) *Something To Be Proud Of: The lives of Asian Disabled People and Carers in Waltham Forest*, London, Borough of Waltham Forest.

NORWICH, B. (1990) *Reappraising Special Education*, London, Cassell.

OFFICE OF POPULATION CENSUSES AND SURVEYS (1987) *Population Trends*, 49, London, HMSO.

PILLING, D. (1990) *Escape from Disadvantage*, London, The Falmer Press.

PUMFREY, P.D. and MITTLER, P. (1989) 'Peeling off the label', *Times Educational Supplement*, No. 3824, pp. 29–30, 13 October.

REYNOLDS, D. (1991) 'School effectiveness and school improvement in the 1990s', *Association for Child Psychology and Psychiatry*, 13, pp. 5–9.

RUTTER, M., MAUGHAM, B., MORTIMORE, P. and OUSTON, J. (1979) *Fifteen Thousand Hours: Secondary Schools and their Effects on Children*, London, Open Books.

SAYER, J. (1987) *Secondary Schools for All?*, London, Cassell.

SMITH, D. and TOMLINSON, S. (1989) *The School Effect: A Study of Multi Racial Comprehensives*, London, Policy Studies Institute.

STRADLING, R. and SAUNDERS, L. (1991) *A Whole School Approach for Raising Attainment*, London, Department of Education and Science and National Foundation for Educational Research.

TOMLINSON, S. (1981) *Educational Subnormality: A Study in Decision Making*, London, Routledge and Kegan Paul.

TOMLINSON, S. (1982) *A Sociology of Special Education*, London, Routledge and Kegan Paul.

TOPPING, K. and WOLFENDALE, S. (1985) *Parental Involvement in Children's Reading*, London, Croom Helm.

TOWNSEND, P. and WHITEHEAD, M. (1988) *Inequalities in Health*, London, Penguin Books.

WEDGE, P. and PROSSER, H. (1973) *Born to Fail?*, London, Arrow Books.

WIDLAKE, P. (1986) *Reducing Educational Disadvantage*, Milton Keynes, Open University Press.

WISEMAN, S. (1964) *Education and Environment*, Manchester, Manchester University Press.

Chapter 13

European Community Understanding

Harry Tomlinson

Context

Which Europe?

Without being pedantic we need to know what we mean by Europe is if there is to be a clear understanding of the curricular implications. The Council of Europe, founded in 1949 by ten countries, now incorporates twenty-four European states. Its aims were to work for greater European unity, to uphold the principles of parliamentary democracy and human rights, and to improve living conditions and promote human values. The European Economic Community (EEC) which was founded in 1958 significantly grew out of the European Coal and Steel Community. A year later Great Britain as one of Europe's 'outer seven states' joined in the European Free Trade Association (EFTA). The EEC became the EC (European Community) but its economic origins remain highly significant, indeed — it could be argued — preeminent. How much of all these developments should be incorporated in the European dimension of the curriculum is unclear.

The political changes in central and eastern Europe have immense implications for any attempt to construct or more accurately impose a new European identity. The revolutionary changes which will follow from the dramatic events of 1989 cannot yet realistically be understood. There is a danger in attempts to incorporate the flux of change in western, central and eastern Europe into some grand new identity, for the purposes of rationalizing the European dimension in the curriculum. At very least this involves immense oversimplification.

The fully integrated market in 1992 will act as a 'motive force for European union' as Jacques Delors stated. The Exchange Rate Mechanism (ERM) is the first stage in a process which is likely to lead to a completed European Monetary System (EMS) with a single currency and a European central bank. The relationship of these centralizing processes in the EC to other developments in all the other European countries is unclear. The implications of a complex and contemporaneous Balkanization in the new Europe is profound.

The Council of Europe

The Council of Europe and its Parliamentary Assembly have focused on education much more purposefully than the European Community where the emphasis has been much more narrowly directed towards training for work and for being a European worker. The Council concentrates on human rights, social and economic affairs, education culture and sport, youth, public health, regional planning and architectural heritage, local and regional authorities, and legal affairs. The Council therefore is evolving in this much wider context.

The Council of Europe has been directly involved in the education field with a strong interest in democracy, human rights, freedom, tolerance and pluralism and Europe's cultural identity. There is a much broader idealism than characterizes the utilitarian emphasis on training for employment on which the EC still concentrates. The Council of Europe's project on second-ary education, 'Preparation of Life' (1978–1982), which was the major intro-duction to the European dimension, was genuinely about a liberal education of the whole person. Their conferences led to a number of extremely valuable and innovatory publications. Those relating to maintaining migrants' links with their country of origin and the training of teachers of migrant workers ensured that the issues of cultural diversity and pedagogy were central. There was a major conference on intolerance in Europe, 'Intolerance — A Threat to Human Rights and Human Dignity', a theme which should not be allowed to go away. The conference and subsequent publications also focused on social and political education for teenagers, the secondary school and the mass media, and the teaching of human rights. The Council of Europe has educational values which encourage cultural diversity.

The inquiry into the preparation of young people for working life in Europe, 'Living Tomorrow', examined evidence from the different experiences within ten countries, including that of the young handicapped. 'Employment and Occupations in Europe' was about the effects of technical and economic changes on employment. The problems of the nature of work and training were given the proper priority, but not made excessively and overwhelmingly important. There was a clear healthy set of values which underlay all this work, built on European cultural achievements, but also a thorough understanding of Europe's darker history.

At the conference held at Donaueschingen in Baden-Wurtemberg in October 1980 there were forty participants from ten countries. 'Education for Parenthood and Family Responsibilities' provided a challenging opportunity to learn from the different cultures, values and educational systems within Europe. What emerged was a fuller understanding of the idiosyncrasies of the different approaches rather than a consensus about some ideal model. Those attending were educated. This was followed by thoughtful and imaginative publications about preparation for family life (Schleicher, 1982), and preparation for personal life and life in society (Befring, 1982). The Council of Europe advertises itself as constructive, peaceful and human. This conference represented this and the creative and liberal approach to education which puts the student and cultural diversity at the centre.

Challenges

In the mid-1980s in Britain ambivalence about the EEC amounted almost to paranoia in high places. Since the EEC was almost synonymous with Europe, this created almost a hostility to teaching about Europe. The major analysis at the time saw education about Europe as part of a long overdue process of breaking down the national insularity of the UK (Goodson and McGivney, 1985). Europe was a convenient 'window on the wider world'. The DES curricular aims for schools, widely accepted in theory, included both:

- to instil respect for religious and moral values, and tolerance of other races;
- to help pupils understand the world in which they live, and the interdependence of individuals, groups and nations.

These were used to persuade teachers to take the European dimension much more seriously. That this focus on Europe might conceivably narrow the internationalism of the curriculum was not apparently appreciated. Similarly unrecognized was the danger, which has probably emerged much more strongly subsequently, that teaching ostensibly about Europe, might be about using the curriculum for cruder ideological purposes.

'European studies' had developed as a subject for the less able as a solution to the problems created by pupils experiencing difficulty in learning foreign languages. The majority of able children therefore received no specific teaching about Europe. Goodson and McGivney (1985) based their book on a survey of what schools were teaching in Britain. Teaching about Europe was concentrated in the hands of linguists. At the same time, modern language teaching was being extended across the ability range. In these circumstances, unless the confusion about the place of the study of Europe in the curriculum was resolved, it was becoming clear that the European dimension in the secondary curriculum would become discredited. There was little discussion about students selling to or even working in Europe at the time.

'European studies' was also a problem in higher education where the power élites determine whether a subject has credibility at school level. Goodson and McGivney insisted that 'European Studies' was a discipline which those in higher education obtusely refused to recognize. However, though there may be considerable uncertainty about what Europe is, it cannot be a discipline in itself. The interdisciplinarity problem and the related low status of 'European studies' at school level required new cross-curricular solutions.

Most schools saw history as potentially the major vehicle for teaching about modern Europe. British history teaching traditionally involved a 'drums and trumpets' approach, though perhaps not significantly more so than in other countries. If understanding the history of the mid and late twentieth century requires a world perspective, an overemphasis on European perspectives could distort rather than clarify this process. It would be possible to reinforce the 'drums and trumpets' European colonialist and racist approaches which have clearly not been eradicated from the National Curriculum (See Volume 1). Most examination syllabuses, historical artefacts themselves, ended their European section around 1954, so the Secretary of State's decision that history ended in 1962 is at least not quite as arbitrary as it appeared. However it does create considerable difficulty in interpreting the new Europe which appears to be the intent of the European dimension.

Geography was the second most important subject for the study of Europe. However the new geography, the descriptive natural science with its study of spatial theory, quantitative data and model building was less obviously related to Europe than the human and physical regional geography, 'capes and bays', which it replaced. Subsequently behavioural geography, liberal geography, phenomenological geography and radical geography, the new phase of developing geography as a subject, reinserted problems of a social, economic and political nature. It was therefore possible to reintroduce Europe. There is nevertheless an artificiality about hunting around the changing nature of a subject in order to import the European dimension. Geography was predominantly taught as a subject in National Curriculum Years 7–9, but examination syllabuses for the minority provided an opportunity for the skill and concept-based courses to refer to regions to illustrate man–environment issues. These could focus at the European level. Geography's special contribution as a subject, apart from dealing with the understanding and communication of spatial information, includes world knowledge, international understanding and environmental awareness, all perhaps more interestingly explored outside the European context.

Modern language teaching was often assumed to convey understanding about the life and culture of other peoples. There is now a clearly recognized potential conflict between emphases on communicative competence and contextual studies. The integration of the teaching of linguistic skills with contemporary background materials should engender understanding of different ways of life. It may also, perhaps much more significantly, improve the learning of the linguistic skills. There remains an issue about how both are related to the European dimension. The literature of the foreign country, and by this we really meant France in practice, was what was understood until

Table 13.1: Challenges: The European Dimension

---

1. What are the implications for cultural pluralism in the National Curriculum of the different interpretations of Europe?
2. Is the European dimension about preparation for life or for work?
3. Is the European dimension about social control?
4. How can the different subjects — history, geography, and modern languages — contribute to the European dimension?
5. Does this distort the nature of the subjects?
6. How does the European dimension relate to the British and world dimensions?
7. How does modern-languages teaching avoid focusing only on another national dimension?
8. What is European about European culture?
9. Is there a European identity and a human identity?
10. Is there a spiritual and religious dimension and is it narrowly Christian?

---

quite recently as culture. If language teaching is centrally concerned with understanding other cultures in the wider sense it would seem particularly inappropriate to select a European language for this purpose. French was in the mid-1980s studied by 90 per cent as their first foreign language, and not centrally in order to sell to France or French-speaking countries, nor to understand the wider European dimension, but because of traditions linked to diplomacy.

Research on the teaching of economics showed that though there had been a common rapid expansion of teaching the subject in western Europe, none of the countries included the teaching of Europe as an economic entity as an aim of their courses. The expansion had been accompanied and stimulated by an increased perception of the subject's value and relevance to each particular society, and also perhaps to individuals but, it would seem, very much in a national context. There was even less interest outside Europe.

'Modern studies' in Scotland was a potentially valuable opportunity to teach about Europe, but the title itself has perhaps already become out of date. There was never quite the same problem about status as for 'European studies' in England and Wales but it was still something of a catch-all subject, with even less academic status than 'European studies' in higher education.

There was clearly no European dimension in the curriculum because no one had established a legitimate justification for a European dimension, and there was no curriculum entitlement debate in 1985. This was most obviously the case in National Curriculum years 10 and 11 with the grandiose option schemes allegedly providing choice but undermining a whole curriculum approach.

Responses

European Secondary Heads Association (ESHA)

The ESHA, which was established at Maastricht in 1988, produced two magazines in 1989 and 1990. Advertised in the second was the publication of a guide to Europe and education with sections on the EC, education, exchange, ESHA, and the European dimension. There was by now no shortage of information about Europe. The inevitable right-binder format anticipated a revision every six months. Jessica Larive, in the same edition, asked how one adapts education to the constantly changing requirements of European industry and commerce without sacrificing basic knowledge subjects (ESHA, 1990). It is not clear whether there is evidence that education needs to be 'adapted' to improve quality. Indeed it may be the incessant adaptations which are the problem. The Community, she suggests, will inevitably 'demand' adaptability, creativity, initiative, communication and linguistic skills. Larive asks how we can instill the 'right' attitudes, capabilities and skills which our youth will need to function in the Community of tomorrow. This language may be interpreted to be about either efficiency or narrowness. One might be equally suspicious about the 'right' attitudes in this brave new Europe in which the Community 'demands'.

Her report to the European Parliament 'Educational policies in the Community: perspectives in the medium term (1989–1992)' she suggests has been the basis of the EC programme. She concentrates on:

- Internationalism — 'integrating' geography, history, social studies, economics and languages/literature, expanded and improved foreign languages courses with a second foreign language obligatory, and the setting up of exchange programmes at secondary level we have a particular national anxiety about sociology and a second foreign language!
- Cooperation — 'I am, of course, opposed to everything and anything being organized by EC institutions'.
- New technologies integrated in education — NEPTUNE (New European Programme for Technology Utilisation in Education) is aimed at secondary schools and recognizes the importance of equal opportunities.

This is a bleak and bureaucratic view of educational perspectives.

ESHA's aim is to raise awareness of a European identity and its advantages by enlarging the knowledge of this historical, cultural, economic and social aspects of the EC. There is emerging an insistent assumption of some European identity which has been arbitrarily created. In practice supranational and indeed national identities emerge slowly from ideologies in conflict, as for example from religious 'wars' or political or economic conflict. In 1992 *Context*, ESHA's new European educational magazine was published to deal with educational practice and to spread information among all those concerned with the education and training of the young Europeans of tomorrow. ESHA's 'School Up Movement' is about the promotion of this same European dimension in education in schools.

The significance of eastern Europe was quickly recognized in *Context* (ESHA, 1992). There is one article by the Deputy Minister of Education of Czechoslovakia. In another, the President of the German Association of Teachers says, 'Europe is no longer limited to the European Community member states . . . Individuality, freedom, individual initiative, individual responsibility, equality before the law, achievement, competition, happiness, prosperity and solidarity', allegedly traditional European values, are experiencing a renaissance in eastern Europe. Fascist movements in western Europe and starvation and brutal intercommunity wars in eastern Europe appear to be unrecognized. This represents a pretty rosey view of a desperately and increasingly divided Britain also (see Volume 1, Chapters 1–3 and Volume 2, Chapters 1–3). Perhaps indeed many of these values are more clearly African or American.

The European Community

An article by Nico van Dijk in *Context* (ibid.) explains that the Treaty of Rome, essentially the Constitution of the EC, makes no mention of education (ESHA, 1992). In the early years of the EC ministers of education simply did not meet. The significance of this is often ignored. The Rome Treaty was not interested in education but does refer to vocational training hence the plethora of new developments in this field, their acronyms explained below. Work experience and work shadowing are the best schools can expect from the EC.

Table 13.2: European Organizations and Programmes

ARION — Programme-of-Study visits for education specialists
CEDEFOP — European centre for the development of vocational training
COMETT — Community programme in education and training for technology
ERASMUS — European Community action scheme for the mobility of university students
EUROTECNET — Community action programme in the field of vocational training and technological change
EURYDICE — The education information network
IRIS — Community network of training programmes for women
LINGUA — Community action programme to promote foreign-language competence in the European Community
PETRA — Community action programme for the vocational training of young people and the preparation for adult and working life

The intervention rules of the European Social Fund (ESF) were clarified in 1989 in relation to the five objectives which relate to resources for further and higher education:

- to promote the development of regions lagging behind;
- to facilitate the redeployment of regions in industrial decline;
- to combat long-term unemployment;

- to facilitate the integration of young people into the labour market in all Community regions; and
- to promote the development of rural areas.

80 per cent of the ESF is devoted to training. In upper-secondary levels attempts are made to seek new funding through the Department of Employment, though this is not easy.

The Department of Education and Science

The 1983 EC Resolution on the European dimension in education required member states to set out their policies for incorporation of the European dimension in education and invites them to implement a number of measures. The UK government prepared its policy statement and report of activities with clearly stated objectives (DES, 1991). The government's policy responses include firstly helping students acquire a view of Europe as a multicultural, multilingual community which is an interesting first priority. It might imply an unusual definition of multicultural in an attempt to take the race issue out of the debate, but it is about cultural diversity. Europe is seen as having histories, geographies and cultures, presumably based on the nation states. Young people are to be prepared to take part in the economic and social development of Europe, with all the opportunities this presents. The commitment to Europe is clear.

Improved competence in other European languages is government policy. The failure to include foreign-language teaching in the primary-school National Curriculum perhaps makes one question this commitment. The government extension, from September 1990, of the availability of special bursaries for trainee teachers to those planning to teach modern foreign languages seems scarcely adequate to the size of the problem. Knowledge about the political, economic and social developments, past, present and future, including knowledge about the origins, workings and role of the EC are seen as important, if difficult to make exciting. A sense of European identity is to be promoted through first-hand experience where appropriate, which requires a more active form of learning and rather more resources than are available. An understanding of the EC's interdependence with the rest of Europe, and with the world is also policy. The EC is the major focus not particularly in its cultural diversity.

The government sees the Centre for Information on Language Teaching (CILT), the Central Bureau for Educational Visits and Exchanges and the UK Centre for European Education (UKCEE) within it, the Education Policy Information Centre (EPIC Europe), but all its curriculum-development agencies, most obviously NCC and SEAC, as being concerned with implementing the European cross-curricular dimension. This should permeate and be integrated into all relevant parts of the curriculum to be effective.

This is how cross-curricular dimensions work. The Programmes of Study, here defined as 'matters, skills and processes' and the Attainment Targets in history, geography and modern foreign languages are means to reflect Britain's place in Europe.

Action A3 asks member states 'to include the European dimension explicitly in their school curricula in all appropriate disciplines, for example literature, languages, history, geography, social sciences, economics and the arts'. There have also been an impressive number of interesting projects in Scotland and Northern Ireland and the language of these government responses seem constructive. There were for example 487 new school and college links established by the Central Bureau in the thirty months before the response was drafted.

It is difficult to judge the quality of work in schools partly because of the lack of clarity as to what the European dimension means. The teaching of history has changed as a result of the National Curriculum but one might argue that it is still too much focused on Britain and Europe (see Volume 1, Chapters 7, 8 and 14). The same could apply to geography to a lesser extent because of the nature of the subject. The changes in modern language teaching will inevitably focus work somewhat on another European country, but this is unlikely to deal with wider European issues to any significant extent.

As the whole curriculum, including the cross-curricular issues, dimensions and themes evolves, environmental issues, economic and industrial understanding and citizenship will become more clearly articulated with the European dimension. Every theme in this book has a European dimension. That we might eventually have an interlocked and coherent planned curriculum in which all the parts interrelate and mutually reinforce seems possible. How students respond to this in their learning is more uncertain.

European society would seem to be manifesting increased racism. Built into the EC resolution and the government's response is an uncritical acceptance either that the new European belongs to a healthy community or that education can create this new ideal European society. A healthy scepticism about a naive acceptance of this new Europeanism is advisable.

The National Curriculum

The traditional specialisms, particularly with any extension beyond history, geography and modern languages, make it difficult to guarantee progression and coherence without sophisticated whole-curriculum planning. In an attempt to create a rationale Shennan (1991) considers sixteen key concepts relevant to the European dimension.

The problem is that these concepts could be applied equally to a wider international context. A similar argument could be extended to knowledge, skills and attitudes. The ten knowledge goals include 'to examine political and economic trends and policies for their present and future effects upon

Table 13.3:   Key Concepts

Unity	Interdependence	Rationality	Naturalism
Diversity	Conflict	Emotionality	Systematization
Change	Liberty	Materialism	Similarity
Continuity	Security	Spirituality	Difference

European society'. The five skill goals include 'to develop social skills in support of linguistic skills as a means of effective communication'. The five attitudes and values include 'to make pupils aware of and help them respect the rich cultural heritage they share with other young Europeans'. This excellent book explains the massive range of opportunities that teaching about Europe presents (Shennan, 1991).

If European history curricula twenty years ago were national political, monocultural and ethnocentric, there is a danger that this may be replaced by an equally unacceptable Eurocentrism which is equally outmoded for the 1990s. President Mary Robinson of the Irish Republic in her inaugural speech suggested that 'As a woman, I want to see women who have felt themselves outside history, to be written back into "history"'. European history can ignore women just as national histories have done. The problem of European colonialism and racism may have been ignored just as completely in the curriculum for the 1990s proposed by the Council of Europe, as the history of British colonialism has been in the National Curriculum. Cultural diversity has perhaps not been given sufficient priority.

In geography the five knowledge goals for the European curriculum would include 'to develop pupil insight and understanding of the location, configuration and diversity of the physical and human environments in Europe'. The three attitudes and values include 'to promote an awareness and empathic understanding of the different ways of life existing within Europe'. The two skill goals include one 'to supplement affective skills by developing practical, active and participatory skills of citizenship'. Not only is understanding Europe important, but Europe itself has some unique meaning.

There are almost mystic overtones. The cultural dimension is interesting. Shennan (1991) suggests that the European experience is based on eight cultural elements:

- currents of religious experience;
- a mode of rational scientific thinking;
- sophisticated political ideologies;
- a range of artistic movements and forms of expression;
- liberal principles of individualism;
- the socio-economic philosophy of capitalism;
- the capacity for linguistic communication; and
- concern for the global environment.

What is particularly European about all of these remains unclear.

Table 13.4: Responses

1. ESHA is encouraging schools to develop a European dimension.
2. The Council of Europe promotes human values in Europe.
3. The European Community provides opportunities to learn about Europe in a work context.
4. The National Curriculum in history, geography and modern languages incorporates a European dimension, but with a limited emphasis on cultural diversity.
5. The DES response to the 1988 EC resolution begins the process of developing a coherent European dimension.
6. The National Curriculum implies a coherent European dimension, not integration.
7. European education now involves:
   - teaching and learning *about* Europe within a global perspective
   - preparing students for life, work and citizenship *in* Europe
   - enriching students' personal and social education *through* direct experience of Europe and contact with Europeans.
8. Attempts to impose a meaning for 'Europe' are premature.
9. The many definitions of European culture make it difficult to teach.
10. The belief that all virtues are European is questionable.

Conclusion

HMI have examined *Education in the Federal Republic of Germany* (HMI, 1985). The aspects of curriculum and assessment covered scarcely mention the European dimension. The preface compared looking at another country's education system with observing other peoples' marriages, allegedly a seductively attractive activity. They found a problem in distinguishing between appearance and reality because of their 'outsider' observer role and the pride of the observed. That HMI, as voyeurs, find such activities seductively attractive the author will refrain from commenting on. There is however a similar problem about the European dimension. As an 'outsider' observer this author finds it difficult to distinguish between appearance and reality. As the observed he is not yet sure he is sufficiently proud of being European.

References

BEFRING, E. (1982) *Preparation for Personal Life and for Life in Society*, Strasbourg, Council of Europe.

COMMISSION OF THE EUROPEAN COMMUNITIES TASK FORCE: HUMAN RESOURCES, EDUCATION, TRAINING AND YOUTH (1989) 'Education Training Youth', Strasbourg, EURYDICE European Unit.

COMMISSION OF THE EUROPEAN COMMUNITIES (1991) 'Education and Training', Strasbourg, Council of Europe.

DEPARTMENT OF EDUCATION AND SCIENCE (1991) 'The European Dimension in Education', London, HMSO.

EUROPEAN SECONDARY HEADS ASSOCIATION, 'Guide to Europe and Education' (1990) Amsterdam, Meulenhoff Publishers, 2, Spring.

EUROPEAN SECONDARY HEADS ASSOCIATION AND EAT (1992) *Context* 1991/1992, Amsterdam, Meulenhoff Publishers.

GOODSON, I.F. and McGIVNEY, V. (1985) *European Dimensions and the Secondary School Curriculum*, Basingstoke, The Falmer Press.

HER MAJESTY'S INSPECTORATE (1986) *Education in the Federal Republic of Germany*, London, HMSO.

SCHLEICHER, P. (1982) *Preparation for Family Life*, Strasbourg, Council of Europe.

SHENNAN, M. (1991) *Teaching about Europe*, Strasbourg, Council of Europe.

Chapter 14

Cultural Diversity and Staff Development

Neil Burtonwood

Context

From 1989–90 the term 'nationally identified needs' has come to mean an almost exclusive concern with INSET intended to support teachers in implementing aspects of the Education Reform Act. In particular there has been an emphasis on developing the curriculum to include the full range of core and foundation subjects and the introduction of local management of schools.

Before concentrating on the INSET issues related to education for pluralism raised by the ERA and National Curriculum, it is helpful to review briefly developments prior to 1988. The future of INSET in relation to cultural diversity builds on the past and the present. The historical perspective is important. One major challenge was to secure sufficient and appropriate INSET when many teachers were yet to be persuaded of the relevance of ethnic diversity and racism when considering the professional task of teaching. Early surveys of course provision found few teachers attending substantial INSET on ethnic-diversity issues (Townsend and Brittan, 1972). In particular, INSET support for teachers of English as a second language (ESL) was considered insufficient to meet the needs of the growing number of non-specialist teachers involved in this field of activity (Townsend, 1971; Taylor, 1974).

INSET in the 1970s tended to emphasize the particular needs of multi-racial areas, especially the apparent underachievement of ethnic-minority children (CRE, 1974) and this pattern of insufficient and heavily localized provision continued into the 1980s (Little and Willey, 1983; Mathews, 1981; Young and Connelly, 1981; Scarman, 1981). The early 1980s saw more of a qualitative analysis of the process and impact of INSET. Eggleston, Dunn and Purewal (1981) stressed the need for the proper targeting of INSET participants, the need for pre-course consultation, better communication of course details and follow up work in school. Their report underlined the value of school-based work and the particular needs of so-called 'white' areas.

The Schools Council (1982) offered the same advice to the Swann committee (DES, 1985) while Brittan's evaluation of the Schools Council project *Education for Multiracial Society* pointed in a similar direction (Brittan, 1983). Developing school-based strategies and adapting approaches so as to meet the particular needs of 'white' areas were to become the major challenges of the 1980s.

The Swann committee responded to the call for more provision of INSET by recommending financial support through the In-Service Teachers Training Grant Scheme (DES, 1985). In January 1986 DES Circular 1/86 identified 'Teaching and the curriculum in a multicultural society' as a national priority area for INSET. This was continued as 'Training in teaching and the planning of the curriculum in a multi-ethnic society' in the Local Education Authority Training Grant Scheme (LEATGS) for 1987–8 and again for school teachers and further education staff in 1988–9. This was to be the last year that multicultural education would feature as a separate national priority area for teachers in schools. From this point INSET came to be predominantly concerned with teachers' responsibilities in delivering the National Curriculum.

Challenges

The period immediately prior to the Education Reform Act 1988 saw major changes in the nature and delivery of in-service education for teachers. In August 1986, Department of Education Circular 6/86 introduced a new LEATGS for the financial year 1987–8. This aimed to promote the professional development of teachers and to support systematic and purposeful planning of INSET. Through the use of specific funding the scheme set out to match staff-development activities with nationally identified needs. A proportion of the funding was also allocated for locally identified needs. Future provision of INSET on ethnic-diversity issues would depend upon successful permeation of National-Curriculum INSET and the awareness of school INSET coordinators when planning the content of school-training days. In areas of very low ethnic-minority population density (often referred to in the INSET literature as 'predominantly white' or 'white Highlands') much came to depend on the work of teams funded by the Education Support Grant (ESG) to pilot INSET programmes in these areas.

Summing up, we can see that the kind of curriculum centralization brought about by the ERA had already taken place in the INSET field through the mechanism of specific funding. In this way INSET was seen as supporting nationally and locally identified curriculum priorities. By 1988 the research literature was pointing to the challenge of developing the school curriculum along multicultural lines. This was seen as particularly sensitive in areas of low ethnic-minority population density where teachers had so far failed to perceive multiculturalism as a curriculum issue. One promising development, however, was already becoming evident. This was the potential benefits to be gained from staff-development activities which were both school-based and involved the whole staff. These aspects will be explored in more detail before turning specifically to the implications of the National Curriculum.

Responses

School-based Work

School-based work has proved particularly valuable in involving the whole staff of a school. The difficulty for individual teachers attempting to implement change following attendance on traditional off-site INSET provision is well documented (Easen, 1985). In addition, school-based INSET can make connections with curriculum development and can proceed from teacher-identified needs. The importance of starting from where teachers are in their professional development is stressed by Wagner (1988). He concluded 'INSET that is in effective, in the sense of becoming part of the school, derives from the school being offered INSET which may not address the school's felt needs (ibid., p.180). One project which has developed through the school-based approach is *World Studies 8–13*. World Studies is defined by Fisher and Hicks (1985, p. 8) as 'studies which promote the knowledge, attitudes and skills that are relevant to living responsibly in a multicultural and interdependent world'. Reviewing the history of this project, the author stresses the need to give teachers a good in-service experience, paying attention both to participants hopes and fears in an affirming person-centred way (Hicks, 1990, p. 77). A number of handbooks are now available which provide ideas and activities for working in this way (Fisher and Hicks, 1985; Development Education Centre, 1986; Pike and Selby, 1988; McLean and Young, 1988; Hicks and Steiner, 1989; Nixon and Watts, 1989; Maitland 1989). What these share is a model of INSET which draws on participants' experiences, sets a climate which provides a combination of security and challenge and entails some form of action planning. It has been strongly argued that this kind of approach is most consistent with democratic cultural pluralism because it seeks to rectify the 'unequal communication rights between teachers and learners on both initial and in-service courses' (Carrington and Short, 1987, p. 11). It is democratic both in recognizing the need for the active participation of learners and in involving learners in defining their own needs and preferred strategies.

School-based work and off-site INSET do not have to be regarded as mutually exclusive. Attendance on external courses often precedes school-based initiatives (Taylor, 1987) and some off-site courses include substantial elements of school-based work (Atkins and Craft, 1988; Galliers, 1988). Successful school-based work also requires trained personnel to act as facilitators and this sets up another kind of training need (Lee, 1987). What is important therefore is a coordinated and coherent INSET provision which starts from staff-identified professional needs, and links into current curriculum development while taking care to avoid an inward-looking parochialism.

A frequent response to this particular challenge has been to include within INSET programmes a major component of action research. Keel (1987) describes an action research project in the north-east of England where the approach is one of collaborative inquiry consistent with teachers' own agenda for change (Biott, Lynch and Robertson, 1984; Lynch, 1985). The role of the outsider is to facilitate a process by which teachers can extend their own criteria for evaluating effectiveness. This kind of approach with its emphasis on a collaborative study of practice is widely regarded as most appropriate in supporting education for pluralism (Bell, 1986; Troyna and Carrington, 1989; Foster, 1990).

Sometimes the role of the outsider has been undertaken by LEA support teams. In describing the work of one such team McGowan (1986) challenges the orthodoxy that teachers must determine their own agenda by arguing that insiders are not always best placed to undertake a needs analysis. The LEA team will also be working within a policy framework and cannot offer a 'pure consultancy' role. In a more recent account of support work in the same city, Chatwin *et al.* (1988) return to the theme of teachers identifying their own needs for staff-development activity.

One form of INSET which has increasingly taken on a school-based dimension is Racism Awareness Training (RAT). Swann (DES, 1985) did call for an evaluation of the effectiveness of RAT, and Pumfrey (1988) has recently reminded us of the need for trainer accountability in this as in any other field. Many RAT programmes have been criticized on the grounds of an illiberal methodology and an overemphasis on individual behaviour while neglecting institutional structures and processes. In reality, individuals and institutions are not separable; it has been shown that RAT can be combined with an organization development perspective to include a strong element of institutional review and action planning for change (Galliers, n.d.; Gorringe, 1987; Further Education Unit, 1988).

Lack of space prohibits a full review of the literature on RAT. Valuable recent sources are available (Avari and Joseph, 1990). It is worth noting that several studies into the effectiveness of RAT stress the need to go beyond personal awareness to the drawing up of practical guidelines for action at institutional level (Gledhill and Heffernan, 1984; Twitchin and Demuth, 1985; Mahony, 1987). Residential courses have proved particularly valuable in providing an appropriate environment for intensive and sustained work (Anti-Racist Strategies Team, 1986; Grant and Grant, 1985; Gaine, 1987). The importance of group work and networking for support is stressed in a recent account in which three headteachers describe the very positive outcome of a RAT course (Abbott, Gilbert and Lawson, 1989). As members of a liaison group, these teachers were able to support each other in implementing strategies for change in their respective schools. This has clear implications for the recruitment of teachers for INSET. Pyramid-based courses will be advantageous where the issue is cross-phase and where continuity, consistency and progression are so important.

The National Curriculum and INSET

The ERA begins by stating that it is an aim of education that all pupils are prepared for their future life as citizens, workers and parents. DES Circular 5/89 elaborates on this by pointing to the importance of preparing all pupils for life in a multicultural society. The concept of *Education for All* requires that INSET for teachers in 'white' areas includes both specific work on cultural diversity and racism and a permeative element throughout the INSET provision (DES, 1985). There is now a considerable amount of material describing the ways that providers in 'white' areas have attempted to respond to this challenge.

A recent account of the historical geography of the regional pattern of multicultural, antiracist education shows how innovations take on regional specific characteristics as they spread. Bonnet (1990, p. 263) argues that advocates of education for pluralism in Tyneside have felt the need to 'filter out the "unacceptable" political content of "London" anti-racism' so that education for pluralism can be presented 'in reformist, individual and consensus-seeking terms'. It is because the agenda for multicultural education was initially drawn up outside 'white' areas that Lynch and his colleagues stressed the importance of starting from the teachers' own agenda (Lynch, 1985). Reports on work in south-west England (Taylor, 1985 and 1987), the east Midlands (Paine and Richards, 1985), Warwickshire (Sharma, 1987), Oxfordshire (Pearse and Despard, 1985) and Manchester (Gledhill and Heffernan, 1984) all indicate the need for attention to style of presentation. One aspect of presentation identified as particularly important by the ESG teams working in 'white' areas is the need to avoid simplistic divisions which suggest that multiculturalism and antiracism constitute mutually exclusive categories (Tomlinson and Coulson, 1988). When classroom practice is investigated it soon becomes evident that material about culture is a necessary, if not sufficient, component of antiracist education (Brandt, 1987; Burtonwood, 1987).

'Discussing the process of change in schools (Fullan, 1982) notes the importance of acknowledging and working from the view of the world held by those who will implement the change'. It is with this in mind that Carrington and Short (1989) call for more attention to the psychology of attitude change and its implications for addressing issues of cultural diversity and racism within staff-development programmes in schools. The 'chicken-and-egg' relationship between behaviour and attitudes underlines the complexities involved.

Permeation and Cross-curricular Themes

The National Curriculum Council has identified multicultural education as a cross-curricular dimension which should permeate all aspects of the curriculum (NCC, 1990a). The importance of cross-curricular issues as an aspect of INSET is stressed by the NCC Professional Development Committee (NCC, 1990b). Permeation does not happen by chance; it has to be planned for and supported. In this context it is disappointing to note the failure to date to publish the findings of the task group set up to 'consider ways in which the National Curriculum can broaden the horizons of all pupils as well as meet the particular needs of pupils from ethnic-minority background' (NCC, 1989). Members of the task group clearly share this sense of disappointment (Tomlinson, 1990) though the NCC does state that it is 'drawing on the work of its multicultural Task Group to ensure its publications and activities take this dimension fully into account (NCC, 1991, p. 3).

It was noted earlier that by 1988 the national priority areas for INSET no longer included multicultural education as a separate category of training for school teachers. DES Circular 20/89 follows the permeation model with cross-curricular issues included for 1990–1 under the heading of 'Training for the basic curriculum and collective worship'. Most recently the DES draft circular identifying the categories of training within the Grant for Education Support and Training (GEST) 1991–2 includes under the category basic curriculum 'Implementing the attainment targets and programmes of study for NC foundation subjects as these are progressively introduced and *with due regard to multicultural and equal opportunities aspects* [my italic]' (DES, 1990). Confirming the shift towards central direction of INSET, the new GEST arrangements differ from the previous LEATGS arrangements by no longer including funding for locally identified priorities. This will undoubtedly threaten school-based work which has been supported through devolution of local funds to schools. These GEST arrangements underline the fact that future provision of INSET dealing with pluralist issues will require that National Curriculum INSET takes seriously the need to take account of cultural diversity.

Effective permeation of INSET will require training the trainers. This was recognized eleven years ago by the House of Commons Home Affairs Committee (1981). Since then a DES-funded evaluation has claimed substantial impact for the 'Training the Trainers' project undertaken in a number of higher-education (HE) institutions (Atkins, 1986). Reference has already been made to the role of HE and LEA support teams in facilitating the process of school-based staff development. Unfortunately, the reducing involvement of HE in INSET and the impact of Local Management of Schools (LMS) on the ability of LEAs to fund support teams is likely to push schools in the direction of self-sufficiency in planning and facilitating staff development. In view of what was said earlier about the value of an external perspective in combatting parochialism, these developments need to be closely monitored.

To conclude this chapter it is intended to explore the challenges for INSET posed by several issues brought into sharp focus by ERA developments. These are assessment, bilingualism, school effectiveness and relationships with parents. Schools Examinations and Assessment Council (1991a) states that it is part of National-Curriculum entitlement that all pupils have their achievements recognized. Teacher assessment, we are told, is the key to this. Concern has often been expressed about the fairness of the assessment process when the school population is culturally and linguistically diverse. It is important that teachers embarking upon the new assessment arrangements take particular account of the need to ensure that children whose first language is not English do have the opportunity to demonstrate the full range of their achievements. It would be reasonable to expect INSET material on assessment to offer some help to teachers in this matter. To date INSET materials have failed to take serious account of the needs of bilingual pupils and their usually monolingual teachers (SEAC, 1991b; SEAC, 1991c). Fortunately others are available (see Chapter 2 and Appendix 3).

Closely related to the issue of assessment is the difficult question of teacher expectation. Eggleston *et al.* (1981) stressed the importance of including teacher perceptions of ethnic-minority children and the assessment implications in the content of INSET programmes. More recently Elton (1989) has returned to this theme. The report of the Records of Achievement national steering committee extends the discussion of stereotyping by noting the importance of INSET which addresses the implications of cultural diversity for Records of Achievement (DES, 1989). Supporting teachers implementing the new assessment arrangements will need to include attention to the requirement that all pupils are given the opportunity to demonstrate the full range of their achievements.

The fullest and most recent survey of provision for bilingual pupils is Bourne's national survey carried out between 1985 and 1988 (Bourne, 1989). As part of her findings, Bourne identifies INSET priorities for teachers involved with bilingual support and the teaching of community languages. She notes how language-support teachers often carry the responsibility of providing INSET for their mainstream colleagues. Here is another area where the provision of training the trainers will be necessary to ensure effectiveness. The survey found little being done for the few language-support teachers in 'white' areas either to help them meet the needs of bilingual children or to respond to the Swann committee and National Curriculum English subject Working Group recommendation that all pupils develop an appreciation of linguistic diversity. Bourne's survey found few mainstream teachers taking advantage of INSET on language support. This proved to be particularly frustrating for support teachers who were involved in programmes intended to help them develop new models of in-class partnership teaching but were unable to develop their classroom work along these lines because the INSET experience was only rarely shared by their mainstream colleagues. The provision of in-service support for teachers of community languages appears to have been equally patchy and instructors have had even less support than teachers. Given the difficulties reported in recruiting appropriately qualified staff in this area, this gap is particularly surprising. Bourne argues for a major expansion of INSET to enable community-languages staff to undertake action research and the production of classroom material (see Chapter 2 and Appendix 3).

In recent years there has been a series of investigations into secondary-school effectiveness (Smith and Tomlinson, 1989). Any investigation which explores school factors in the underachievement of any group of pupils is likely to be more relevant to school-focused staff development than earlier investigations into achievement which tended to focus more on pupil background. This recent work answers the Swann committee's call for more research on school factors in underachievement. Work which claims to demonstrate that the school attended by a pupil does make a difference to the level of attainment reached must be of interest to those who plan INSET material. One interesting extension of this is provided by Gill (1989). He argues that antiracist educators face the challenge of articulating their principles in a way which addresses the general issue of school effectiveness. Gill sees institutional performance indicators as a useful analytical tool in pursuing racial equality. Criteria for assessing effectiveness, he says, should include race-equality dimensions. To exemplify this approach, Gill demonstrates the operationalization of parental involvement as a performance indicator. This kind of exercise could make a useful contribution to school-based INSET.

The quality of relationships between schools and parents is an area highlighted by several aspects of the ERA. In 1989 the publication of the report concerning Burnage High School, Manchester, provided a reminder of the importance of involving parents in school policy-making for multicultural, antiracist education (MacDonald, Bhavnani, Khan and John, 1989). Reviewing the research project on 'Pupils, Race and Education in Primary Schools' Grugeon and Woods (1990) stress the value of including parents and the wider community as part of the strategy of collaboration cited throughout this chapter. The requirements of the ERA relating to religious education and collective worship add another dimension to community consultation. Recent press reports indicate that this will continue to be a difficult area for teachers (Lodge, 1990). Religious education is just one of the controversial professional issues where INSET support is required. The Commission for Racial Equality called for INSET support to help teachers deal with the classroom conflict brought about by the Gulf War (*Times Educational Supplement*, 22 February 1991). These specifics highlight the general point that neither initial training nor INSET offer real support to teachers in handling controversial issues in the classroom (Carrington and Troyna, 1989).

Since the mid-1980s the structural context within which INSET takes place has changed radically. The research studies reviewed in this chapter would support a move towards school-based staff development linked to school-development plans for the curriculum and associated assessment. Several studies reported here would emphasize that there is still a role for both HE and LEA support teams both in offering an outsider perspective and in training trainers.

The ERA poses a number of challenges, not least the need to plan and monitor the implementation of cultural diversity as a cross-curricular dimension. In multilingual schools assessment will require particular attention if bilingual children are to enjoy equal opportunities to demonstrate their knowledge, skills and understanding. The ERA has put institutional evaluation on the agenda. School-effectiveness studies provide useful data for exploring how schools deliver equal opportunities for all their pupils. These are major concerns facing those who plan INSET for the 1990s. This review of developments to date suggest that there are some promising responses while major gaps in provision remain. What is needed now is a funding mechanism for INSET which provides a positive lead from the centre while allowing flexibility to foster locally developed initiatives matched to the needs identified by teachers themselves.

References

ABBOTT, B., GILBERT, S. and LAWSON, R. (1989) 'Towards anti-racist awareness: confessions of some teacher converts', in WOODS, P. (1989) *Working For Teacher Development*, Dereham, Peter Francis.

ANTI-RACIST STRATEGIES TEAM (1986) 'The ILEA Anti-Racist Strategies Team racism awareness course', *Multi-Ethnic Education Review*, 5, 2, pp. 31–2.

ATKINS, M.J. (1986) *Final Report of the DES Funded Evaluation: 'Training the Trainers: Education for a Multicultural Society'*, Newcastle-Upon-Tyne, University of Newcastle-Upon-Tyne.

ATKINS, M.J. and CRAFT, M. (1988) 'Training the trainers in multicultural education: the evaluation of a national programme', *British Journal of In-Service Education*, 14, pp. 81–91.

AVARI, B. and JOSEPH, G.G. (1990) 'Race relations training: the state of the art', in PUMFREY, P.D. and VERMA, G.K. (1990) *Race Relations and Urban Education*, Lewes, The Falmer Press.

BELL, G.H. (1986) 'Developing intercultural understanding; an action research approach', Sheffield Polytechnic (mimeo).

BIOTT, C., LYNCH, J. and ROBERTSON, W. (1984) 'Supporting teachers' own progress towards multicultural education', *Multicultural Teaching*, 2, 2, pp. 39–41.

BONNETT, A. (1990) 'Anti-racism as a radical educational ideology in London and Tyneside', *Oxford Review of Education*, 16, 2, pp. 255–67.

BOURNE, J. (1989) *Moving Into Mainstream*, Windsor, NFER-Nelson.

BRANDT, G. (1987) *The Realization of Anti-Racist Education*, Lewes, The Falmer Press.

BRITTAN, E. (1983) *Education For A Multiracial Society: An Evaluation*, London, Schools Council.

BURTONWOOD, N. (1987) 'Anti-racist education: a scientific revolution?', *New Community*, 14, 1, 2, pp. 210–7.

CARRINGTON, B. and SHORT, G. (1987) 'Breakthrough to political literacy: political education, anti-racist teaching and the primary school', *Journal of Education Policy*, 2, 1, pp. 1–13.

CARRINGTON, B. and SHORT, G. (1989) 'Policy or presentation? The psychology of anti-racist education', *New Community*, 15, 2, pp. 227–40.

CARRINGTON, B. and TROYNA, B. (1989) *Children and Controversial Issues*, Lewes, The Falmer Press.

CHATWIN, R., TURNER, M. and WICK, T. (1988) 'School-focused INSET and the external team', *British Journal of In-Service Education*, 14, pp. 129–37.

COMMISSION FOR RACIAL EQUALITY (1974) *In-Service Education of Teachers in Multi-Racial Areas*, London, CRE.

DEPARTMENT OF EDUCATION AND SCIENCE (1985) *Education for All* (the Swann Report), London, HMSO.

DEPARTMENT OF EDUCATION AND SCIENCE (1989) *The Report of the Records of Achievement Steering Committee*, London, HMSO.

DEPARTMENT OF EDUCATION AND SCIENCE (1990) *Draft Circular, Grants for Education Support and Training*, London, HMSO.

DEVELOPMENT EDUCATION CENTRE (1986) *A Sense of School: An Active Learning Approach To In-Service*, Birmingham, Development Education Centre.

EASEN, P. (1985) *Making School-Centred INSET Work*, Beckenham, Croom Helm/ Open University.

EGGLESTON, S.J., DUNN, D.K. and PUREWAL, A. (1981) *In-Service Teacher Education In A Multi-Racial Society*, Keele, University of Keele.

ELTON, Lord (1989) *Discipline in Schools*, London, HMSO.

FISHER, S. and HICKS, D. (1985) *World Studies 8–13; A Teachers Handbook*, Edinburgh, Oliver and Boyd.

FOSTER, P. (1990) *Policy and Practice in Multicultural and Anti-Racist Education*, London, Routledge.

FULLAN, M. (1982) 'Planning, doing and coping with change', in MOON, B., MURPHY, P. and RAYNOR, J. (Eds) *Policies For The Curriculum*, London, Hodder and Stoughton.

FURTHER EDUCATION UNIT (1988) *Staff Development For A Multicultural Society: Introductory Module*, London, FEU.

GAINE, C. (1987) *No Problem Here*, London, Hutchinson.

GALLIERS, D. (n.d.) *Anti-Racist In-Service Teacher Education*, Walsall, West Midlands College of Higher Education (mimeo).

GALLIERS, D. (1988) 'Staff development and GRIST', *Multicultural Teaching*, 6, 3, pp. 19–21.

GILL, B. (1989) 'Indicators and institutional evaluation', *Multicultural Teaching*, 8, 1 pp. 8–12.

GLEDHILL, M. and HEFFERNAN, M. (1984) 'Racism awareness workshops for teachers', *Educational and Child Psychology*, 1,1 pp. 46–59.

GORRINGE, R. (1987) 'Staff development in multicultural Britain: a way forward', in MEBRAHTU, T. (Ed) *Swann and the Global Dimension*, Bristol, Youth Education Service.

GRANT, C.A. and GRANT, G.W. (1985) 'Staff development and education that is multicultural', *British Journal of In-Service Education*, 12, pp. 6–18.

GRUGEON, E. and WOODS, P. (1990) *Educating All*, London, Routledge.

Neil Burtonwood

HICKS, D. (1990) 'Project: a short history 1980–1989', *The World Studies 8–13, Westminter Studies in Education*, 13 pp. 61–80.
HICKS, D. and STEINER, M. (1989) *Making Global Connections: A World Studies Workbook*, Edinburgh, Oliver and Boyd.
HOUSE OF COMMONS (1981) *Racial Disadvantage*, 5th Report from the Home Affairs Committee, 1, London, HMSO.
KEEL, P. (1987) 'Action research as a medium for curriculum development in multicultural education', in CHIVERS, T.S. (Ed) *Race and Culture in Education*, Windsor, NFER-Nelson.
LEE, D. (1987) 'Towards a coherent strategy for INSET: a systematic approach to implementation', *Multicultural Teaching*, 5, 3, pp. 36–8.
LITTLE, A. and WILLEY, P. (1983) *Studies In The Multi-Ethnic Curriculum*, London, Schools Council.
LODGE, B. (1990) 'Bradford complaint tests RE reforms', the *Times Educational Supplement*, 23 February.
LYNCH, J. (1985) 'An initial typology of perspectives on staff development for multicultural teacher development', in MODGIL, S. *et al.* (Eds), *Multicultural Education: The Interminable Debate*, Lewes, The Falmer Press.
MACDONALD, I., BHAVNANI, R., KHAN, L. and JOHN, G. (1989) *Murder In The Playground: The Burnage Report*, London, Longsight Press.
MAHONEY, E. (1987) 'RAT in an "all white" School', *Multicultural Teaching*, 5, 2, p. 9.
MAITLAND, S. (1989) *Multicultural INSET: A practical Handbook For Teachers*, Stoke, Trentham Books.
MATTHEWS, A. (1981) *Advisory Approaches To Multicultural Education*, London, Runnymede Trust.
McGOWAN, P. (1986) 'INSET partnerships: insiders and outsiders', *British Journal of In-Service Education*, 13, pp. 35–9.
McLEAN, B. and YOUNG, J. (1988) *Multicultural Anti-Racist Education: A Manual For Primary Schools*, London, Longman.
NATIONAL CURRICULUM COUNCIL (1989) *Annual Report 1988–1989*, York, NCC.
NATIONAL CURRICULUM COUNCIL (1990a) *Curriculum Guidance No. 3 the Whole Curriculum*, York, NCC.
NATIONAL CURRICULUM COUNCIL (1990b) *Annual Report 1989–90*, York, NCC.
NATIONAL CURRICULUM COUNCIL (1991) *NCC News Issue No. 5*, York, NCC.
NIXON, J. and WATTS, M. (1989) *INSET Workshops for Schools: Whole School Approaches To Multicultural Education*, London, Macmillan.
PAINE, J. and RICHARDS, K. (1985) 'The East Midlands: it's not a problem here . . .', in CARTER, A. (Ed) *Teachers For A Multicultural Society*, York, SCDC Publications.
PEARSE, S. and DESPARD, A. (1985) 'Oxfordshire: approaching multicultural education', in CARTER, A. (Ed) *Teachers For A Multicultural Society*, York, SCDC Publications.
PIKE, G. and SELBY, D. (1988) *Global Teacher, Global Learner*, London, Hodder and Stoughton.
PUMFREY, P.D. (1988) 'Racism awareness: training, education and accountability', in PUMFREY, P.D, and VERMA, G.K. (Eds) *Educational Attainment: Issues and Outcomes In Multicultural Education*, Lewes, The Falmer Press.
SCARMAN, LORD (1981) *The Brixton Disorders*, Cmnd., 8427, London, HMSO.
SCHOOLS COUNCIL (1982) *Education of Children From Ethnic Minority Groups, Evidence to Swann*, London, Schools Council.

SCHOOLS EXAMINATION AND ASSESSMENT COUNCIL (SEAC) (1991a) *Teacher Assessment at Key Stage 3*, London, SEAC.

SCHOOLS EXAMINATION AND ASSESSMENT Council (1991b) *Teacher Assessment at Key Stage 3: An In-Service Resource, Mathematics*, London, SEAC.

SCHOOLS EXAMINATION AND ASSESSMENT COUNCIL (1991c) *Teacher Assessment at Key Stage 3: An In-Service Resource, Science*, London, SEAC.

SHARMA, S. (1987) 'EFA on wheels: the intercultural mobile unit', *Multicultural Teaching*, 5, 2, pp. 13–16.

SMITH, D. and TOMLINSON, S. (1989) *The School Effect*, London, Policy Studies Institute/Heinemann.

TAYLOR, B. (1985) *Multicultural Education For All: Perspectives 22*, Exeter, University of Exeter.

TAYLOR, B. (1987) *Ethnicity and Prejudice in 'White Highlands' Schools: Perspectives 35*, Exeter, University of Exeter.

TAYLOR, F. (1974) *Race, School and Community: A Study of Research and Literature* Slough, NFER.

TOMLINSON, S. (1990) Letters, the *Times Educational Supplement*, 30 November.

TOMLINSON, S. and COULSON, P. (1988) *Education For A Multicultural Society: A Descriptive Analysis Of A Sample of Projects Funded By ESG In Mainly White Areas*, Lancaster, University of Lancaster.

TOWNSEND, H.E.R. (1971) *Immigrant Pupils In England: The LEA Response*, Slough, NFER.

TOWNSEND, H.E.R. and BRITTAN, E.M. (1972) *Organisation In Multiracial Schools*, Slough, NFER.

TROYNA, B. and CARRINGTON, B. (1989) 'Whose side are we on? Ethical dilemmas in research on "race" and education', in BURGESS, R.G. (Ed) *The Ethics of Educational Research*, London, The Falmer Press.

TWITCHIN, J. and DEMUTH, C. (1985) *Multicultural Education: Views From The Classroom*, London, BBC Publications.

WAGNER, P. (1988) 'Developing cooperative learning in the primary school', in LANG, P. (Ed) (1988) *Thinking About PSE In The Primary School*, Oxford, Basil Blackwell.

YOUNG, K. and CONNELLY, N. (1981) *Policy and Practice In The Multiracial City*, London, Policy Studies Institute.

Chapter 15

Accountability and the Local Management of Schools

Alex B. Robertson

Context

The contributions to this series are firmly rooted in the subjects and cross-curricular themes and dimensions specified by the National Curriculum and also address ways in which schools can respond to pressures to extend what is offered to students through the concept of the whole curriculum. Emphasis is placed squarely on the contribution subject specialists can make to the effective delivery of a curriculum which takes into account the character of a pluralistic society. However, even the most enterprising and skilled of practitioners will not have a free hand to achieve such an ambitious aim. This chapter selects for inquiry two underlying factors, local management of schools and the doctrine of accountability, both of which are subject-neutral but have immense implications for how successful or not the subjects will be as change agents. The purpose of this contextual and speculative chapter is to identify possible ways in which the introduction of such important innovations as devolved financing and a sense of corporate responsibility to the community interact with the aims and organization of the school. Although the recent introduction of LMS and procedures to ensure account-ability rule out an empirically argued case, there is an underlying hypothesis. This is, that as power to make potentially very significant, resource-based decisions is devolved to schools, a new framework must be evolved, both conceptual and organizational, to replace traditional oversight by central and local government in order that decisions are not idiosyncratic, parochial and therefore threatening to the legitimate interests of some in a community. How to create a 'bottom-up' culture in which schools and community interact as never before is the challenge, and it is a formidable one. A recent study from the United States, *Bureaucracy and Professionalism* (Glanz, 1991) traces the relationship of what are called 'supervisory' roles to the development of teacher professionalism and, as a historical perspective is taken, the problems of creating a balance are powerfully revealed.

Initiative and enterprise have costs; decisions by teachers have to be set within an appropriate ideological or ethical framework as well as within the more readily recognized financial constraints. No stronger imperative has developed in Britain, albeit slowly and painfully over the last half century, than that of enhancing the opportunities of the nation's children through education, and in this context the rights and needs of ethnic groups have increasingly made a significant contribution to new thinking about education as a whole. It is inevitable that a time of radical change in the organization of the education system will create concern to ensure that what the late-nineteenth-century constitutional historian, Dicey, called in a striking phrase when the process was emerging, 'the equalisation of advantages', will not be jeopardized (Dicey, 1905). It is a contention of this chapter that it will be a greater challenge for the profession to respond to the ethical and in the most general sense, political demands of the new curriculum, than it will for teachers to find strategies to enhance their technical delivery of what the law requires.

The intensity of educational reform over the last decade is unprecedented in its radicalism and variety, as is the sustained level of public and professional debate. Historians of education can point to periods of significant change which engendered intense feeling, but there is no comparable example of a government, over a succession of administrations, continuing the process of change so energetically. The assertively ideological stance of Conservatism over the last decade made it inevitable that reform would occur against a very polarized background. As a result it will be some time before teachers can stand back unemotionally from professional involvement in order to assess the outcome of the sequence of changes which, cumulatively, is transforming the nature of their profession — for transformed it will be.

Two examples from the past are sufficient to demonstrate the intimate relationship, already referred to in the American context, which exists between the regulatory powers of government to maintain the efficiency of the system and the perception of professionalism which develops. Perhaps it needs to be recalled that teaching has never possessed the authority and independence of the classical professions to create its own identity, but has been shaped to a marked degree by its response to a framework created from outside. When government introduced in 1862 the important pioneering attempt to define the principle of public accountability in education, it failed to select an appropriate administrative instrument, choosing instead the crude and restrictive device known ever since as 'payment by results', with all its well-known negative implications for the emergent profession. By way of contrast, the creation of local educational authorities in 1902, the first example in our educational history of universal, powerful and efficient local agencies on which central government could rely, and to which for most of the century it has been content to devolve major responsibilities, demonstrated a more constructive and sophisticated approach which provided many opportunities for the profession to develop a new and more complex identity. This was particularly so in respect of the difficult areas of autonomy and accountability.

Since 1979, legislation has profoundly reshaped the structure of the system and even the internal practices of schools, including their management styles and teaching methods, have not escaped scrutiny and redefinition (Maclure, 1989). This attack on the powerful, if exaggerated myth of teacher independence, particularly in regard to curriculum selection and delivery, gave rise among opponents to charges of almost dictatorial centralism which, because it coincided with the emergence of a new policy towards local government in general, became exceptionally acrimonious and even involved those who would otherwise have been the government's allies (Muffet, 1988). The government asserted, on the other hand, that its reforms were designed to enlarge opportunities, improve standards and devolve to parents and local communities greater rights and responsibilities for their own affairs. The profession, through the strategy of grant-aided status and local financial management, was promised autonomy beyond anything previously experienced. In fact, it is inevitable in the British system that there will be a rather uncomfortable mix, at least for those who like tidiness, of centralist and devolved power groupings. What has changed, perhaps dramatically, is the relative priority given to the limited number of strategies available to any government to achieve its aims. The juggler, using the same number of balls, is capable of intricate changes of pattern. While strengthening its hold over the most powerful levers of control, the examining and moderating processes of the curriculum, the DES has rediscovered the faith of nineteenth-century liberals in the dynamic of the market and the aspirations and characteristics of communities, to infuse energy into the running of schools and oversee the performance of practitioners.

Gradually, and no doubt painfully, a new synthesis of teacher professionalism will evolve. The most significant government policies to influence this remain unclear. The new contractual arrangements will certainly be significant as will, perhaps, the powerful, and potentially assertive, new governing bodies. But less obvious elements will play a part, such as perhaps the notion of continuity of development from 5 to 16 with its implications for rethinking the traditional, and very unsatisfactory, relationship between primary and secondary teachers. Certainly the subtle effects of working to more prescribed syllabuses and examining procedures will have an effect on self-image, and already the requirement to negotiate with students — the unfamiliarity of the phrase is itself significant — over their studies and assessments is causing some teachers no small adjustment to their previous concept of professionalism. Whatever future historians determine were the most significant catalysts, of two things we can be sure. The issue of accountability will have a significant place and will evolve against the background of an increasingly consumer-orientated and litigious society to which all professions will have difficulty adapting. Also, the decision to devolve to schools financial responsibilities far beyond the freedom to decide on simple repairs, or even the right of virement, but involving major decisions on school organization, staffing and professional development, will profoundly change the attitudes of teachers to their work. What these devices will not of themselves do, is change attitudes about the nature of our society in, for example, such profoundly sensitive matters as gender and race. In other words, the profession and the community, interacting through the interface of reformed governing bodies, working for the first time in a very exposed and high-profile way, will have to take responsibility for relating administrative and professional decisions to the ill-defined but none the less powerful signals coming from the community.

Challenges

The issues raised in this book demand that the profession seeks a new synthesis. Autonomy can be a powerful encouragement to a dynamic, outward-looking and creative profession; it can also lead to professionalism preoccupied with status and power which creates a very successful form of unionism, impenetrable to the laity. The archetypal professions of law and medicine have exhibited both characteristics and there has always been a significant school of thought in the teaching profession warning of the dangers of exclusivity and arguing that education must be diffused among society in the most open way possible. In a book of great foresight published in 1940, *Education and Social Change*, Professor Fred Clarke argued that the nature of British society had prevented the emergence of 'a genuine popular philosophy of education such as exists in the United States and some Commonwealth countries . . . the mass of the English people have never yet evolved genuine schools of their own. Schools have always been provided for them from above', a view borne out by the image of schooling in the literature of this country. Fifty years later, the system has become much more open but there is still a notable indirectness in the relationship of most parents to the school system. If a genuine dialogue is to take place, and it is surely a prerequisite of the concept of accountability, let alone decisions about scarce resources, any last traces of this lack of involvement must be ended (Sockett, 1980; Elliott *et al.*, 1981).

In fact, it was to be many years before teaching was to be permitted sufficient autonomy for the issue of accountability to be strongly addressed. While central government and the local education authorities in particular circumscribed the freedom of action of schools — through, for example, the packing of governing bodies, zoning, and most potent of all, control of the money supply — the focus of pressure groups, of which the ethnic minorities were the most notable and long a particular preoccupation of educationists, was diverted away from the schools, except in specific incidents of believed racism, to where the power was seen really to lie.

It is to be expected that under the very considerable freedom of action given to schools by LMS, particularly when associated with the new governing bodies, this focus will change. It will change even more if grant-maintained schools become characteristic of our society as is likely (DFE, 1992). Schools have new opportunities to influence a range of activities and provision which cumulatively over a period could decisively change the character of the institution. Parents have statutory rights of access to information and decision-making; and most important of all, the character of society is changing and the local community is increasingly interested in educational matters. The 'market-forces' emphasis of the Conservatives has only reinforced an evolving new orientation which is recognized by all the political parties in their interest in one form or another of citizen or consumer rights. The White Paper, 'Choice and Diversity: A new framework for schools' (DFE, 1992) indicates the next stage.

The synthesis to be addressed involves the complex interaction of three principal groups with others whose role is not yet clear. Of this latter group the reorganized national inspectorate and the courts can be expected to play a significant part. The three major components are, the teaching profession, the local authorities, and the community, interacting with the others through the governing bodies, but also through a web of disparate interest groups. The three groupings have major adjustments to make to their traditional view of the educational world. Teachers, it must be remembered, are historically recent converts to the idea of activist parent or community participation; LEAs have also been resentful of power-sharing and community pressure groups, for understandable political and strategic reasons, have been reluctant to merge their individuality in cooperative ventures. In this latter regard it will be of the utmost importance to monitor how the extremely interesting initiative of the SACREs evolves (see Volume 1, Chapter 4).

The country, then, far beyond the educational world narrowly defined, is having to learn new ways. The Secretary of State, in an interview with Brian Walden, (13 October 1991, Channel 3) accepted that there will be difficulties in harnessing the interest and active participation of the whole community. Nonetheless, he asserted that the mechanisms being set up, in particular the provision of clear information, would empower parents, and he insisted that central government would take measures to ensure the quality of the data to be disseminated. If, however, there is greater professional leadership, as Walden suggested could occur if community engagement was not secured, decisions which affect the community, decisions which go far beyond financial management in the rather accountant-orientated perception some have of LMS, would be made by small groups of professionals. If this is thought improper, ways must be found to open up the processes to scrutiny. Everything has a cost; every decision in a school involves resources. The distribution of these resources, particularly in those aspects of the school's life which fall outside the statutory obligations of the National Curriculum, could have profound implications for the education and future development of each child in the school. It is inevitable that groups which have grave suspicions of the motives of society towards them, or feel themselves to be marginalized, will be watching developments over the next five years with concern as the National Curriculum and the accompanying administrative strategies are implemented.

Well before public debate was complicated by the greatly enhanced strength of feeling which accompanies most political initiatives in education, the complexities of educational provision in a pluralist society were already being explored. In a significant article of 1982, Dorn and Troyna analysed the thesis that multiracial education had never been a significant part of policy-making at the DES and concluded, 'fragmentation of responsibility has meant that multiracial education considerations remain outside the official structure and that, consequently, the development of any national policy is stillborn'. The argument derived from this was that schools and local authorities were inhibited in positive action by lack of leadership from the centre. In the same journal, Kowalczewski, arguing for a more sophisticated theoretical underpinning of multiracial education, asserted, 'many teachers desperately need the support and guidance of central and local authorities in terms of policy directives, resources, finance and in-service training, otherwise the long-term prospects of black children in British schools will be even bleaker' (Kowalczewski, 1982).

Two years earlier, John Wyatt, seeking in a modernized concept of traditional liberal education, a generous framework in which modern educational accountability might be set, observed that, 'Although considerable effort and even more considerable verbal flow has gone into the quest for expression of individuality in modern education, equal attention has not been paid to how different people with different cultures and different beliefs may still gain access to life chances in our society' (Wyatt, 1980). These quotations have not been selected with any thought to their representativeness, but to emphasize the point that an educational system which, despite its traditional dispersal of power, has been hugely influenced from the centre, in this case negatively, must make a most determined effort to counteract the tendency at school and community level to feel that initiatives for change reside elsewhere if accountability and local management are to succeed.

Responses

The importance and difficulty of this challenge should not be underestimated. Success will have been achieved when teachers, governors, LEAs and the DES recognize the fears and aspirations of minority groups and assimilate them into their planning, no longer regarding them as an element to be bolted on to an existing framework if resources allow. This will necessitate the DES and the LEAs, some of which have already played a distinguished part in setting the parameters of a culturally diverse society, cooperating to signal that in performance indicators, staff appraisal, school audits and planning strategies, the allocation of funds, in the presentation of individual subjects, and in that most influential and difficult of all factors to monitor, the individual beliefs of teachers, a heightened awareness must exist of the need to create a school ethos of cultural pluralism. This must be as distinct and unselfconscious as the child-centredness associated with primary schools, the academic ethos of the old grammar schools or the sense of openness to the community of the best comprehensive schools.

It can be generally agreed that it would be desirable for the national government to speak out powerfully and consistently about the nature of the relationship of the education system to the kind of society it desires. But just as, for example, the equal-opportunities legislation of the 1970s was a crucial assertion of national will, little would have been achieved without the internalization of its principles by the various power bases in the community, most notably by local government. A study published in 1978 argued that the formation of national policy was as likely to be motivated by such outcomes as managerial efficiency and financial stringency as it was by more profound aims (Lucas and Richards, 1978). This truism has significant implications for the debate about accountability and the effects of local management. It may indeed be suggested that it is the growing uncertainty about the relationship of local and central government to the schools, which is at the heart of anxiety about LMS which, in general, finds many supporters in the profession. The wary or hostile response to the likely effects on special needs and social deprivation in critiques of LMS (extending in 1993 to Special Schools-LMSS) has probably intensified the concerns of ethnic minorities and others who feel themselves disadvantaged, about uncertainty as to whether individual schools will have the will or resources to build upon those advances in community relationships and equal opportunities which have been painfully constructed so far. Changes in Section 11 funding also bear on this point (see Appendix 3).

Lee, interpreting a report of the Centre for the Analysis of Social Policy, which among other themes drew attention to large disparities of allocation among LEA formulae, wrote, 'Formula funding is all about rationing money. Schools are, quite literally, competing for resources: they will be calling for more to be allocated on the basis of age weighted pupil numbers, premises costs, or to protect small schools, whichever is likely to benefit them most. Every time that one school receives more, others must lose money to balance the books' (Lee, 1990).

Even when the sum has been agreed for a school, the intentions which might have gone into its determination may be somewhat reassessed by the governors of the school as they determine their own priorities. It is self-evident that in any system dependent upon the reflection of local, as opposed to national guidelines, there will be a danger of parochialism, both institutional and communal. The same fear is evident in those who regret the erosion of the ideal of public-service broadcasting or the introduction into the National Health Service of new financing models. A statement in April 1990 by the then Secretary of State, Mr MacGregor, that 'we shall see schools becoming much more sensitive to the needs of the community which they serve. They will have to respond efficiently and effectively to pupils' needs and parents' concerns.' (MacGregor, 1990) will not reassure those who have little faith in the capacity of society to understand their aspirations and which, on occasion, seem fundamentally to disapprove of them. Events in areas where minority-ethnic group pupils are in a majority, such as at the grant-maintained Stratford school in east London, highlight the complexities and the controversies in putting a policy into practice.

Nor will the analysis of a respected commentator who is convinced of the positive potential of LMS reassure them. Michael Duffy wrote that LMS 'carried into faculties and departments and into the forum of the staffroom, could help break down the time-worn habits and assumptions that are the real restrictive practices of our profession'. But he recognized that as with the 1862 code, the philosophical side effects on which government set such store could diminish and distort the opportunities. Under the 'politician's rhetoric' there were harsh realities. 'Efficiency is not the same thing as effectiveness, however, and it often depends on factors that are beyond a school's control. State schools are not businesses. They cannot change their product, or choose their location or social environment, and they cannot (except slowly, patiently and in the long term) change the community that they serve' (Duffy, 1990). Geoffrey Morris, Chief Education Officer of Cambridgeshire, the LEA which pioneered local financial management, raised another concern in analysing the present state of his county's adaptation to the government's LMS scheme. He feared that the emphasis on simple, clear criteria underpinning the formula would greatly diminish the opportunity for the locality or authority to respond to their diagnosis of the needs of the area (O'Boyle, 1990). This is, in fact, from the small amount of literature on LMS which addresses the possible impact on ethnic groups, the most serious concern. It permeates articles in the journal *Multicultural Teaching* and often identifies the composition of governing bodies as a key aspect in the building of public confidence. It is incumbent on members of all bodies where important decisions with resource implications are taken, but on which all interested parties are not represented, to exercise great sensitivity and even-handedness if trust is to be built up. The old precept of English law, that justice should not only be done, but be seen to be done, could scarcely be bettered as a guide in this case also. On the question of trust, Morris recounted how at a meeting of a local teachers' consultative committee which had pressed for extra money for non-contact time in primary schools, he had to explain that even if available, the money would have had to be distributed via the formula across the LEA. The government he contended 'don't trust the discretion of folks like us'.

If it is the case that new patterns of power are evolving and new relationships between central and local government are being forged, the kind of accusation made by Morris will send ripples of alarm through the politically aware pressure groups. The implications of this point are sharpened by the trend in relationships between minority and majority groups identified by Tomlinson. She observes that since the Swann report, the nature of multicultural education has shifted to a preoccupation with how, 'to offer an appropriate and relevant education to young white people, so that they will leave school able to accept that their non-white fellow pupils are their equal fellow citizens with equal rights and responsibilities' (Tomlinson, 1990). As she points out, the potential of the National Curriculum to address this is considerable, and it is the function of this book to suggest that technically this is within the control of teachers with a minimum of resource implication. But it must be recognized that successful exploitation of the opportunities provided depends upon a concerted effort by all the agencies of education, government, teacher associations and community groups as well as the schools themselves. In other words, an education system conducive to a 'multicultural and global' view of society must be as clear an aim as improving the efficiency of teaching and the creativity of school management (Tomlinson, 1990). The question is whether, in the emphasis on market forces and under the strain of maintaining standards and attracting students, schools and their governing bodies will be able to emphasize sufficiently this particular aspect of accountability.

Troyna has little faith in the traditional view that if the majority white population has revealed to it the rightness of a world outlook through the medium of a liberal, multicultural element in teaching or, it may be added, through the rather contrived rituals of school assemblies, enlightenment will dawn. He would prefer that an 'imperative to move beyond the identification of tactics and reliance on opportunism . . . must aim to formulate an interventionist strategy which has a clearly specified *raison d'être* . . . must try to ensure that our various initiatives cohere into an organized model which has a distinctive theoretical base and is invested with intellectual rigour and rationality' (Troyna, 1989). Those sympathetic to such a view may find that as national and local government disengage from the policy-making of schools and as teachers enter a new relationship with their clients, such consensus will be even more difficult to achieve than before. It could be argued also, that a time of economic recession, with its attendant societal pressures, is the worst time to begin an initiative so dependent on goodwill, by removing most of the constraints or conventions which have guided public policy on education. Whatever strategy is adopted, the need for a rigorous and rational approach can hardly be denied. How far the hazards of an energetic response to one of the most sensitive issues in the search for a more just society will be addressed against a likely response to LMS of economic retrenchment, with its accompanying tensions and arguments over priorities, as well as the preoccupation of schools with other competing demands, is a matter of real concern.

It is here that the concern about formula-funding occurs again. If an LEA is unable or unwilling to prioritize multicultural education in the discretion it currently has over some 25 per cent of the aggregated budget, perhaps in respect of language support, aspects of social deprivation or in-service train-ing, schools which make these a feature of their development plans might well find the going difficult. Ironically, the energetic school which has an ambitious plan to offset deficit and raise funds, say through letting its pre-mises, might well disadvantage local ethnic groups which would find the facilit-ies of the school helpful, but could not pay the price. A related issue is the access of children — all children — to the advantages of the wide provision of activities which historically British schools have provided. While it is vital that all children have this opportunity, it is also clear that because of the social distribution of many ethnic groups in inner-city areas where schools have always been hard pressed to provide the benefits of a generous curriculum and out-of-school activities, it will become extremely difficult for the governors of such schools, beset with the need to counter the effects of falling rolls as a result of parental choice and low income, to maintain, let alone extend, such an enriching experience.

It was remarked above that there is little reference to the possible effects on ethnic-minority groups in the growing literature on LMS. This is true both of the training manuals and general surveys. Perhaps this is not surpris-ing as anxiety derived less from LMS or the notion of accountability *per se*, than from fear that groups which had not succeeded well under the former system, would be particularly likely to lose out when the variables deter-mining the availability of funds and courses were increased. There is, on the other hand, a growing literature on the possible effects of LMS on special-needs provision. There is nothing inherent in the local management idea which associates it with one social group or another, with indeed the question of enlarging opportunities at all. It would be a worrying outcome if the rights and expectations of ethnic-minority groups became mixed inextricably with the issue of special needs in education which, in this country, tend to be associated with handicap, slow learning and low achievement (see Chapter 12). It has been pointed out that ethnic groups have already some ground for suspicion that deficit models of education persist and that stereotypes of educational inadequacy are still far too common (Mittler, 1989). If this feeling is general, the advent of LMS could have unfortunate results. Quite apart from perhaps diminishing support from *all* who need special consideration or attention, the pressure to achieve results and to 'sell' the school to parents, no bad things in themselves, could cause a school, in the more highly charged atmosphere of social expectations, to be suspected of attempting to manip-ulate the entry or to play down the needs or rights of those who were believed to present a negative image. The recent interest by the Commission for Racial Equality in school exclusions, suspensions and expulsions, demon-strates that this has long been a concern of Afro-Caribbean groups and great care will be needed in the newer, more market-orientated context, to ensure fairness.

The writer has been led, perhaps, to identify the potential problems too exclusively. This may be no bad thing, for if schools are to function effectively in their communities and if what might be called the new professionalism is to emerge, or if at a more practical level, performance indicators and development plans are to have any meaning, they must be based on realistic understanding of what is at stake. The implications for intelligent school management are formidable. Fifty years ago a notable British educationist published a book which he called, *To Whom do Schools Belong?* and found the answer difficult to determine (Smith, 1943). It is no less of a problem now and the American experience reinforces this. However, at the time of the question posed above, an American professor of education at least identified a way forward in the relationship between the curriculum and those (whoever they were) who controlled or 'supervised' the system.

> the fact that the new curriculum presents a challenge to supervision is clear . . . Supervision must meet this challenge . . . Supervision faces a two-fold task, one, to provide leadership in adapting the curriculum to the needs of this society, and two, to adjust and adapt its own philosophy and methods so that they will harmonize with this developing curriculum and improve its vitality and functioning quality. (Mackenzie, 1937)

A modern authority complements this exactly.

> Attainment of cultural pluralism is lodged squarely in the policy, structures, practices and beliefs not only in the educational system but in society at large. It is not an individual problem; it requires both a political commitment and institutional efforts. The school should not and cannot remain neutral in these matters. (Verma, 1989)

References

CLARKE, F. (1940) *Education and Social Change*, The University of London Press, London.

DEPARTMENT FOR EDUCATION AND THE WESH OFFICE (1992) *Choice and Diversity: A new framework for schools*, Cmnd., 2021, London, HMSO.

DUFFY, M. (1990) 'Heresy and Magic', The *Times Educational Supplement*, 16 February.

DICEY, A.V. (1905) *Law and Public Opinion in England*, London, Macmillan, p. 275.

DORN, A. and TROYNA, B. (1982) Multiracial Education and the Politics of Decision-Making; *Oxford Review of Education*, 8, 2.

ELLIOTT, J. *et al.* (1981) *School Accountability*, London, Grant McIntyre.

GLANZ, J. (1991) *Bureaucracy and Professionalism*, London/Toronto, Fairleigh Dickinson.

KOWALCZEWSKI, P.S. (1982) 'Race and Education: Racism, Diversity, and Inequality: Implications for Multicultural Education'; *Oxford Review of Education*, 8, 2.

LAWTON, D. (1980) *The Politics of the School Curriculum*, London, RKP.

LEE, T. (1990) 'A Cash Flow that is Likely to Leave Little in Reserve', The *Times Educational Supplement*, 29 June.

LUCAS, B.K. and RICHARDS, P.G. (1978) *A History of Local Government in the Twentieth Century*, London, Allen and Unwin.
MACGREGOR, J. (1990) 'Comment on LMS', *Public Finance and Accountancy*, 6 April, p. 20.
MACLURE, S. (1989) *Education Re-formed*, London, Hodder and Stoughton.
MITTLER, P. (1989) 'Warlock and Swann: Similarities and Differences', in VERMA, G.K. (Ed) *Education for All*, London, The Falmer Press.
MUFFET, D. (1988) *The Times Educational Supplement*, 19 August.
O'BOYLE, C. (1990) 'The Business of Education', *Public Finance and Accountancy*, 6 April, pp. 21–4.
SMITH, L. (1943) 'To Whom Do the Schools Belong', London, Blackwell.
SOCKETT, H. (1980) *Accountability in the English Educational System*, London, Hodder and Stoughton.
TOMLINSON, S. (1990) *Multicultural Education in White Schools*, London, Batsford.
TROYNA, B. (1989) 'A New Planet? Tackling Racial Inequality in All-White Schools and Colleges', in VERMA, G.K. (Ed) *Education for All*, London, The Falmer Press.
VERMA, G.K. (1989) 'Cultural Pluralism: Strategies for Change', in VERMA, G.K. (Ed), *Education for All*, London, The Falmer Press.
WYATT, J. (1980) 'Accountability Means More Than Coping', *Oxford Review of Education*, 6, 1.

Appendix 1: Implications of Race-Relations Legislation

Prabodh Merchant

Earlier chapters have provided ethnic and cultural contexts which should be taken into account if the educational needs and aspirations of all students are to be properly fulfilled. In an increasingly competitive environment with the ever present scarcity of resources it is particularly important that those with the primary responsibility of education are also aware of the legal context in relation to race and culture within which they need to carry out their work. It will be helpful therefore to look briefly at the development of race-relations law in this country over the past twenty to thirty years, resulting from the changing racial, cultural and religious composition of the population.

Background to the Laws

While it is true to say that the UK has always had migrants who have been assimilated into the social and economic life of the country, these have been, up to the mid 1950s, generally of white-European origins. For these migrants, difficulties in the main were those resulting from differences in language, religion and those flowing from newness: i.e., lack of contacts, availability of, and access to, goods and services. It was assumed that most, if not all, of the problems likely to be encountered by these migrants would resolve themselves without any special intervention by the State in a matter of a generation or two at most. The differences such as those relating to religion, custom and practice could be accommodated within the existing legal framework. Problems of race discrimination were thought to be virtually non-existent and could similarly be left to be dealt with by the common-sense application of existing public-order legislation supported by the innate sense of fair play on the part of the majority of the British people.

Post-war reconstruction of shattered cities and economies and the scarcity of labour in all the European countries necessitated a wider search for suitable labour. Thus, throughout the 1950s, various European countries actively encouraged recruitment of labour from their colonies or from countries newly given their independence. For the United Kingdom the most fruitful sources of labour were the islands of the Caribbean, and the newly independent countries of the Indian subcontinent. People from these countries were already familiar to the British and, as members of the Commonwealth, were free to enter the mother country without any restrictions. Throughout the 1950s people came to work and mostly returned to the countries of origin to visit the families whom they supported. As their prime concern was to obtain work, they were attracted to towns and cities offering opportunities for unskilled and semi-skilled work. Again, with the responsibility of supporting their families in their country of origin, it was important that living expenses in this country were kept to a minimum. This typically meant living in Victorian terraced housing shared with friends and relatives in the cheapest areas of town, close to mills, factories and transport depots where they worked. Inevitably, differences in priorities, culture, language, religion, and so forth caused friction between these newcomers and the white working-class residents.

Towards the end of the 1950s, in response to public clamour, the government made known its intention to introduce restrictions on the entry of Commonwealth citizens. This intention was translated in 1962 into the Commonwealth Immigrants Act. Commonwealth citizens entering the UK for work after the passing of the Act in mid-1962 needed vouchers. Dependents of those already in UK were, however, allowed to come without vouchers. This had a significant impact on the nature of immigration and the pattern of their settlement in the UK. Initially there was a rush to beat the deadline of unrestricted entry. This was followed by a need for entrants of both pre and post-period of the 1962 Act to take up permanent settlement and make arrangements for their families to join them here in the United Kingdom. Thus, by introducing an element of sponsorship, the voucher system reinforced bonds of friendship and kinship and provided a further incentive for the new entrants to settle among existing communities and into similar work areas. This change in the composition and pattern of migration had, in its turn, implications for the various services including the education service. The arrival of families with school-age young people into areas which were already the poorest in terms of housing, education, and social and environmental amenities created further tensions and friction.

The 1962 Act was followed in 1965 by the first of the three Race Relations Acts. The 1965 Race Relations Act created a race relations board with powers to take up individual cases of overt discrimination in a very limited sphere of public life. The emphasis of the Act was on conciliation, with the reserve power to take those few who behaved in an illegal way to court. As yet there was no official acceptance of racial discrimination as a significant factor in the continuing disadvantage and harassment suffered by those who were now being euphemistically referred to as 'new-Commonwealth immigrants'.

The task of helping the newcomers to adjust to British society was largely left to the newcomers and voluntary groups such as the Joint Council for the Welfare of Immigrants, the National Committee for Commonwealth Immigrants and concerned individuals. However, the extra burden on local authorities with substantial populations of migrants from the new Commonwealth was recognized. Section 11 of the Local Government Act 1966 therefore provides that the Secretary of State may pay grants towards expenditure on additional staff to those 'local authorities who in his opinion are required to make special provision in the exercise of any of their functions in consequence of the presence within their areas of substantial numbers of immigrants from the Commonwealth whose language or customs differ from those of the community'. Up to 75 per cent of salary costs of approved posts was payable. By far the largest proportion of this grant was used to fund posts in education[1]. Thus, in 1986–87, of the estimated £100m Section 11 expenditure, 79.5 per cent went towards funding posts in education mainly as generalist teachers, ESL school-based peripatetic teachers and classroom assistants'.

The next substantial piece of legislation covering race relations was the second Race Relations Act in 1968. This act extended the powers of the race relations board to cover employment, housing, education, and the provision of goods, facilities and services, and the publication or display of discriminatory advertisements and notices. The board was also given the power to investigate suspected unlawful discrimination where there was no individual complainant. Due to inadequate resources and the absence of any provision to tackle indirect discrimination, in practice the board's investigations were largely confined to individual complaints. The 1968 Act also established the Community Relations Commission (CRC) and charged it with the responsibility for creating better understanding and harmonious relations between peoples of different races and cultures. The CRC in turn provided funds to local voluntary committees to employ officers to undertake work in pursuance of these objectives. Both the Race Relations Board and the Community Relations Commission did some very valuable work in tackling the difficulties experienced by new-Commonwealth migrants.

However, by the early 1970s, it was apparent that the law needed widening to include indirect discrimination and strengthening to allow a proactive rather than a merely reactive approach to be taken to counter the continuing high levels of direct and indirect discrimination based largely on colour. It was also recognized that equality of opportunity and treatment could not be made conditional upon the total abandonment of cultural and ethnic identity by racial minorities, increasing proportions of whose members were either born here or had been substantially brought up in the United Kingdom.

The Current Law

With these considerations and the experience and lessons learned from the 1965 and 1968 Race Relations Acts, a new Race Relations Act was enacted in 1976. The Act merged the Race Relations Board and the Community Relations Commission to form a new body, the Commission for Racial Equality, with new and stronger powers for the creation of a society based on equality of opportunity for all racial groups. The Commission has a duty of:

- Working towards the elimination of discrimination;
- Promoting equality of opportunity and good relations between persons of different racial groups generally; and
- Keeping under review the workings of the Act and, when required by the Secretary of State, or when it otherwise thinks it necessary, drawing up and submitting to the Secretary of State proposals for amending it.

The 1976 Act gave a wider definition of unlawful discrimination to include traditional practices and procedures which, although they may not be intended to discriminate or disadvantage, nevertheless had that effect on ethnic minorities. A requirement or condition which although applied equally, or would be applied equally, to all racial groups constitutes unlawful indirect discrimination if:

- A considerably smaller proportion of persons of a racial group can comply with it as compared with the proportion of persons of another racial group;
- It cannot be shown to be justifiable irrespective of colour, race, nationality or ethnic or national origins of the person or persons to whom it is applied; and
- It is to the detriment of the person who cannot comply with it.

Thus unnecessarily demanding educational qualifications for jobs which do not require such high qualifications could be indirectly discriminatory. Similarly, unjustifiable dress or language requirements could constitute unlawful indirect discrimination. The 1976 Act also enables measures to be taken to meet the special needs of particular racial groups in regard to their education, training or welfare, or any other ancillary benefits. Additionally, the Act allows provision to be made for training and encouragement to apply for work in which particular racial groups are underrepresented. Actual selection for a job must, of course, be on merit.

The two basic objectives of the Race Relations Act 1976 can therefore be stated as follows: firstly to regulate behaviour by laying down minimum acceptable standards which should govern relations between groups and individuals in any civilized society. The second objective is to encourage behaviour and actions necessary to overcome the effects of discrimination and disadvantage and thereby help to create a society in which groups and individuals enjoy genuine equality of opportunity. As both objectives aim to bring about a qualitative change in society their importance to educationalists cannot be overstated.

This then, is the broad legal context in terms of race relations, within which the education service has to operate. Detailed guidance on the implementation of the Race Relations Act with specific reference to every section is, of course, available from a variety of sources. Thus, for example, the Commission for Racial Equality's code of practice for the elimination of racial discrimination in education sets out the implications of every relevant section of the 1976 Act to help those involved with education to provide it without discrimination made unlawful by the Act. Other publications provide detailed guidance on important issues relating to the encouragement of awareness and initiatives necessary for the creation of an education service which is capable of meeting the needs and aspirations of a multiracial, multicultural and multifaith society. However, it may perhaps be useful to consider, albeit very briefly, one or two important avenues for making progress towards achieving these objectives within the framework of the Race Relations Act.

Multicultural Education

Clearly this has been, and continues to be, important in disseminating information relating to the culture, traditions, and beliefs of various groups within society. However, the need is to build on the understanding and tolerance which will, hopefully, result from greater awareness of other ways of living by ensuring that the more positive aspects of different systems and values are identified and respected.

Antiracist Education

A careful and sympathetic review of teaching materials and methods is necessary to ensure that they are as free as possible of cultural and racial bias based on negative and/or stereotypical images and assumptions. Their replacement by appropriately based materials and methods will be helpful in promoting self-development and mutual respect amongst students and teachers. Encouragement can also be given to underrepresented groups to apply for work in the Education Service, especially in teaching posts. This would not only provide much needed role models, but could also be an additional cultural resource.

The National Curriculum

Implementing some of the initiatives discussed above within the constraints of the National Curriculum is inevitably going to pose challenges for both resources and commitment. As far as may be practicable, attempts should be made to ensure that teaching materials and methods in various subjects within the National Curriculum are such as to enable the various minority groups to understand and value their particular ethnic identities.

Finally, there are also other Acts which impose various duties and obligations on those involved in providing education. For example, the 1988 Education Reform Act with its provision for the Local Management of Schools (LMS), opting out, the National Curriculum, and the character of religious worship. All of these issues have racial as well as cultural and religious dimensions. Similarly, the right of parents to a school of their choice for their children poses challenges, which sometimes may be in conflict with obligations under other legislation. Consider, for example, the recent test cases in Dewsbury and Cleveland. In both, the High Court upheld the right of parental choice under the 1988 Education Reform Act, even though such judgments appeared to undermine the 1976 Race Relations Act. Under the terms of the latter, LEAs are not allowed to act in any way that would constitute racial discrimination. The parents won the right to have their children transferred to other schools from the ones to which they had been originally allocated. The parents were white[2] and the schools had a high proportion of Asian pupils (see Chapter 2 in this volume about parental choice).

Section 18 (I) of the Race Relations Act 1976 as originally enacted made it unlawful for a local education authority (LEA) to discriminate racially in carrying out those functions under the Education Acts 1944 to 1975 which do not fall under Section 17 of the 1976 Act. The Education Acts of 1980 and 1981 updated Section 18 so that it covers functions under those Education Acts also. There is no similar reference in the 1986 or 1988 Education Acts. There is a suggestion that the words in Section 235 (7) of the 1988 Act that it 'shall be construed as one with the 1944 Act' are intended to deal with this point. But the position is not clear.

As with all laws, race-relations legislation must be kept under review to ensure that it addresses contemporary concerns adequately. The Commission for Racial Equality (CRE) undertook a review of the Race Relations Act 1976 in 1985, and made recommendations to which the government made no formal response. In the light of subsequent events, the CRE undertook a second review and published a consultation document in 1991 entitled *Second Review of the Race Relations Act 1976: A Consultative Document* (CRE, 1991). The review is in two sections. In the first of these, the CRE sets out proposals for changes in the legislation which it considers will improve the effectiveness of the law-enforcement process. The second part of the consultation document reflects on issues closely related to race relations and on ways in which society might better manage the many and varied tensions that occur across the boundaries of race, religion and sex, bearing in mind the implications of the move towards a more integrated Europe[3].

It should be mentioned that what we have learned as a result of twenty years' experience is that the law is a necessary but not a sufficient condition of solving the problems of race relations. The aims of legislation have to be translated into practice by various institutions in our society (e.g., courts, industries, universities, schools, politicians, employers, and all citizens).

Footnotes

1   A Scrutiny of Grants under Section 11 of Local Government Act 1966 — Final Report, December, 1988.
2   In the Cleveland case one parent was of Afro-Caribbean origins.
3   The final version was published in 1992.

References

COMMISSION FOR RACIAL EQUALITY (1991) *Second Review of the Race Relations Act 1976: A Consultative Document*, London, CRE.
COMMISSION FOR RACIAL EQUALITY (1992) Second Review of the Race Relations Act, London, CRE.

Appendix 2

Appendix 2a

Lists of Recent ERA-related Publications (secondary-schools orientation): National Curriculum Council (NCC); School Examinations and Assessment Council (SEAC): Department of Education and Science (DES) (Department for Education since July, 1992); and Her Majesty's Inspectorate (HMI).

(For lists of National Curriculum subject-related publications, see Volume 1, Appendix 2).

In 1992 a joint publication by DES/DFE, NCC and SEAC *Schools Update for Teachers and Governors*, to be published termly, replaced the separate newsletters *ERA Bulletin, NCC News* and *SEAC Recorder*. It provides details of NC publications and activities.

Section A: National Curriculum Council

Key: (CR) = Consultation Reports
     (CG) = Curriculum Guidance
     (N-S G) = Non-Statutory Guidance
     (NOP OPs) = National Oracy Project, Occasional Papers
     (INSET) = In-Service Education for Teachers

General Publications

NCC (1989) *An Introduction to the National Curriculum* (INSET).
NCC (1989) *NCC News, No 1, June*.
NCC (1989) *NCC News, No 2, December*.

NCC (1989) *Developing INSET Activities.*

NCC (1989) *The National Curriculum: A Guide for Employers.*

NCC (1989) *NCC Annual Report 1988–89*, December.

NCC (1989) *A Curriculum for All — Special Educational Needs in the National Curriculum.*

NCC (1989) *National Curriculum: Developing INSET Activities*, Video (37 mins) (INSET).

NCC (1990) *NCC News: Newsletter of the National Curriculum Council, No. 3*, April.

NCC (1990) *NCC News, No. 4*, October.

NCC (1990) *A guide for Employers.*

NCC (1990) *Circular 10: The National Curriculum at Key Stage 4.*

NCC (1990) *The National Curriculum at Key Stage 4: A digest.*

NCC (1990) *Incorporating Programmes of Study into Schemes of Work.*

NCC (1990) *Corporate Plan 1990–91.*

NCC (1990) *The Whole Curriculum*, March (CG).

NCC (1990) *The National Curriculum: A Guide for Parents of Secondary Pupils*, May (also published in Greek, Turkish, Chinese, Bengali, Gujerati, Hindi, Punjabi and Urdu).

NCC (1991) *NCC Annual Report 1990–1991*, December.

NCC (1991) *The National Curriculum and the Initial Training of Student Articled and Licensed Teachers.*

NCC (1991) *Teacher Placements and the National Curriculum.*

NCC (1991) *NCC News, No. 5*, February.

NCC (1991) *NCC News, No. 6*, June.

NCC (1991) *NCC News, No. 7*, November.

NCC (1991) *NCC Consultation Report.*

NCC (1992) *The National Curriculum and Pupils with Severe Learning Difficulties* (CG).

NCC (1992) *The National Curriculum and Pupils with Severe Learning Difficulties* (INSET).

NCC (1992) *The National Curriculum Corporate Plan 1992–95.*

NCC (1992) *NCC Annual Report 1991–1992*, December.

National Curriculum Council

Lists of recent publications relating to cross-curricular themes in the National Curriculum in Secondary Schools

NCC (1989) *An Introduction to the National Curriculum* (INSET).

NCC (1989) *Video Developing INSET Activities* (INSET).

NCC (1989) *Developing INSET Activities* (INSET).

NCC (1989) *Curriculum Guidance No. 2. A Curriculum for All — Special Educational Needs in the National Curriculum* (CG).

NCC (1989) *The National Curriculum: A Guide for Employers*.

NCC (1989) *Curriculum Guidance No. 2: A Curriculum for All*, October (CG).

NCC (1990) *The Whole Curriculum*, March (CG).

NCC (1990) *Education for Economic and Industrial Understanding*, April (CG).

NCC (1990) *Circular 10: The National Curriculum at Key Stage 4*.

NCC (1990) *Education for Economic and Industrial Understanding* (CG).

NCC (1990) *Health Education*, July (CG).

NCC (1990) *Careers Education and Guidance*, August (CG).

NCC (1990) *Environmental Education* (CG).

NCC (1990) *Education for Citizenship* (CG).

NCC (1991) *Assessment through Talk in Key Stages 3 and 4 Beyond* (NOP OPs).

NCC (1991) *Managing Economic and Industrial Understanding in Schools*.

NCC (1991) *Education for Work: A Guide for Industry and Commerce*.

NCC (1991) *Work Experience and the School Curriculum*.

NCC (1991) *Linguistic Diversity and the National Curriculum*.

NCC (1992) *Education for work: A Guide for Industry and Commerce*.

NCC (1992) *English and Economic and Industrial Understanding at Key Stages 3 and 4* (INSET).

NCC (1992) *Mathematics and Economic and Industrial Understanding at Key Stages 3 and 4* (INSET).

NCC (1992) *Science and Economic and Industrial Understanding at Key Stages 3 and 4* (INSET).

NCC (1992) *Design and Technology and Economic and Industrial Understanding at Key Stages 3 and 4* (INSET).

NCC (1992) *History and Economic and Industrial Understanding at Key Stages 3 and 4* (INSET).

NCC (1992) *Geography and Economic and Industrial Understanding at Key Stages 3 and 4* (INSET).

NCC (1992) *Modern Foreign Languages and Economic and Industrial Understanding at Key Stages 3 and 4* (INSET).

NCC (1992) *Information Technology and Economic and Industrial Understanding at Key Stages 3 and 4* (INSET).

Section B: School Examinations and Assessment Council

Key: (AAS) = A level/A level Special
      (ASSM) = Assessment Matters
      (EMU) = Evaluation and Monitoring Unit
      (GCSE) = General Certificate of Secondary Education
      (KS3) = Key Stage 3
      (KS4) = Key Stage 4

Appendix 2

General Publications

SEAC (1989) *The Recorder* (Autumn).
SEAC (1989) *Teacher Assessment in the Classroom*, Pack A.
SEAC (1989) *Teacher Assessment in the School*, Pack B.
SEAC (1989) *A Source Book for Teachers*, Pack C.
SEAC (1990) *Examining GCSE: First General Scrutiny Report* (GCSE).
SEAC (1990) *GCSE AS level Chief Examiners' Conference Report* (AAS).
SEAC (1990) *Your Questions Answered* (ASSM).
SEAC (1990) *A Sourcebook for Teacher Assessment* (ASSM).
SEAC (1990) *The Recorder* (Spring).
SEAC (1990) *The Recorder* (Summer).
SEAC (1990) *The Recorder* (Autumn).
SEAC (1991) *National Curriculum Assessment; Responsibility of LEAs in 1991–92.*
SEAC (1991) *Decision Analytic Aids to Examining — The DAATE Report* (EMU).
SEAC (1991) *Examining GCSE: Second General Scrutiny Report* (GCSE).
SEAC (1991) *A and AS Examinations 1989: General Scrutiny Report* (AAS).
SEAC (1991) *Coursework: Learning from GCSE Experience — An Account of the Proceedings of a SEAC Conference* (GCSE).
SEAC (1991) *A and AS Level Results 1990* (AAS).
SEAC (1991) *Key Stage 4 Assessment: Quality Assured* (KS4).
SEAC (1991) *Teacher Assessment at Key Stage 3 1992* (KS3).
SEAC (1991) *National Pilot for Mathematics and Science KS3: End of Key Stage Assessment Arrangements 1992* (KS3).
SEAC (1991) *NCA Arrangements — National Pilot Leaflets for LEAs* (KS3).
SEAC (1991) *Chief Examiners' Conferences 1991 Evaluation Report* (EMU).
SEAC (1991) *National Curriculum Assessment at Key Stage 3: A Review of the 1991 Pilots with Implications for 1992* (EMU).
SEAC (1991) *The Recorder* (Spring).
SEAC (1991) *The Recorder* (Summer).
SEAC (1991) *The Recorder* (Autumn).
SEAC (1991) *Timetable for Assessment Cycle 1991–92* (ASSM).
SEAC (1991) *Information and Guidance for LEAs and Governing Bodies of Non-LEA Maintained Schools* Autumn, (KS3).
SEAC (1991) *The Parents' Charter.*
SEAC (1991) *Teacher Assessment in Practice 1992* (KS3).
SEAC (1992) *Briefing Note 2: Tests for 14-year-olds* (KS3).
SEAC (1992) *A and AS Level Results 1991* (AAS).
SEAC (1992) *GCSE Criteria: Welsh First Language.*
SEAC (1992) *GCSE Criteria: Welsh Literature and Welsh Second Language.*
SEAC (1992) *GCSE Criteria: English, English Literature, Mathematics, Science (Biology, Chemistry, Physics).*
SEAC (1992) *GCSE/KS4: Standards for Assessment and Certification.*

Schools Examination and Assessment Council

List of recent publications relating to cross-curricular themes in the National Curriculum in Secondary Schools

SEAC (1991) *Sciences — Cross-Curricular Implications*

Section C: Department of Education and Science (DFE after 1 July 1992)

Key: (NCSO) = National Curriculum Statutory Orders
(SI) = Statutory Instruments
(SO) = Statutory Orders
(C) = Circulars
(TGATR) = Task Group on Assessment and Testing Reports

General Publications

DES (1985) *Better Schools.*
DES (1986) *Children at School and Problems Related to AIDS.*
DES (1987) *Task Group on Assessment and Testing: A Report.*
DES (1988) *Education at Work — A Guide for Schools.*
DES (1988) *Education at Work — A Guide for Employers.*
DES (1988) *National Curriculum Task Group on Assessment and Testing* (TGATR).
DES (1989) *Report of the Task Group on Assessment and Testing* (TGATR).
DES (1989) *National Curriculum: From Policy to Practice*, February.
DES (1989) *Further Education.*
DES (1989) *Higher Education — the Next 25 Years.*
DES (1989) *School Governors — How to Become a Grant-Maintained School*, 2nd edition.
DES (1989) *National Curriculum: A Guide for Parents.*
DES (1989) *Education (National Curriculum) (Temporary Exceptions for Individual Pupils Regulations* (SI).
DES (1989) *Education (School Curriculum and Related Information) Regulations* (SI).
DES (1989) *Education (School Curriculum and Related Information) (Amendment) Regulations* (SI).
DES (1989) *Education (School Records) Regulations* (SI).
DES (1989) *Planning for School Development 1.*
DES (1990) *Good Behaviour and Discipline in Schools*, revised.
DES (1990) *HMI Short Courses: 1990.*

DES (1990) *National Curriculum for 14–16-year-olds.*
DES (1990) *National Curriculum and Assessment.*
DES (1990) *Records of Achievement* (C).
DES (1990) *The Education Reform Act 1988: The Education (National Curriculum) (Assessment Arrangements for English, Mathematics and Science) Order 1990*, July (C).
DES (1990) *Education (Individual Pupil's Achievements) (Information) Regulations* (SI).
DES (1990) *Education (Special Educational Needs) (Amendment) Regulations* (SI).
DES (1990) *Education (School Curriculum and Related Information) (Amendment) Regulations* (SI).
DES (1990) *Education (National Curriculum) (Assessment Arrangements for English, Mathematics and Science) Order* (SI).
DES (1991) *Development Planning — A Practical Guide.*
DES (1991) *Education Statistics for the UK 1990 Edition.*
DES (1991) *School Governors — The School Curriculum.*
DES (1991) *Your Child and the National Curriculum: A Parent's Guide to What Is Taught in Schools.*
DES (1991) *The Parent's Charter: You and Your Child's Education.*
DES (1992) *HIV and AIDS: A Guide for the Education Service.*
DES (1992) *Education Statistics for the UK 1991 Edition.*
DFE (1992) *Are You Interested in Becoming a School Inspector?*
DFE (1992) *Education Europe.*
DFE (1992) *Your Child and the National Curriculum* (2nd Ed).
DFE (1992) *Choice and Diversity: A New Framework for Schools.*

Department of Education and Science

List of recent publications relating to cross-curricular themes in the National Curriculum in Secondary Schools

DES (1985) *Better Schools.*

Section D: Her Majesty's Inspectorate

Key: (CMS) = Curriculum Matters Series

Each year, several hundred HMI inspection and survey reports are published by the Department of Education and Science. These contain evidence and evaluative comment relevant to schools' preparedness for, and implementation of, National Curriculum requirements.

General Publications

HMI (1985) *Quality in Schools — Education and Appraisal.*
HMI (1986) *The Curriculum from 5–16* (CMS).
HMI (1987) *Teaching Poetry in the Secondary School: An HMI View.*
HMI (1987) *The New Teacher in School.*
HMI (1988) *Secondary Schools: An Appraisal by HMI.*
HMI (1989) *Education Observed 10: Curriculum at 11-plus.*
HMI (1989) *Education Observed 12: The Lower Attaining Pupils' Programme 1982–88.*
HMI (1989) *The Curriculum from 5–16* (2nd Ed) (CMS).
HMI (1990) *Education Observed 14: Girls Learning Mathematics.*
HMI (1990) *Standards in Education 1989–90: The Annual Report of the Chief Inspector of Schools.*
HMI (1990) *Special Needs Issues.*
HMI (1991) *Standards in Education 1990–91: The Annual Report of the Chief Inspector of Schools.*
HMI (1991) *Assessment, Recording, and Reporting.*
HMI (1991) *National Curriculum and Special Needs.*
HMI (1992) *Standards in Education 1991–92: The Annual Report of the Chief Inspector of Schools.*
HMI (1992) *Getting in on the Act. Provision for Pupils with Special Educational Needs: the National Picture.*

Her Majesty's Inspectorate

List of recent publications relating to cross-curriculum themes in the National Curriculum in Secondary Schools

HMI (1988) *Careers Education and Guidance from 5 to 16.*
HMI (1988) *Secondary Schools: An Appraisal by HMI.*

Appendix 2b

National Educational Resources Information Services (NERIS)

Information concerning cross-curricular elements, themes, dimensions and skills: An alternative source.

The following section describes briefly a recently developed source of educational information. Publications identified using the system are presented. These are intended both as a resource in their own right and also to indicate the scope and potential of the system. References presented include many of those listed in Volume 1, Appendix 2 and in Volume 2, Appendix 2a earlier, *but are in a different grouping and format*. Because of the breadth of the descriptors used in the search, there is also overlap between categories. The groupings presented derive from electronic searches based on cross-curricular **elements**, pp. 231–240 **themes**, pp. 241–253 **dimensions** pp. 253–256 and **skills** pp. 256–271. The School of Education of the University of Manchester is a subscriber to the system. The listings are reproduced with the permission of NERIS.

During the 1990s, it is anticipated that the uses of computer-based technology in the storing and retrieval of educational information will expand rapidly. A major potential growth point is represented by the National Educational Resources Information Service (NERIS). NERIS was established in 1987 with the purpose of helping those who were experiencing difficulties in obtaining information about available teaching materials and other resources. The aim was to establish a major resource, mainly for educationalists. Originally NERIS concentrated on sciences, mathematics, social and personal education and geography, but this has been greatly extended to include additional information related to the National Curriculum. It is supported by the DES, NCC, SEAC, CCW (Wales), NICC (Northern Ireland), SCC (Scotland) and the Training Agency.

NERIS uses commonly available educational computers, a modem and some specially written software that enables users to locate information on learning materials and the curriculum. Discs containing the database, or sections of it, can also be obtained, rather than subscribing to the complete on-line system. The NERIS database includes copyright-free materials that can be reproduced or adapted for use in schools. Institutions using Prestel, Prestel Education and Campus (the successor to the Times Network system) can access the NERIS database.

Initially, the system was subsidized in respect of both the network charges and overheads and was grant-aided by the DTI. In June 1990, it was reported that some 5,750 schools were using the database which contained some 33,000 items at that time. The service now has to function within a market environment. By June 1992, the number of items on the database had risen to 53,000 and is continuing to increase rapidly. The number of schools subscribing to the service has fallen to about 3,000.

The flexibility of the database is one of its great strengths. Another is that additional information concerning the whole curriculum is continuously being added. In combination, these attributes allow subscribers to search the database efficiently and rapidly for materials that are central to their concerns, whether these be particular subjects or cross-curricular elements, themes, dimensions or skills.

Only bibliographic references are presented. Users can obtain further details about each by using the system. Using various descriptors, such as primary, secondary, etc., it is possible to identify materials specific to particular stages of education.

Further information concerning NERIS can be obtained from:

The Director,
NERIS,
Maryland College,
Leighton Street,
Woburn,
Milton Keynes,
Buckinghamshire,
MK17 9JD.
(tel: 0525 290 663).

Statement of Search: Elements

Search for documents containing NATIONAL and CURRICULUM in free text and also containing CROSS and CURRICULAR in free text and also containing **ELEMENTS** in free text (pp. 231–240).

Source: Reproduced from NERIS on CD-ROM Summer 1992

Ref: 1037063231
TITLE: NATIONAL YOUTH PARLIAMENT COMPETITION
MEDIA: Information sheet
PUBLISHER: Citizenship Foundation
PUBLISHED: Annually

Ref: 1037062880
TITLE: CHILDREN FIRST
MEDIA: Booklet; 4 vol. A4.
AUTHOR: Allen P., Harris M., Tozer H.
PUBLISHER: Wheaton Publishers Ltd
PUBLISHED: 1990

Ref: 1037061197
TITLE: CROSS CURRICULAR THEMES: THE SCHOOL AND THE COMMUNITY
MEDIA: TV broadcast; 15 mins, teacher's booklet
SERIES: Programmes for Primary Teachers
PUBLISHER: ITV Schools, Central Independent Television
PUBLISHED: 1992 (Spring Term)

Ref: 1037060604
TITLE: GARDEN FESTIVAL WALES 1992
MEDIA: Visit

Ref: 1037060238
TITLE: CURRICULUM OVERVIEW SCOTLAND
MEDIA: Booklet; 10pp A4, photo illustrations
AUTHOR: Preece J.
SERIES: Enterprising Classroom, Book 1A
PUBLISHER: School Curriculum Industry Partnership (SCIP),
Mini-Enterprises in Schools Project
PUBLISHED: 1991

Ref: 1037060234
TITLE: CASE STUDIES IN ENGLISH
MEDIA: Booklet; 26pp A4, photo illustrations
AUTHOR: Stock J.
SERIES: Enterprising Classroom, Book 5
PUBLISHER: School Curriculum Industry Partnership (SCIP),
Mini-Enterprises in Schools Project
PUBLISHED: 1991

Ref: 1037060089
TITLE: SCHOOL CURRICULUM INDUSTRY PARTNERSHIP (SCIP)/
MINI-ENTERPRISES IN SCHOOLS PROJECT (MESP)
MEDIA: Information sheet
SERIES: SCIP Network
PUBLISHER: School Curriculum Industry Partnership (SCIP)
PUBLISHED: 1990

Ref: 1037059921
TITLE: LANGUAGE LEARNING FOR THE NEXT CENTURY
MEDIA: Article; 2pp A4, colour photographs
SERIES: NCC News, Issue 7
PUBLISHER: National Curriculum Council (NCC)
PUBLISHED: 1991 (Autumn)

Ref: 1037058623
TITLE: FOOD FOR THOUGHT: FISH FARMING IN THE
HIGHLANDS AND ISLANDS
MEDIA: Multi media pack; teacher notes, pupil notes, tape-slide
presentation, video, audio tapes, computer software, supplementary
materials
PUBLISHER: Highlands and Islands Enterprise, in association with Scottish
Council for Educational Technology (SCET) and Primary Education
Development Project
PUBLISHED: 1991

Ref: 1037057996
TITLE: DELIVERY OF PROCESS SKILLS AND KEY ELEMENTS OF
PERSONAL AND SOCIAL DEVELOPMENT: FIVE CASE STUDIES
MEDIA: Booklet; 42pp A4
SERIES: Curriculum Design for the Secondary Stages
PUBLISHER: Scottish Consultative Council on the Curriculum (SCCC)
PUBLISHED: 1991

Ref: 1037057931
TITLE: GEOGRAPHY AND CROSS-CURRICULAR THEMES
MEDIA: Article
SERIES: Teaching Geography, Vol. 16, No. 4, pp. 147–154
PUBLISHER: The Geographical Association
PUBLISHED: 1991 (October)

Ref: 1037057382
TITLE: CURRICULUM GUIDANCE
MEDIA: Booklet; set of 8, pp. 18–54 A4
PUBLISHER: National Curriculum Council (NCC)
PUBLISHED: 1989/90

Ref: 1037057380
TITLE: EDUCATION FOR CITIZENSHIP
MEDIA: Booklet; 26pp A4
SERIES: Curriculum Guidance, 8
PUBLISHER: National Curriculum Council (NCC)
PUBLISHED: 1990

Ref: 1037057377
TITLE: THE WHOLE CURRICULUM
MEDIA: Booklet; 18pp. A4
SERIES: Curriculum Guidance, 3
PUBLISHER: National Curriculum Council (NCC)
PUBLISHED: 1990

Ref: 1037057376
TITLE: EDUCATION FOR ECONOMIC AND INDUSTRIAL
UNDERSTANDING
MEDIA: Booklet; 54pp. A4, colour illus.
SERIES: Curriculum Guidance, Number 4
PUBLISHER: National Curriculum Council (NCC)
PUBLISHED: 1990

Ref: 1037057375
TITLE: HEALTH EDUCATION
MEDIA: Booklet; 34pp A4
SERIES: Curriculum Guidance, Number 5
PUBLISHER: National Curriculum Council (NCC)
PUBLISHED: 1990

Ref: 1037057374
TITLE: CAREERS EDUCATION AND GUIDANCE
MEDIA: Booklet; 44pp A4
SERIES: Curriculum Guidance, Number 6
PUBLISHER: National Curriculum Council (NCC)
PUBLISHED: 1990

Ref: 1037057373
TITLE: ENVIRONMENTAL EDUCATION
MEDIA: Booklet; 49pp A4
SERIES: Curriculum Guidance, Number 7
PUBLISHER: National Curriculum Council (NCC)
PUBLISHED: 1990

Ref: 1037057358
TITLE: COORDINATION OF TECHNOLOGY DOES NOT EQUAL
COORDINATION OF IT; ON MISPERCEPTION AND
MALADAPTATION
MEDIA: Discussion paper
AUTHOR: Passey D., Ridgeway J.
PUBLISHER: STAC Project
PUBLISHED: 1991

Ref: 1037057357
TITLE: A VIEW OF IT ACROSS THE CURRICULUM
MEDIA: Information sheet; posters
PUBLISHER: STAC Project
PUBLISHED: 1990 (June)

Ref: 1037057152
TITLE: WEATHER
MEDIA: Poster; set of 6, A2, 12pp teacher's booklet
AUTHOR: Paul J.
SERIES: Poster Packs
PUBLISHER: Scholastic Educational
PUBLISHED: 1992

Ref: 1037056715
TITLE: MANAGEMENT OF CROSS-CURRICULAR ISSUES
MEDIA: Information sheet
AUTHOR: Waring M.
SERIES: FL North West Region
PUBLISHED: 1989

Ref: 1037056678
TITLE: FLEXIBLE LEARNING CASE STUDY — GRAEME HIGH
SCHOOL — THE USE OF IT
MEDIA: Report
AUTHOR: Gray C.
SERIES: FL Scottish Region
PUBLISHED: 1991

Ref: 1037056677
TITLE: FLEXIBLE LEARNING CASE STUDY — INFORMATION
TECHNOLOGY IN MUSIC (DUMFRIES AND GALLOWAY)
MEDIA: Report
AUTHOR: Davies L.
SERIES: FL Scottish Region
PUBLISHED: 1991

Ref: 1037055815
TITLE: THE NATIONAL CURRICULUM — CONSTRUCTION AND
THE BUILT ENVIRONMENT
MEDIA: Book; 51pp A4, loose leaf, ringbinder
PUBLISHER: Construction Industry Training Board (CITB)
PUBLISHED: 1991

Ref: 1037054335
TITLE: PERSONAL AND SOCIAL DEVELOPMENT (PSD)
MEDIA: Article; 1p A4
SERIES: NCC News, Issue 6
PUBLISHER: National Curriculum Council (NCC)
PUBLISHED: 1991 (June)

Ref: 1037053899
TITLE: MAPPING OF INFORMATION TECHNOLOGY: A VIEW
ACROSS THE CURRICULUM
MEDIA: Teacher notes
AUTHOR: Passey D.
PUBLISHER: University of Lancaster STAC Project
PUBLISHED: 1990

Ref: 1037052614
TITLE: 5–14 UPDATE: ISSUE NO 5
MEDIA: Periodical; 4pp A4
PUBLISHER: Scottish Office Education Department (SOED)
PUBLISHED: 1991 (January)

Ref: 1037050880
TITLE: CROSS CURRICULAR ISSUES: AN INSET MANUAL FOR
SECONDARY SCHOOLS
MEDIA: Book; ring binder 104pp 297 x 210mm
AUTHOR: Tilly G. (Ed)
PUBLISHER: Longman
PUBLISHED: (planned) 1991

Ref: 1037047214
TITLE: WORK EXPERIENCE AND THE SCHOOL CURRICULUM
MEDIA: Booklet; 43pp A4, colour illus.
PUBLISHER: National Curriculum Council (NCC)
PUBLISHED: 1991

Ref: 1037047212
TITLE: GEOGRAPHY NON-STATUTORY GUIDANCE ENGLAND
MEDIA: Book; loose-leaf, 54pp A4
PUBLISHER: National Curriculum Council (NCC)
PUBLISHED: 1991 (June)

Ref: 1037047209
TITLE: PLANNING THE GEOGRAPHY CURRICULUM: PART 2
MEDIA: Information sheet; 17pp A4
SERIES: Geography Non-Statutory Guidance, England
PUBLISHER: National Curriculum Council (NCC)
PUBLISHED: 1991 (June)

Ref: 1037047085
TITLE: HISTORY NON-STATUTORY GUIDANCE ENGLAND
MEDIA: Book; loose-leaf, 102pp A4
PUBLISHER: National Curriculum Council (NCC)
PUBLISHED: 1991 (June)

Ref: 1037047083
TITLE: EXAMPLES OF PLANNING GRIDS
MEDIA: Information sheet; 3pp A4
SERIES: History Non-Statutory Guidance, England
PUBLISHER: National Curriculum Council (NCC)
PUBLISHED: 1991 (June)

Ref: 1037047079
TITLE: PLANNING SCHEMES OF WORK FOR STUDY UNITS
MEDIA: Information sheet; 8pp A4
SERIES: History Non-Statutory Guidance, England
PUBLISHER: National Curriculum Council (NCC)
PUBLISHED: 1991 (June)

Ref: 1037047078
TITLE: IMPLEMENTING NATIONAL CURRICULUM HISTORY:
PART 2
MEDIA: Information sheet; 19pp A4
SERIES: History Non-Statutory Guidance, England
PUBLISHER: National Curriculum Council (NCC)

Ref: 1037044558
TITLE: HISTORY PROGRAMME OF STUDY FOR KEY STAGE 3
(ENGLAND) LEVELS 3-7
MEDIA: Information sheet
AUTHOR: Department of Education and Science (DES)
SERIES: History in the National Curriculum (England)
PUBLISHER: HMSO
PUBLISHED: 1991 (March)

Ref: 1037044557
TITLE: HISTORY PROGRAMME OF STUDY FOR KEY STAGE 4
(ENGLAND) MODEL 1 AND MODEL 2 LEVELS 4-10
MEDIA: Information sheet
AUTHOR: Department of Education and Science (DES)
SERIES: History in the National Curriculum (England)
PUBLISHER: HMSO
PUBLISHED: 1991 (March)

Ref: 1037043978
TITLE: A PROBLEM OF TIME — A REVIEW OF CURRICULUM
GUIDANCE 6
MEDIA: Review
AUTHOR: Birchall P.
SERIES: Teaching Geography, Vol. 16, No.1, p. 31
PUBLISHER: The geographical Association
PUBLISHED: 1991 (January)

Ref: 1037046831
TITLE: CITIZENSHIP EDUCATION: CROSS-CURRICULAR
THEMES AND THE COMMUNITY
MEDIA: Course; 1 day

Ref: 1037046824
TITLE: PARENTAL INVOLVEMENT IN SCHOOL HEALTH
EDUCATION
MEDIA: Course; 1 day

Ref: 1037046774
TITLE: INSET MATERIALS IN INFORMATION TECHNOLOGY
MEDIA: TV broadcast; 30 mins
PUBLISHER: ITV Schools, Yorkshire Television
TRANSMISSION DATE: 1991 (Autumn Term)

Ref: 1037046755
TITLE: SUPPLEMENTARY REPORT OF THE CROSS-CURRICULAR
WORKING GROUP ON INFORMATION TECHNOLOGY (CCIT)
MEDIA: Report; 6pp A4
SERIES: Cross-Curricular Themes: Consultation Report
PUBLISHER: Northern Ireland Curriculum Council (NICC)
PUBLISHED: 1989

Ref: 1037046752
TITLE: HOME ECONOMICS
MEDIA: Information sheet; 3pp A4
SERIES: Cross-Curricular Themes: Consultation Report
PUBLISHER: Northern Ireland Curriculum Council (NICC)
PUBLISHED: 1989

Ref: 1037046746
TITLE: ART AND DESIGN
MEDIA: Information sheet; 5pp A4
SERIES: Cross-Curricular Themes: Consultation Report
PUBLISHER: Northern Ireland Curriculum Council (NICC)
PUBLISHED: 1989

Ref: 1037046742
TITLE: SCIENCE
MEDIA: Information sheet; 7pp A4
SERIES: Cross-Curricular Themes: Consultation Report
PUBLISHER: Northern Ireland Curriculum Council (NICC)
PUBLISHED: 1989

Ref: n/a
TITLE: A MATTER OF VALUES — A REVIEW OF CURRICULUM
GUIDANCE 4
MEDIA: Article
AUTHOR: Carter R.
SERIES: Teaching Geography, Vol. 16, No. 1, p. 30
PUBLISHER: The Geographical Association
PUBLISHED: 1991 (January)

Ref: 1037043398
TITLE: ENVIRONMENTAL EDUCATION AS A CROSS
CURRICULAR THEME FOR PUPILS FROM 5 TO 16
MEDIA: Course
SERIES: HMI Short Courses

Ref: 1037042702
TITLE: A FRAMEWORK FOR THE WHOLE CURRICULUM 5–16
AND DEVELOPING THE WHOLE CURRICULUM
MEDIA: Information sheet
SERIES: The Whole Curriculum 5–16 in Wales
PUBLISHER: Curriculum Council for Wales (CCW)
PUBLISHED: 1991 (Feb)

Ref: 1037041947
TITLE: FAMILY EDUCATION AND THE SCHOOL CURRICULUM
MEDIA: Article; 4pp A4
AUTHOR: Bailey G.
SERIES: Journal of Community Education, Vol. 8, No. 4, pp. 13–16.
PUBLISHER: Community Education Development Centre
PUBLISHED: 1990

Ref: 1037038057
TITLE: TECHNOLOGY ACROSS THE CURRICULUM — THE
WIGAN PROJECT
MEDIA: Report
AUTHOR: Yates C.
SERIES: DATER 89
PUBLISHER: Loughborough University of Technology
PUBLISHED: 1989

Ref: 1037028851
TITLE: THE NATIONAL CURRICULUM AND WHOLE
CURRICULUM PLANNING: PRELIMINARY GUIDANCE
MEDIA: Information sheet; 4pp A4
SERIES: NCC Circulars, Number 6
PUBLISHER: National Curriculum Council (NCC)
PUBLISHED: 1989 (Oct)

Ref: 1037023166
TITLE: MULTI-MEDIA APPROACHES TO ELEMENTS OF THE
NATIONAL CURRICULUM
MEDIA: Project
SERIES: FL West Midlands Region

Ref: 1037021716
TITLE: NATHE'S RESPONSE TO THE DESIGN AND
TECHNOLOGY WORKING GROUP'S FINAL REPORT
MEDIA: Information sheet
PUBLISHER: National Association of Teachers of Home Economics and
Technology
PUBLISHED: 1989 (Oct)

Ref: 1037021511
TITLE: HARTWELL HOME MADE JAMS
MEDIA: Article; case study
AUTHOR: Broughton J.
SERIES: SCIP News 24
PUBLISHER: School Curriculum Industry Partnership (SCIP)
PUBLISHED: 1989

Ref: 1037008964
TITLE: MATHEMATICS IN THE NATIONAL CURRICULUM
MEDIA: Book; 83pp A4, loose leaf, ringbinder
AUTHOR: Department of Education and Science (DES), Welsh Office
PUBLISHER: HMSO
PUBLISHED: 1989 (March)

Ref: 1031080072
TITLE: HUNTING DOWN TECHNOLOGY IN SCHOOLS: WHO
TEACHES IT? HOW AND WHY?
MEDIA: Article
AUTHOR: Clegg A.
SERIES: ASE School Science Review Vol. 69, No. 246, pp. 34–41
PUBLISHER: Association for Science Education (ASE)
PUBLISHED: 1987 September

Ref: 1030250073
TITLE: A COMMON PURPOSE
MEDIA: Book; 57pp. illus.
AUTHOR: Adams E. *et al*.
PUBLISHER: WWF UK
PUBLISHED: 1988

Statement of Search: Themes

Search for documents containing NATIONAL and CURRICULUM in free text and also containing CROSS and CURRICULAR in free text and also containing **THEMES** in free text (pp. 241–253).

Source: Reproduced from NERIS on CD-ROM Summer 1992.

Ref: 1037063517
TITLE: CITIZENSHIP EDUCATION
MEDIA: Information sheet; 4pp A4
SERIES: CSCS Broadsheet No. 31
PUBLISHER: CSCS/Centre for Citizenship Studies in Education

Ref: 1037062995
TITLE: ARC-EN-CIEL STAGE 3
MEDIA: Resource pack; pupil book, 192pp, teacher's book, 128 x A4
repromasters, 6 cassettes, 48 OHP transparency repromasters
PUBLISHER: Mary Glasgow Publications Ltd

Ref: 1037062593
TITLE: SCIPSIMS — SCIP SIMULATIONS AND OTHER ACTIVE
LEARNING RESOURCES
MEDIA: Booklet; set of 13, teacher's notes, pupil-learning materials
PUBLISHER: School Curriculum Industry Partnership (SCIP)

Ref: 1037062589
TITLE: SPONSORSHIP — A NEGOTIATION EXERCISE
MEDIA: Booklet; teacher's notes, pupil-learning materials, 16pp A4
AUTHOR: Turner D., Whitaker M.
SERIES: SCIPSIMS No. 4
PUBLISHER: School Curriculum Industry Partnership (SCIP)
PUBLISHED: 1990

Ref: 1037062585
TITLE: THE GREEN CAR COMPANY — A TRADING SIMULATION
MEDIA: Booklet; 16pp A4
AUTHOR: Humphrey B., Walsh P.
SERIES: SCIPSIMS No. 8
PUBLISHER: School Curriculum Industry Partnership (SCIP), Mini-
Enterprises in Schools Project
PUBLISHED: 1991

Ref: 1037062583
TITLE: CRISIS — A SIMULATION GAME
MEDIA: Booklet; 17pp A4
AUTHOR: Humphrey B., Walsh P.
SERIES: SCIPSIMS No. 10
PUBLISHER: School Curriculum Industry Partnership (SCIP), Mini-Enterprises in Schools Project
PUBLISHED: 1991

Ref: 1037062569
TITLE: CHRISTIANITY TOPIC BOOK ONE
MEDIA: Book; 117pp A4, line drawings, photocopiable
AUTHOR: Cooling M.
SERIES: Christianity Topic Books
PUBLISHER: Association of Christian Teachers, Religious and Moral Education Press
PUBLISHED: 1991

Ref: 1037061202
TITLE: MANAGING THE WHOLE CURRICULUM
MEDIA: TV broadcast; 15 mins, teacher's booklet
SERIES: Programmes For Primary Teachers
PUBLISHER: ITV Schools, Central Independent Television
TRANSMISSION DATE: 1991/92

Ref: 1037061197
TITLE: CROSS CURRICULAR THEMES: THE SCHOOL AND THE COMMUNITY
MEDIA: TV broadcast; 15 mins, teacher's booklet
SERIES: Programmes for Primary Teachers
PUBLISHER: ITV Schools, Central Independent Television
PUBLISHED: 1992 (Spring Term)

Ref: 1037060849
TITLE: THE NATIONAL CURRICULUM CORPORATE PLAN 1992–1995
MEDIA: Booklet; 10pp A4
PUBLISHER: National Curriculum Council (NCC)
PUBLISHED: 1991

Ref: 1037060706
TITLE: PREPARING A SCHEME OF WORK: THE SECONDARY
SCHOOL
MEDIA: Information sheet
SERIES: Non Statutory Guidance for Welsh and Welsh as a Second Language
in the National Curriculum
PUBLISHER: Curriculum Council for Wales (CCW)
PUBLISHED: 1990 (November)

Ref: 1037060611
TITLE: WELSH MOUNTAIN ZOO — EDUCATIONAL FACILITIES
MEDIA: Information sheet
PUBLISHER: Welsh Mountain Zoo

Ref: 1037060274
TITLE: A WHOLE SCHOOL POLICY FOR WORKING WITH
INDUSTRY IN SPECIAL SCHOOLS
MEDIA: Article; case study
AUTHOR: Jordan A., Matthews M.
SERIES: SCIP News, No. 30, p. 40
PUBLISHER: School Curriculum Industry Partnership (SCIP),
Mini-Enterprises in Schools Project
PUBLISHED: 1991

Ref: 1037060239
TITLE: CURRICULUM OVERVIEW
MEDIA: Booklet; 20pp A4, photo illustrations
AUTHOR: Preece J.
SERIES: Enterprising Classroom, Book 1
PUBLISHER: School Curriculum Industry Partnership (SCIP),
Mini-Enterprises in Schools Project
PUBLISHED: 1991

Ref: 1037060234
TITLE: CASE STUDIES IN ENGLISH
MEDIA: Booklet; 26pp A4, photo illustrations
AUTHOR: Stock J.
SERIES: Enterprising Classroom, Book 5
PUBLISHER: School Curriculum Industry Partnership (SCIP),
Mini-Enterprises in Schools Project
PUBLISHED: 1991

Ref: 1037057376
TITLE: EDUCATION FOR ECONOMIC AND INDUSTRIAL
UNDERSTANDING
MEDIA: Booklet; 54pp A4, colour illus.
SERIES: Curriculum Guidance, Number 4
PUBLISHER: National Curriculum Council (NCC)
PUBLISHED: 1990

Ref: 1037057375
TITLE: HEALTH EDUCATION
MEDIA: Booklet; 34pp A4
SERIES: Curriculum Guidance, Number 5
PUBLISHER: National Curriculum Council (NCC)
PUBLISHED: 1990

Ref: 1037057374
TITLE: CAREERS EDUCATION AND GUIDANCE
MEDIA: Booklet; 44pp A4
SERIES: Curriculum Guidance, Number 6
PUBLISHER: National Curriculum Council (NCC)
PUBLISHED: 1990

Ref: 1037057373
TITLE: ENVIRONMENTAL EDUCATION
MEDIA: Booklet; 49pp A4
SERIES: Curriculum Guidance, Number 7
PUBLISHER: National Curriculum Council (NCC)
PUBLISHED: 1990

Ref: 1037057150
TITLE: MATHS PROJECTS
MEDIA: Book; paperback 128pp 283 x 210mm, line drawings
AUTHOR: Bell D.
SERIES: Bright Ideas
PUBLISHER: Scholastic Educational
PUBLISHED: 1992

Ref: 1037056715
TITLE: MANAGEMENT OF CROSS-CURRICULAR ISSUES
MEDIA: Information sheet
AUTHOR: Waring M.
SERIES: FL North West Region
PUBLISHED: 1989

Ref: 1037060089
TITLE: SCHOOL CURRICULUM INDUSTRY PARTNERSHIP
(SCIP)/MINI-ENTERPRISES IN SCHOOLS PROJECT (MESP)
MEDIA: Information sheet
SERIES: SCIP Network
PUBLISHER: School Curriculum Industry Partnership (SCIP)
PUBLISHED: 1990

Ref: 1037059921
TITLE: LANGUAGE LEARNING FOR THE NEXT CENTURY
MEDIA: Article; 2pp A4, colour photographs
SERIES: NCC News, Issue 7
PUBLISHER: National Curriculum Council (NCC)
PUBLISHED: 1991 (Autumn)

Ref: 1037057931
TITLE: GEOGRAPHY AND CROSS-CURRICULAR THEMES
MEDIA: Article
SERIES: Teaching Geography, Vol. 16, No. 4, pp. 147–154
PUBLISHER: The Geographical Association
PUBLISHED: 1991 (October)

Ref: 1037057644
TITLE: GREENPRINT FOR ACTION
MEDIA: Book; set of 8, 32pp A4 each, illus, storage case
AUTHOR: Huckle J. *et al.*
PUBLISHER: National Extension College, NALGO Education
PUBLISHED: 1990

Ref: 1037057382
TITLE: CURRICULUM GUIDANCE
MEDIA: Booklet; set of 8, pp. 18–54 A4
PUBLISHER: National Curriculum Council (NCC)
PUBLISHED: 1989/90

Ref: 1037057380
TITLE: EDUCATION FOR CITIZENSHIP
MEDIA: Booklet; 26pp A4
SERIES: Curriculum Guidance, Number 8
PUBLISHER: National Curriculum Council (NCC)
PUBLISHED: 1990

Ref: 1037057377
TITLE: THE WHOLE CURRICULUM
MEDIA: Booklet; 18pp A4
SERIES: Curriculum Guidance, Number 3
PUBLISHER: National Curriculum Council (NCC)

Ref: 1037055689
TITLE: NATHE EDUCATIONAL SUPPLEMENTS
MEDIA: Information sheet
PUBLISHER: National Association of Teachers of Home Economics and Technology
PUBLISHED: 1991

Ref: 1037054496
TITLE: FOOD FOR THOUGHT
MEDIA: Booklet; 12pp.
PUBLISHER: Oxfam
PUBLISHED: 1991

Ref: 1037054343
TITLE: WORKING WITH INDUSTRY
MEDIA: Article; 1p A4
SERIES: NCC News, Issue 6
PUBLISHER: National Curriculum Council (NCC)
PUBLISHED: 1991 (June)

Ref: 1037054341
TITLE: HISTORY AND GEOGRAPHY: NON-STATUTORY GUIDANCE
MEDIA: Article; 2pp A4
SERIES: NCC News, Issue 6
PUBLISHER: National Curriculum Council (NCC)
PUBLISHED: 1991 (June)

Ref: 1037054339
TITLE: STARTING OUT WITH THE NATIONAL CURRICULUM
MEDIA: Article; 2pp A4
SERIES: NCC News, Issue 6
PUBLISHER: National Curriculum Council (NCC)
PUBLISHED: 1991 (June)

Ref: 1037054335
TITLE: PERSONAL AND SOCIAL DEVELOPMENT (PSD)
MEDIA: Article; 1p A4
SERIES: NCC News, Issue 6
PUBLISHER: National Curriculum Council (NCC)
PUBLISHED: 1991 (June)

Ref: 1037053977
TITLE: OUR WORLD
MEDIA: TV broadcast; 28 x 15 min programmes, teacher's booklet
PUBLISHER: ITV Schools, Yorkshire Television
TRANSMISSION DATE: 1991–92

Ref: 1037053000
TITLE: TECHNOLOGY — THE USE OF FELT IN DIFFERENT
CULTURES
MEDIA: Resource pack; teacher's notes, pupil activity sheets, 40pp A4
AUTHOR: Spyrou M.
PUBLISHER: Commonwealth Institute
PUBLISHED: 1992

Ref: 1037052678
TITLE: ENTERPRISE EDUCATION AND THE NATIONAL
CURRICULUM
MEDIA: Book
AUTHOR: Crompton K., Turner D.
PUBLISHER: Community Service Volunteers Mini-Enterprises in Schools
Project
PUBLISHED: 1990

Ref: 1037047209
TITLE: PLANNING THE GEOGRAPHY CURRICULUM: PART 2
MEDIA: Information sheet; 17pp A4
SERIES: Geography Non-Statutory Guidance, England
PUBLISHER: National Curriculum Council (NCC)
PUBLISHED: 1991 (June)

Ref: 1037047115
TITLE: CROSS CURRICULUM THEMES, DIMENSIONS, SKILLS
AND THEIR ASSESSMENT
MEDIA: Course
AUTHOR: Mathews H. (Course Director)
SERIES: WJEC INSET on assessment courses

Ref: 1037047078
TITLE: IMPLEMENTING NATIONAL CURRICULUM HISTORY:
PART 2
MEDIA: Information sheet; 19pp A4
SERIES: History Non-Statutory Guidance, England
PUBLISHER: National Curriculum Council (NCC)
PUBLISHED: 1991 (June)

Ref: 1037046831
TITLE: CITIZENSHIP EDUCATION: CROSS-CURRICULAR
THEMES AND THE COMMUNITY
MEDIA: Course; 1 day

Ref: 1037046755
TITLE: SUPPLEMENTARY REPORT OF THE CROSS-CURRICULAR
WORKING GROUP ON INFORMATION TECHNOLOGY (CCIT)
MEDIA: Report; 6pp A4
SERIES: Cross-Curricular Themes: Consultation Report
PUBLISHER: Northern Ireland Curriculum Council (NICC)
PUBLISHED: 1989

Ref: 1037046752
TITLE: HOME ECONOMICS
MEDIA: Information sheet; 3pp A4
SERIES: Cross-Curricular Themes: Consultation Report
PUBLISHER: Northern Ireland Curriculum Council (NICC)
PUBLISHED: 1989

Ref: 1037046746
TITLE: ART AND DESIGN
MEDIA: Information sheet; 5pp A4
SERIES: Cross-Curricular Themes: Consultation Report
PUBLISHER: Northern Ireland Curriculum Council (NICC)
PUBLISHED: 1989

Ref: 1037046742
TITLE: SCIENCE
MEDIA: Information sheet; 7pp A4
SERIES: Cross-Curricular Themes: Consultation Report
PUBLISHER: Northern Ireland Curriculum Council (NICC)
PUBLISHED: 1989

Ref: 1037046588
TITLE: TEACHING AND LEARNING PROCEDURES — ISSUES FOR
INSET
MEDIA: Video; VHS, 20 mins, teacher's notes
SERIES: Design and Technology Starters
PUBLISHER: TVS Education, Kent Educational Television
PUBLISHED: 1990

Ref: 1037046551
TITLE: DTI FUNDS SCHOOLS–INDUSTRY PROJECTS
MEDIA: Article; 1p A4
SERIES: NCC News, Issue 5
PUBLISHER: National Curriculum Council (NCC)
PUBLISHED: 1991 (Feb)

Ref: 1037046253
TITLE: ABOUT CONSERVATION AND DEVELOPMENT
MEDIA: Booklet; 51pp A4, 8pp A4 teacher's notes
SERIES: Finding out
PUBLISHER: Hobsons
PUBLISHED: 1990

Ref: 1037046088
TITLE: PROJECT EARTH STATION
MEDIA: Resource pack; slide, activity sheets, information sheets
SERIES: Materials for Secondary Education
PUBLISHER: BT Education Service
PUBLISHED: 1990

Ref: 1037043398
TITLE: ENVIRONMENTAL EDUCATION AS A CROSS
CURRICULAR THEME FOR PUPILS FROM 5 TO 16
MEDIA: Course
SERIES: HMI Short Courses

Ref: 1037042935
TITLE: BIBLIOGRAPHY
MEDIA: Information sheet; 1p A4, loose-leaf punched
SERIES: Science Guidance Materials
PUBLISHER: Northern Ireland Curriculum Council (NICC)
PUBLISHED: 1990 (August)

Ref: 1037042702
TITLE: A FRAMEWORK FOR THE WHOLE CURRICULUM
5–16 AND DEVELOPING THE WHOLE CURRICULUM
MEDIA: Information sheet
SERIES: The Whole Curriculum 5–16 in Wales
PUBLISHER: Curriculum Council for Wales (CCW)
PUBLISHED: 1991 (Feb)

Ref: 1037041811
TITLE: DEVELOPING LINKS — DEVELOPING CURRICULA
MEDIA: Course notes
AUTHOR: Harris M.
SERIES: Mathematics Outside School, Unit 9
PUBLISHER: University of London Institute of Education
PUBLISHED: 1990

Ref: 1037041769
TITLE: BIRDS AND MATHEMATICS IN THE NATIONAL
CURRICULUM
MEDIA: Teacher's notes
AUTHOR: Cutler B., Hughes M.
SERIES: Birds and Mathematics
PUBLISHER: The Royal Society for the Protection of Birds (RSPB)
PUBLISHED: 1989

Ref: 1037038858
TITLE: SCHOOL LINKS
MEDIA: Article
AUTHOR: Zwaga K.
SERIES: Network Newsletter No. 11
PUBLISHER: European Development Education Curriculum Network
PUBLISHED: 1989

Ref: 1037037040
TITLE: PRACTICAL PROJECTS WITH MATHEMATICS: A
RESOURCE PACK OF APPLICATIONS TO THE PHYSICAL WORLD
MEDIA: Resource pack; book, paperback 160pp 297 x 210mm, 270 line
diagrams, 8 A2 posters, teacher's notes
AUTHOR: Cherouvim N. *et al.*
PUBLISHER: Cambridge University Press
PUBLISHED: 1990

Ref: 1037036763
TITLE: ECONOMIC AWARENESS
MEDIA: Information sheet; 2pp A4, loose-leaf punched
SERIES: Cross-curricular Themes Guidance Materials
PUBLISHER: Northern Ireland Curriculum Council (NICC)

Ref: 1037036008
TITLE: STUDENTS INTO INDUSTRY
MEDIA: Resource pack; 136pp (approx) A4, illustrated
AUTHOR: McKay F., Lawlor S.
PUBLISHER: Framework Press
PUBLISHED: 1909

Ref: 1037035141
TITLE: PROPOSALS FOR THE SCIENCE CURRICULUM IN
NORTHERN IRELAND
MEDIA: Article
AUTHOR: McGarvey B.
SERIES: ASE Education in Science, No. 137, pp. 29–30
PUBLISHER: The Association for Science Education (ASE)
PUBLISHED: 1990 (April)

Ref: 1037034838
TITLE: NOISE POLLUTION FACT PACK
MEDIA: Review
PUBLISHER: Chemical Industry Education Centre
PUBLISHED: 1990

Ref: 1037033464
TITLE: PROMOTING TECHNOLOGY ACROSS THE WHOLE
CURRICULUM
MEDIA: Leaflet; 4pp A4
SERIES: Technology Within and Across the Curriculum
PUBLISHER: Six Counties Technology Project
PUBLISHED: 1990

Ref: 1037030568
TITLE: BUSINESS EDUCATION — A HANDBOOK FOR SCHOOLS
MEDIA: Book
AUTHOR: Eraut M.R., Cole G.A.
PUBLISHER: Training Agency
PUBLISHED: 1990

Ref: 1037030517
TITLE: ENERGY: ECONOMIC AWARENESS AND
ENVIRONMENTAL EDUCATION
MEDIA: Resource pack; 4, A4 booklets, illustrated, folder, poster
AUTHOR: Webster K.
PUBLISHER: WWF UK
PUBLISHED: 1990

Ref: 1037028851
TITLE: THE NATIONAL CURRICULUM AND WHOLE
CURRICULUM PLANNING: PRELIMINARY GUIDANCE
MEDIA: Information sheet; 4pp A4
SERIES: NCC Circulars, Number 6
PUBLISHER: National Curriculum Council (NCC)
PUBLISHED: 1989 (Oct)

Ref: 1037027826
TITLE: YOUNG ENTERPRISE BUSINESS COMPANY SCHEME:
INTO BUSINESS PROGRAMME
MEDIA: Place

Ref: 1037026885
TITLE: FLEXIBLE LEARNING (FL) IN ESSEX AND BEDFORDSHIRE
MEDIA: Project
SERIES: FL Eastern Region

Ref: 1037025270
TITLE: CAMBRIDGE PRIMARY MATHS LEVEL 6, TEACHER'S
RESOURCE BOOK
MEDIA: Book; Paperback
AUTHOR: Edwards R., Edwards M., Ward A.
PUBLISHER: Cambridge University Press
PUBLISHED: 1990

Ref: 1037024287
TITLE: THE INDUSTRIAL DIMENSION AND THE NATIONAL
CURRICULUM: SOME PRACTICAL PROPOSALS
MEDIA: Article; case study
AUTHOR: Peffers J.
SERIES: SCIP News 19 pp. 3–6
PUBLISHER: School Curriculum Industry Partnership (SCIP)
PUBLISHED: 1987

Ref: 1037022402
TITLE: ENTERPRISING PEOPLE
MEDIA: Resource pack; colour photographs, test, 12pp booklet.
PUBLISHER: BP Educational Service

Ref: 1037021109
TITLE: SCIENCE EDUCATION AND THE ENVIRONMENT
MEDIA: Article
AUTHOR: Gayford C.
SERIES: ASE Education in Science No. 131, pp. 22–23
PUBLISHER: Association for Science Education (ASE)
PUBLISHED: 1989

Ref: 1037018746
TITLE: FARM DEVELOPMENT SIMULATION
MEDIA: Resource pack; teacher's notes, pupil information sheets
AUTHOR: Atterton G.
PUBLISHER: Resources for Learning Development Unit

Ref: 1037018744
TITLE: ACCENTUATE THE POSITIVE
MEDIA: Article
AUTHOR: Hewitt M.
SERIES: Teaching Geography, Vol 14, No. 3, pp. 104–105
PUBLISHER: The Geographical Association
PUBLISHED: 1989 (June)

Ref: 1037016044
TITLE: LEARNING ABOUT WORK IN THE NATIONAL
CURRICULUM
MEDIA: Article
AUTHOR: Law B., Barry M.
SERIES: SCIP News 23 pp. 38–40.
PUBLISHER: School Curriculum Industry Partnership (SCIP)
PUBLISHED: 1989

Ref: 1037009583
TITLE: SOCIAL AND VOCATIONAL SKILLS (SVS) AGAIN
MEDIA: Video; VHS, 16 min.
AUTHOR: Central Support Group (CSG) for SVS
SERIES: Standard Grade Starter Materials
PUBLISHER: Scottish Consultative Council on the Curriculum (SCCC)
PUBLISHED: 1988

Ref: 1037008964
TITLE: MATHEMATICS IN THE NATIONAL CURRICULUM
MEDIA: Book; 83pp A4, loose leaf, ringbinder
AUTHOR: Department of Education and Science (DES), Welsh Office
PUBLISHER: HMSO
PUBLISHED: 1989 (March)

Ref: 1037007571
TITLE: SCHOOLS OLYMPUS BROADCASTING ASSOCIATION
(SOBA)
MEDIA: Organisation

Ref: 1031240046
TITLE: LEARNING GEOGRAPHY WITH COMPUTERS
MEDIA: Computer software; BBC B, Master, Research Machinese,
Nimbus, books, 7 x A4
PUBLISHER: National Council for Educational Technology (NCET)
PUBLISHED: 1989 (Rev. ed)

Statement of Search: Dimensions

Search for documents containing NATIONAL and CURRICULUM in free
text and also containing CROSS and CURRICULAR in free text and also
containing **DIMENSIONS** in free text (pp. 253–256).

Source: Reproduced from NERIS on CD-ROM Summer 1992.

Ref: 1037061202
TITLE: MANAGING THE WHOLE CURRICULUM
MEDIA: TV broadcast; 15 mins, teacher's booklet
SERIES: Programmes For Primary Teachers
PUBLISHER: ITV Schools, Central Independent Television
TRANSMISSION DATE: 1991/92

Ref: 1037060849
TITLE: THE NATIONAL CURRICULUM CORPORATE PLAN 1992–
1995
MEDIA: Booklet; 10pp A4
PUBLISHER: National Curriculum Council (NCC)
PUBLISHED: 1991

Ref: 1037060238
TITLE: CURRICULUM OVERVIEW SCOTLAND
MEDIA: Booklet; 10pp A4, photo illustrations
AUTHOR: Preece J.
SERIES: Enterprising Classroom, Book 1A
PUBLISHER: School Curriculum Industry Partnership (SCIP), Mini-
Enterprises in Schools Project
PUBLISHED: 1991

Ref: 1037056715
TITLE: MANAGEMENT OF CROSS-CURRICULAR ISSUES
MEDIA: Information sheet
AUTHOR: Waring M.
SERIES: FL North West Region
PUBLISHED: 1989

Ref: 1037054335
TITLE: PERSONAL AND SOCIAL DEVELOPMENT (PSD)
MEDIA: Article; 1p A4
SERIES: NCC News, Issue 6
PUBLISHER: National Curriculum Council (NCC)
PUBLISHED: 1991 (June)

Ref: 1037047209
TITLE: PLANNING THE GEOGRAPHY CURRICULUM: PART 2
MEDIA: Information sheet; 17pp A4
SERIES: Geography Non-Statutory Guidance, England
PUBLISHER: National Curriculum Council (NCC)
PUBLISHED: 1991 (June)

Ref: 1037047115
TITLE: CROSS CURRICULUM THEMES, DIMENSIONS, SKILLS
AND THEIR ASSESSMENT
MEDIA: Course
AUTHOR: Mathews H. (Course Director)
SERIES: WJEC INSET on assessment courses

Ref: 1037043398
TITLE: ENVIRONMENTAL EDUCATION AS A CROSS
CURRICULAR THEME FOR PUPILS FROM 5 TO 16
MEDIA: Course
SERIES: HMI Short Courses

Ref: 1037042702
TITLE: A FRAMEWORK FOR THE WHOLE CURRICULUM 5–16
AND DEVELOPING THE WHOLE CURRICULUM
MEDIA: Information sheet
SERIES: The Whole Curriculum 5–16 in Wales
PUBLISHER: Curriculum Council for Wales (CCW)
PUBLISHED: 1991 (Feb)

Ref: 1037040466
TITLE: TECHNOLOGY WITHIN AND ACROSS THE CURRICULUM
MEDIA: Leaflet, Series of 24, each 4pp A4
PUBLISHER: Six Counties Technology Project
PUBLISHED: 1990

Ref: 1037030943
TITLE: ENERGY
MEDIA: Videodisc
PUBLISHER: Interactive Learning Project
PUBLISHED: 1990

Ref: 1037028851
TITLE: THE NATIONAL CURRICULUM AND WHOLE
CURRICULUM PLANNING: PRELIMINARY GUIDANCE
MEDIA: Information sheet; 4pp A4
SERIES: NCC Circulars, Number 6
PUBLISHER: National Curriculum Council (NCC)
PUBLISHED: 1989 (Oct)

Ref: 1037028685
TITLE: MANY CULTURES TOGETHER
MEDIA: Booklet; 124pp A4
AUTHOR: Fortune H.H.
SERIES: Resources for Environmental and Social Studies Teaching (RESST)
No. 36
PUBLISHER: Moray House College of Education
PUBLISHED: 1983

Statement of Search: Skills

Search for documents containing NATIONAL and CURRICULUM in free text and also containing CROSS and CURRICULAR in free text and also containing **SKILLS** in free text (pp. 256–271).

Source: Reproduced from NERIS on CD-ROM Summer 1992.

Ref: 1037063517
TITLE: CITIZENSHIP EDUCATION
MEDIA: Information sheet; 4pp A4
SERIES: CSCS Broadsheet No. 31
PUBLISHER: CSCS/Centre for Citizenship Studies in Education

Ref: 1037063231
TITLE: NATIONAL YOUTH PARLIAMENT COMPETITION
MEDIA: Information sheet
PUBLISHER: Citizenship Foundation
PUBLISHED: Annually

Ref: 1037062995
TITLE: ARC-EN-CIEL STAGE 3
MEDIA: Resource pack; pupil book, 192pp, teacher's book, 128 x A4
repromasters, 6 cassettes, 48 OHP transparency repromasters
PUBLISHER: Mary Glasgow Publications Ltd

Ref: 1037062880
TITLE: CHILDREN FIRST
MEDIA: Booklet; 4 vol. A4
AUTHOR: Allen P., Harris M., Tozer H.
PUBLISHER: Wheaton Publishers Ltd
PUBLISHED: 1990

Ref: 1037062585
TITLE: THE GREEN CAR COMPANY — A TRADING SIMULATION
MEDIA: Booklet; 16pp A4
AUTHOR: Humphrey B., Walsh P.
SERIES: SCIPSIMS No. 8
PUBLISHER: School Curriculum Industry Partnership (SCIP),
Mini-Enterprises in Schools Project
PUBLISHED: 1991

Ref: 1037061202
TITLE: MANAGING THE WHOLE CURRICULUM
MEDIA: TV broadcast; 15 mins, teacher's booklet
SERIES: Programmes For Primary Teachers
PUBLISHER: ITV Schools, Central Independent Television
TRANSMISSION DATE: 1991/92

Ref: 1037061197
TITLE: CROSS CURRICULAR THEMES: THE SCHOOL AND
COMMUNITY
MEDIA: TV broadcast; 15 mins, teacher's booklet
SERIES: Programmes for Primary Teachers
PUBLISHER: ITV Schools, Central Independent Television
PUBLISHED: 1992 (Spring Term)

Ref: 1037061115
TITLE: SEA BIRDS
MEDIA: TV broadcast; 15 minute programme, teacher's notes
PRODUCER: Stanier T.
SERIES: WATCH
PUBLISHER: BBC Education
TRANSMISSION DATE: 1992 (Summer Term)

Ref: 1037060849
TITLE: THE NATIONAL CURRICULUM CORPORATE PLAN
1992–1995
MEDIA: Booklet; 10pp A4
PUBLISHER: National Curriculum Council (NCC)
PUBLISHED: 1991

Ref: 1037060800
TITLE: NEOMATICA
MEDIA: CD ROM; IBM PC and compatibles
PUBLISHER: Boston Spa Training
PUBLISHED: 1991

Ref: 1037060239
TITLE: CURRICULUM OVERVIEW
MEDIA: Booklet; 20pp A4, photo illustrations
AUTHOR: Preece J.
SERIES: Enterprising Classroom, Book 1
PUBLISHER: School Curriculum Industry Partnership (SCIP),
PUBLISHED: 1991

Ref: 1037060238
TITLE: CURRICULUM OVERVIEW SCOTLAND
MEDIA: Booklet; 10pp A4, photo illustrations
AUTHOR: Preece J.
SERIES: Enterprising Classroom, Book 1A
PUBLISHER: School Curriculum Industry Partnership (SCIP),
Mini-Enterprises in Schools Project
PUBLISHED: 1991

Ref: 1037060221
TITLE: ECONOMIC AND INDUSTRIAL UNDERSTANDING AND
SKILLS FOR THINKING
MEDIA: Article; case study
AUTHOR: Craft A.
SERIES: SCIP News, No. 28, pp. 40–42
PUBLISHER: School Curriculum Industry Partnership (SCIP)
PUBLISHED: 1991

Ref: 1037060196
TITLE: THE ENTERPRISE FILE
MEDIA: Resource pack; teacher's notes, work sheets
PUBLISHER: Mini Enterprises in Schools Project
PUBLISHED: 1990

Ref: 1037060176
TITLE: EDUCATING FOR ECONOMIC AND INDUSTRIAL
UNDERSTANDING — CURRICULUM PLANNING AND INSET
CARD SET
MEDIA: Booklet; 12pp A4, INSET materials, card set
AUTHOR: Miller A.D.
PUBLISHER: School Curriculum Industry Partnership (SCIP)
PUBLISHED: 1990

Ref: 1037059921
TITLE: LANGUAGE LEARNING FOR THE NEXT CENTURY
MEDIA: Article; 2pp A4, colour photographs
SERIES: NCC News, Issue 7
PUBLISHER: National Curriculum Council (NCC)
PUBLISHED: 1991 (Autumn)

Ref: 1037058623
TITLE: FOOD FOR THOUGHT: FISH FARMING IN THE
HIGHLANDS AND ISLANDS
MEDIA: Multi-media pack; teacher's notes, pupil notes, tape-slide
presentation, video, audio tapes, computer software, supplementary materials
PUBLISHER: Highlands and Islands Enterprise, in association with Scottish
Council for Educational Technology (SCET) and Primary Education
Development Project
PUBLISHED: 1991

Ref: 1037058559
TITLE: INSPIRATIONS FOR SCIENCE
MEDIA: Review
AUHOR: Batchelor M.C., Calvert R.O. (Nottingham Polytechnic)
PUBLISHER: Nottingham Technology Education Development Group
PUBLISHED: 1991

Ref: 1037057996
TITLE: DELIVERY OF PROCESS SKILLS AND KEY ELEMENTS OF
PERSONAL AND SOCIAL DEVELOPMENT: FIVE CASE STUDIES
MEDIA: Booklet; 42pp A4
SERIES: Curriculum Design for the Secondary Stages
PUBLISHER: Scottish Consultative Council on the Curriculum (SCCC)
PUBLISHED: 1991

Ref: 1037057965
TITLE: DEVELOPING THE 'COMMUNITY ACTIVE' CURRICULUM
MEDIA: Article; 1p A4
AUTHOR: Billington L.
SERIES: Network, Vol. 11, No. 2, p. 9
PUBLISHER: Community Education Development Centre
PUBLISHED: 1991

Ref: 1037057931
TITLE: GEOGRAPHY AND CROSS-CURRICULAR THEMES
MEDIA: Article
SERIES: Teaching Geography, Vol. 16, No. 4, pp. 147–154
PUBLISHER: The Geographical Association
PUBLISHED: 1991 (October)

Ref: 1037057594
TITLE: MANAGING THE CURRICULUM
MEDIA: Multi-media pack; module overview, tutor's handbook, 4 course units, workshop materials (set of 7), VHS video
AUTHOR: MTHT Module Group *et al*.
SERIES: Management Training for Headteachers, Module No. 3
PUBLISHER: Scottish Office Education Department (SOED)
PUBLISHED: 1990

Ref: 1037056715
TITLE: MANAGEMENT OF CROSS-CURRICULAR ISSUES
MEDIA: Information sheet
AUTHOR: Waring M.
SERIES: FL North West Region
PUBLISHED: 1989

Ref: 1037056677
TITLE: FLEXIBLE LEARNING CASE STUDY — INFORMATION TECHNOLOGY IN MUSIC (DUMFRIES AND GALLOWAY)
MEDIA: Report
AUTHOR: Davies L.
SERIES: FL Scottish Region
PUBLISHED: 1991

Ref: 1037056455
TITLE: FLEXIBLE LEARNING EXPERIENCES IN GEOGRAPHY
MEDIA: Report
SERIES: FL North West Region
PUBLISHED: 1990/1991

Ref: 1037055835
TITLE: THINGS YOU NEED TO KNOW
MEDIA: Review
AUTHOR: Batchelor M.C., Calvert R.O. (Nottingham Polytechnic)
PUBLISHER: Nottingham Technology Education Development Group
PUBLISHED: 1991 (October)

Ref: 1037055692
TITLE: NATIONAL CURRICULUM AND LEARNING SKILLS
MEDIA: Information sheet; 13pp A4
PUBLISHER: The Library Association
PUBLISHED: 1991

Ref: 1037054339
TITLE: STARTING OUT WITH THE NATIONAL CURRICULUM
MEDIA: Article; 2pp A4
SERIES: NCC News, Issue 6
PUBLISHER: National Curriculum Council (NCC)
PUBLISHED: 1991 (June)

Ref: 1037054335
TITLE: PERSONAL AND SOCIAL DEVELOPMENT (PSD)
MEDIA: Article; 1p A4
SERIES: NCC News, Issue 6
PUBLISHER: National Curriculum Council (NCC)
PUBLISHED: 1991 (June)

Ref: 1037054017
TITLE: START THE DAY
MEDIA: TV broadcast; 28 x 10 min programmes, teacher's booklet
PUBLISHER: ITV Schools, Yorkshire Television
TRANSMISSION DATE: 1991–92

Ref: 1037053977
TITLE: OUR WORLD
MEDIA: TV broadcast; 28 x 15 min programmes, teacher's booklet
PUBLISHER: ITV Schools, Yorkshire Television
TRANSMISSION DATE: 1991–92

Ref: 1037052678
TITLE: ENTERPRISE EDUCATION AND THE NATIONAL
CURRICULUM
MEDIA: Book
AUTHOR: Crompton K., Turner D.
PUBLISHER: Community Service Volunteers Mini-Enterprises in Schools
Project
PUBLISHED: 1990

Ref: 1037052414
TITLE: INFORMATION SKILLS AND THE NATIONAL
CURRICULUM: A SUMMARY SHEET
MEDIA: Leaflet
AUTHOR: NCET
PUBLISHER: NCET
PUBLISHED: 1990 (2nd ed)

Ref: 1037050946
TITLE: TEACHER'S RESOURCE PACK: 1
MEDIA: Book; ring binder 96pp 296 x 210mm, b&w illustrations
AUTHOR: Greasley B. *et al.*
SERIES: Enquiry Geography
PUBLISHER: Hodder and Stoughton Educational
PUBLISHED: 1991

Ref: 1037049410
TITLE: TECHNOLOGICAL LITERACY AND THE CURRICULUM: VOL 2
MEDIA: Book; hardback 224pp 243 x 156mm
AUTHOR: Beynon J. (Ed)
PUBLISHER: Falmer Press
PUBLISHED: 1991

Ref: 1037046742
TITLE: SCIENCE
MEDIA: Information sheet; 7pp A4
SERIES: Cross-Curricular Themes: Consultation Report
PUBLISHER: Northern Ireland Curriculum Council (NICC)
PUBLISHED: 1989

Ref: 1037046687
TITLE: GOOD HEALTH
MEDIA: TV broadcast; 14 x 15 min programmes, teacher's booklet, 3 pupil books
PUBLISHER: ITV Schools, Central Independent Television
TRANSMISSION DATE: 1991–92

Ref: 1037046546
TITLE: LEARNING TOGETHER: GLOBAL EDUCATION 4–7
MEDIA: Book; paperback 104pp 240 x 165mm, b&w and colour photographs, b&w illus.
AUTHOR: Fountain S.
PUBLISHER: Stanley Thornes, WWF UK, York University
PUBLISHED: 1990

Ref: 1037046088
TITLE: PROJECT EARTH STATION
MEDIA: Resource pack; slide, activity sheets, information sheets
SERIES: Materials for Secondary Education
PUBLISHER: BT Education Service
PUBLISHED: 1990

Ref: 1037043977
TITLE: A MATTER OF VALUES — A REVIEW OF CURRICULUM
GUIDANCE 4
MEDIA: Article
AUTHOR: Carter R.
SERIES: Teaching Geography, Vol. 16, No. 1, p. 30
PUBLISHER: The Geographical Association
PUBLISHED: 1991 (January)

Ref: 1037043471
TITLE: WATCHING THE WORLD
MEDIA: Review
AUTHOR: Mann L.
SERIES: The English Magazine 23, p. 45
PUBLISHER: The English and Media Centre
PUBLISHED: 1990

Ref: 1037043410
TITLE: ORGANISING FOR THE NATIONAL CURRICULUM (11–16)
MEDIA: Course
SERIES: HMI Short Courses

Ref: 1037041947
TITLE: FAMILY EDUCATION AND THE SCHOOL
CURRICULUM
MEDIA: Article; 4pp A4
AUTHOR: Bailey G.
SERIES: Journal of Community Education, Vol. 8, No. 4, pp. 13–16.
PUBLISHER: Community Education Development Centre
PUBLISHED: 1990

Ref: 1037041811
TITLE: DEVELOPING LINKS — DEVELOPING CURRICULA
MEDIA: Course notes
AUTHOR: Harris M.
SERIES: Mathematics Outside School, Unit 9
PUBLISHER: University of London Institute of Education
PUBLISHED: 1990

Ref: 1037041769
TITLE: BIRDS AND MATHEMATICS IN THE NATIONAL
CURRICULUM
MEDIA: Teacher's notes
AUTHOR: Cutler B., Hughes M.
SERIES: Birds and Mathematics
PUBLISHER: The Royal Society for the Protection of Birds (RSPB)
PUBLISHED: 1989

Ref: 1037039212
TITLE: USING AIR
MEDIA: Teacher's notes
SERIES: Science and Technology Education in Primary Schools (STEPS)

Ref: 1037038775
TITLE: CDT: IS IT 'HANDS ON' OR 'HANDS OFF'?
MEDIA: Article
AUTHOR: West D.J. (St Paul's School for Girls, Birmingham)
SERIES: Studies in Design Education Craft and Technology Vol. 22, No. 1
PUBLISHER: Trentham Books limited
PUBLISHED: 1990 (Winter)

Ref: 1037036763
TITLE: ECONOMIC AWARENESS
MEDIA: Information sheet; 2pp A4, loose-leaf punched
SERIES: Cross-curricular Themes Guidance Materials
PUBLISHER: Northern Ireland Curriculum Council (NICC)

Ref: 1037036444
TITLE: COMMUNICATION FOR ALL — A CROSS CURRICULAR
SKILL INVOLVING INTERACTION BETWEEN 'SPEAKER AND
LISTENER'
MEDIA: Book; paperback 32pp 297 x 210mm, line drawings
AUTHOR: Fagg S. *et al.*
PUBLISHER: David Fulton Publishers
PUBLISHED: 1990

Ref: 1037036256
TITLE: CURRICULAR LINKS
MEDIA: Teacher's notes; 52pp A4
AUTHOR: Pressley M. (CDO–Grampian Region)
SERIES: Grampian Resources
PUBLISHER: Grampian Regional Council (GRC) Department of Education
in association with Moray TVEI
PUBLISHED: 1989

Ref: 1037036011
TITLE: DEVELOPING SKILLS FOR TVEI: CO-OPERATIVE
WORKING, PLANNING AND ORGANISING, USING
INFORMATION VOLUME 2
MEDIA: RESOURCE PACK; 128pp A4, illustrated
AUTHOR: Clark H.R., Onslow N., Sage L.R.
PUBLISHER: Framework Press
PUBLISHED: 1990 (Autumn)

Ref: 1037036010
TITLE: DEVELOPING SKILLS FOR TVEI: CO-OPERATIVE
WORKING, PLANNING AND ORGANISING, USING
INFORMATION VOLUME 1
MEDIA: Resource pack; 128pp A4, illustrated
AUTHOR: Clark H.R., Onslow N., Sage L.R.
PUBLISHER: Framework Press
PUBLISHED: 1990

Ref: 1037033880
TITLE: APPROPRIATE TECHNOLOGY IN THE DESIGN AND
TECHNOLOGY NATIONAL CURRICULUM
MEDIA: Report
AUTHOR: Mulberg C.
SERIES: DATER 89
PUBLISHER: Loughborough University of Technology
PUBLISHED: 1989

Ref: 1037031404
TITLE: SPREADSHEETS ACROSS THE CURRICULUM
MEDIA: Review
AUTHOR: Warburton J.
PUBLISHER: Avon County Council

Ref: 1037030943
TITLE: ENERGY
MEDIA: Videodisc
PUBLISHER: Interactive Learning Project
PUBLISHED: 1990

Ref: 1037030915
TITLE: SHOPPING LIST PADS
MEDIA: Worksheet; 4 x A5, 2 x A4
PUBLISHER: Resources for Learning Difficulties, The Consortium

Ref: 1037030882
TITLE: MATHEMATICS AND ENVIRONMENTAL EDUCATION
MEDIA: Book; 72pp, 210 x 210mm
AUTHOR: Collins J.D. (Maths Advisor for Devon LEA) (Ed)
PUBLISHER: WWF UK
PUBLISHED: 1990 (March)

Ref: 1037030672
TITLE: THE UNEMPLOYED: MODERN STUDIES UNIT
MEDIA: Booklet; teacher's notes, 14pp A4, pupil materials, 176pp A4,
glossary, statistics
AUTHOR: Central Support Group (CSG) for Modern Studies, Tayside
Regional Council (TRC) Department of Education
SERIES: Standard Grade, Exemplar Materials
PUBLISHER: Scottish Consultative Council on the Curriculum (SCC) in
association with Tayside Regional Council (TRC)
PUBLISHED: 1989

Ref: 1037030517
TITLE: ENERGY: ECONOMIC AWARENESS AND
ENVIRONMENTAL EDUCATION
MEDIA: Resource pack; 4, A4 booklets, illustrated, folder, poster
AUTHOR: Webster K.
PUBLISHER: WWF UK
PUBLISHED: 1990

Ref: 1037029673
TITLE: PEOPLE WHO HAVE HELPED THE WORLD
MEDIA: Book; set of 6, hardback, pp. 76–84
PUBLISHER: Learning Development Aids

Ref: 1037028851
TITLE: THE NATIONAL CURRICULUM AND WHOLE
CURRICULUM PLANNING: PRELIMINARY GUIDANCE
MEDIA: Information sheet; 4pp A4
SERIES: NCC Circulars, Number 6
PUBLISHER: National Curriculum Council (NCC)
PUBLISHED: 1989 (Oct)

Ref: 1037027834
TITLE: CONSTRUCTING A SCHEME OF WORK
MEDIA: Information sheet; 12pp A4
SERIES: Non-Statutory Guidance for Design and Technology
PUBLISHER: National Curriculum Council (NCC)
PUBLISHED: 1990 (April)

Ref: 1037027826
TITLE: YOUNG ENTERPRISE BUSINESS COMPANY SCHEME:
INTO BUSINESS PROGRAMME
MEDIA: Place

Ref: 1037026959
TITLE: HEALTH EDUCATION FROM 5 TO 16
MEDIA: Booklet; 11pp A5
SERIES: Curriculum Matters, 6, The Responses
PUBLISHER: Her Majesty's Inspectorate (HMI), Department of Education and Science (DES)
PUBLISHED: 1990 (Jan)

Ref: 1037026887
TITLE: FLEXIBLE LEARNING IN NORFOLK AND CAMBRIDGESHIRE
MEDIA: Project
SERIES: FL Eastern Region

Ref: 1037024532
TITLE: WHOLE SCHOOL APPROACH: APPROACHES TO TEACHING INFORMATION HANDLING SKILLS
MEDIA: Booklet
AUTHOR: Haines C.G., Owen-Evans S.
SERIES: FL London Region

Ref: 1037024374
TITLE: IT ACROSS THE NATIONAL CURRICULUM — SUPPORT MATERIALS
MEDIA: Book; loose leaf, ring file
AUTHOR: Lincolnshire ESG IT Team
PUBLISHER: Curriculum Support Services, Lincolnshire CC
PUBLISHED: 1989 (Nov)

Ref: 1037023532
TITLE: INITIAL PRINCIPLES UNDERLYING THE APPROVAL OF SYLLABUSES AND SYLLABUS CRITERIA
MEDIA: Information sheet; 5pp A4
SERIES: SEAC Guidance Notes, Number 2
PUBLISHER: School Examinations and Assessment Council (SEAC)
PUBLISHED: 1989 (May)

Ref: 1037023108
TITLE: RESOURCE BASED LEARNING IN ACTION
MEDIA: Book; 100pp A4
AUTHOR: Smith I., Togneri C.
SERIES: SCET Publications
PUBLISHER: Scottish Council for Educational Technology (SCET)
PUBLISHED: 1989

Ref: 1037022954
TITLE: THE EASY ENTERPRISE PUBLISHING KIT
MEDIA: Resource pack; guide book, activity book, pupil information sheets
AUTHOR: Worley J.
PUBLISHER: North Eastern Evening Gazette and Cleveland LEA
PUBLISHED: 1989

Ref: 1037022402
TITLE: ENTERPRISING REOPLE
MEDIA: Resource pack; colour photographs, text, 12pp booklet
PUBLISHER: BP Educational Service

Ref: 1037021511
TITLE: HARTWELL HOME MADE JAMS
MEDIA: Article; case study
AUTHOR: Broughton J.
SERIES: SCIP News 24
PUBLISHER: School Curriculum Industry Partnership (SCIP)
PUBLISHED: 1989

Ref: 1037021220
TITLE: IT CURRICULUM SUPPORT MATERIAL
MEDIA: Book
PUBLISHER: MEDUSA
PUBLISHED: 1988

Ref: 1037021109
TITLE: SCIENCE EDUCATION AND THE ENVIRONMENT
MEDIA: Article
AUTHOR: Gayford C.
SERIES: ASE Education in Science No. 131, pp. 22–23
PUBLISHER: Association for Science Education (ASE)
PUBLISHED: 1989

Ref: 1037018739
TITLE: THE MATHEMATICS CURRICULUM: IMPLICATIONS FOR TEACHING MAP SKILLS
MEDIA: Article
AUTHOR: Boardman D.
SERIES: Teaching Geography, Vol. 14, No. 3, pp. 116–119
PUBLISHER: The Geographical Association
PUBLISHED: 1989 (June)

Ref: 1037013976
TITLE: SMILE'S COVERAGE OF THE NATIONAL CURRICULUM
MEDIA: Information sheet
AUTHOR: Wrigley A.
PUBLISHED: 1989

Ref: 1037011272
TITLE: WHOLE SCHOOL POLICY ON STUDY SKILLS
MEDIA: Article
AUTHOR: Tabberer R.

Ref: 1037010431
TITLE: THE DESIGN COUNCIL
MEDIA: Organisation;

Ref: 1037010426
TITLE: HEALTH EDUCATION WITHIN THE CURRICULUM 5–19
MEDIA: Booklet; 67pp A4
AUTHOR: Northern Ireland Council for Education Development (NICED)
PUBLISHER: NICED
PUBLISHED: 1989

Ref: 1037010028
TITLE: INTRODUCTION TO DISCUSSION
MEDIA: Curricular package; A4, 20pp
AUTHOR: Brady J., Young J.
SERIES: CAST Publications. APSD project
PUBLISHER: Curriculum Advice and Support Team
PUBLISHED: 1978

Ref: 1037009587
TITLE: CO-ORDINATOR'S HANDBOOK: SVS UNIT
MEDIA: Teacher's notes; 136pp A4 (ring binder format)
AUTHOR: Central Support Group (CSG) for SVS
SERIES: Standard Grade Staff Development Materials
PUBLISHER: Scottish Consultative Council on the Curriculum (SCCC)
PUBLISHED: 1988

Ref: 1037009583
TITLE: SOCIAL AND VOCATIONAL SKILLS (SVS) AGAIN
MEDIA: Video; VHS, 16 min.
AUTHOR: Central Support Group (CSG) for SVS
SERIES: Standard Grade Starter Materials
PUBLISHER: Scottish Consultative Council on the Curriculum (SCCC)
PUBLISHED: 1988

Ref: 1037008964
TITLE: MATHEMATICS IN THE NATIONAL CURRICULUM
MEDIA: Book; 83pp A4, loose leaf, ring binder
AUTHOR: Department of Education and Science (DES), Welsh Office
PUBLISHER: HMSO
PUBLISHED: 1989 (March)

Ref: 1037007631
TITLE: MODERN STUDIES: STARTER PACK
MEDIA: Multi-media pack; teacher's notes (5 looseleaf packs, booklet 12pp
A5, leaflet 5pp A4), pupil information sheet, VHS video, 24 min.
AUTHOR: Central Support Group (CSG) for Modern Studies in association
with Scottish Council for Educational Technology (SCET) and Modern
Studies Association (MSA)
SERIES: Standard Grade. Starter Materials
PUBLISHER: Scottish Consultative Council on the Curriculum (SCCC)
PUBLISHED: 1988

Ref: 1037006203
TITLE: THE ENTERPRISE PUBLISHING KIT
MEDIA: Multi-media pack; teacher's guidebook, book of activities, pupil
reference sheets, planning wallchart, storage box
AUTHOR: Worley J.
PUBLISHER: North Eastern Evening Gazette
PUBLISHED: 1988

Ref: 1037004193
TITLE: FINANCIAL PLANNING AND MANAGEMENT OF DESIGN
AND TECHNOLOGY PROJECTS
MEDIA: Multi-media pack; 60 min VHS video, computer software, BBC
Master, RML Nimbus, Acorn Archimedes and IBM PC (but RML and IBM
formats resource BBC Basic 86 to run) resource cards, teacher's notes
AUTHOR: Gleave B., Allman G.
PUBLISHER: Banking Information Service
PUBLISHED: 1988

Ref: 1037003964
TITLE: DEVELOPMENT OF ST MODAN'S HIGH SCHOOL LIBRARY
MEDIA: Report
AUTHOR: St Modan's High School, Stirling

Ref: 1037003962
TITLE: DEVELOPING INFORMATION SKILLS — ONE SCHOOL'S
APPROACH
MEDIA: Teacher's notes
AUTHOR: Markless S.

Ref: 1032090016
TITLE: ECONOMIC AWARENESS
MEDIA: Information sheet; 4pp A4
AUTHOR: Northern Ireland Council for Educational Development
(NICED)
PUBLISHER: NICED
PUBLISHED: 1988

Ref: 1031930008
TITLE: MODULAR HUMANITIES SCHEME: I
MEDIA: Examination scheme; rationale
SERIES: WJEC Modular Humanities

Ref: 1031080072
TITLE: HUNTING DOWN TECHNOLOGY IN SCHOOLS: WHO
TEACHES IT? HOW AND WHY?
MEDIA: Article
AUTHOR: Cleeg A.
SERIES: ASE School Science Review Vol. 69, No. 246, pp. 34–41
PUBLISHER: Association for Science Education (ASE)
PUBLISHED: 1987 September

Ref: 1030250073
TITLE: A COMMON PURPOSE
MEDIA: Book; 57pp. illus.
AUTHOR: Adams E. *et al.*
PUBLISHER: WWF UK
PUBLISHED: 1988

Appendix 3

Section 11 of Local Government Act 1966: Background and Current (1990) Administrative Arrangements

The Local Government Act 1966 was passed when it was considered that additional costs were being imposed on local authority budgets by the arrival of a considerable number of immigrants from the Commonwealth (see Volume 1, Chapter 3; Volume 2, Chapter 2). For understandable reasons, immigrants were not evenly dispersed across the country. They tended to go to places where accommodation and jobs were likely to be found. Frequently this meant their going to places where previous arrivals from the same ethnic minority group had established themselves. Some areas of the country, particularly the large conurbations, received a disproportionate number of immigrants. This uneven distribution continues in 1992, and is unlikely to change other than slowly. In contrast to most grants by the Department of Education and Science, the Local Government Act 1966 provision initially did not have cash limits set on it.

Section 11 of the Local Government Act was the first government intervention to provide assistance to multiracial areas. Originally such a grant was at the rate of 50 per cent of expenditure but this was later increased to 75 per cent. This grant, administered by the Home Office, has been used primarily by social services and education authorities although it was designed to cover all staff employed by local authority departments.

The purpose of Section 11 as set out in the document is:

1   Subject to the provision of this section the Secretary of State may pay to local authorities who in his opinion are required to make special provision in the exercise of any of their functions in consequence of the presence within their areas of substantial numbers of immigrants from the Commonwealth whose language or customs differ from those of the community, grants of such amounts as he may with the consent of the Treasury

determine on account of expenditure of such description (being expenditure in respect of the employment of staff) as he may so determine.

2 No grant shall be paid under this section in respect of expenditure incurred before 1st April 1967.

Although Section-11 grant has been interpreted as 'the only government finance earmarked directly and exclusively for combatting racial disadvantage' (Home Affairs Committee, 1981, par. 48), many aspects of the grant's operation have been criticized. The main criticisms of Section-11 grant include its low take-up by some local authorities and the absence of any monitoring of Section-11 funded staff by the Home Office.

In response to various criticisms of Section-11 grant, the government issued revised administrative arrangements for the payment of this grant, which came into force on 1 January 1983. The changes in the arrangements were announced in the government's White Paper 'Racial Disadvantage' (circ. 8476) and were set out in detail in the Home Office circular 97/1982. The revised guidelines issued by the Home Office in 1982 were sound in principle, but were not taken in the same spirit by many LEAs. This was, in part, because of the 25 per cent of costs incurred. There was still a great deal of reluctance and inability to identify and account for Section 11 post-holders at local and central government levels.

In March 1986 the Home Office issued a further draft circular and proposed further adjustments for the administration of the grant. The suggested changes implied that Home Office earlier circular had been less effective than had been anticipated. The new circular 72/1986 came into force on 1 October 1986. The latest review of Section 11 was conducted from October 1988. As a result Home Office issued circular 78/1990. By 1988 100 million pounds per annum were being spent on Section 11 funding by the Home Office. Of this, eighty-two million were committed to the education service. The 1988 review team was extremely critical of the uses being made of Section 11 funding. Major criticisms included:

- absence of clear objectives for grants;
- no effective system for evaluating the results;
- the 12,000 post funded under the scheme continued with virtually no scrutiny;
- the administrative system was bureaucratic and wasteful;
- some subsidized ethnic minority posts appeared tokenistic; and
- little consultation concerning application took place with ethnic-minority communities.

A range of recommendations was proposed by the review team so as to address the weaknesses identified. One of the most important was to amend the target group from New Commonwealth immigrants and their descendants to 'meeting ethnic minority needs arising from racial disadvantage'. Other proposals were designed to clarify the objectives of grants by making the primary aim 'to open up mainstream services and opportunities of the ethnic minorities'. Local authorities were to be made more accountable for the funding and an increased ethnic minority community involvement in the whole process was to be required.

After consultation, new policy criteria were published in October 1990. These *retained* the criticized definition of the target group whereby ethnic minorities originating from outside the New Commonwealth remained excluded from Section 11 funding provision. A cash limit was set. In education, Section 11 funding was only to be made available for work in specified schools on approved schemes that met the Home Office's criteria. Guidance is provided in Home Office Circular No. 78/1990.

Extracts from the Home Office Circular No. 78/1990: Section 11 of the Local Government Act 1966

1.   This Circular sets out the new arrangements for the administration of grant under Section 11 of the Local Government Act 1966. Separate guidance is being issued to Training and Enterprise Councils (TECs) to take account of their new responsibilities for the administration of arrangements (see para 14 below) in connection with the payment of grant to ethnic minority voluntary sector organisations presently outside the scope of Section 11. A copy of that guidance is also enclosed for information.

2.   Under Section 11 of the Local Government Act 1966, the Secretary of State may pay grant in respect of the employment of staff to those local authorities who, in his opinion, have to make special provision in the exercise of any of their functions in consequence of the presence within their areas of substantial numbers of people from the Commonwealth whose language or customs differ from those of the rest of the community.

3.   For the purposes of grant under Section 11 the qualifying group includes:
(i)   All those born in a country of the New Commonwealth however long they have been resident in the UK; and
(ii) their direct descendants.
There is no quantitative definition of what is meant by 'substantial numbers'. The essential requirement is to demonstrate a special need in the target group of sufficient size that it cannot be properly addressed without the additional help that may be obtained through Section 11 funding. Applications for grant should make clear the level of need.

Scrutiny Report

4. Following the publication in July 1989* of the report of an efficiency scrutiny of the current arrangements for the administration of grant, the Government confirmed its agreement with the conclusion that there was a continuing need for specific grant provision but that the present system of grant allocation needed substantial improvement in order to ensure that the available money was used to the best effect; that there should be established a clear framework of policy statements, approved by Ministers of the appropriate Government Departments, within which allocation of grant could take place. The Government has given full consideration to a number of other recommendations of the scrutiny, together with comments made in response to the consultation period which preceded the issue of this Circular. This Circular sets out the details of the new arrangements which supersede those in Home Office Circular 72/1986.

Principal Changes

5.   (i)   All provision must fall within the new criteria for grant as contained in the statement of policy accompanying this Circular.
   (ii)   The grant is subject to an overall cash limit.
   (iii) Local authorities will in future be required to bid for provision within a fixed timetable (details at Annex A); bids to be project-based, the first bids — to cover the period commencing 1 April 1992 — to be submitted by 30 April 1991.
   (iv)   All projects approved for funding will in future be time-limited; they will be annually reviewed and monitored against recognisable performance targets.
   (v)   Local authorities will be required to identify, within their bids, a proportion of provision for the voluntary sector.
   (vi)   Payment of grant will be quarterly in arrears.

Section 11 Grant and the Government's Race Relations Policy

6. The Government's fundamental objective is to enable everyone, irrespective of ethnic origin, to participate fully and freely in the life

---

* Copies of the report are available through HMSO, ISBN No. 0113409702.

of the nation while having the freedom to maintain their own cultural identity.

The achievement of this objective involves central and local government; the private and voluntary sectors; and the ethnic minority communities themselves. The Government believes that at present there is a continuing need for specific grant to meet needs particular to ethnic minorities of Commonwealth origin that prevent full participation in the mainstream of national life. Barriers to opportunity arise in a number of areas, particularly through differences of language, in educational attainment, and through economic, social and cultural differences.

7. Genuine equality of opportunity is a Government priority. It is right that individuals from minority communities are given the assistance and encouragement necessary to enable them to participate fully in the wider community. The Government believes that improved arrangements for Section 11 grant will help to achieve this objective. These aims and framework are set out more fully in the policy document which accompanies this Circular and which forms the basis for the future use of Section 11 funding.

New Administrative Arrangements

8. The grant is subject to a cash limit reviewable annually. Future bids for funding will be invited on an annual basis to a fixed time-table geared to the financial year (Annex A). Existing provision approved under previous arrangements (i.e., posts approved following application up to 31 May 1990) will continue, subject to their being filled/not having been vacant for more than six months, to receive funding up to 31 March 1992. Bids under the new system may include bids both for existing Section 11 provision (submitted in project form) and for new provision, but *all* bids must be within the new criteria for grant. Bids may also be made for projects that are presently funded by central government and other similar agencies where that funding is due to run out, but must be submitted well before the final date of existing funding. Grant will *not* be approved for provision that is already receiving mainstream funding. Bids will need to include the following details:
(i) How the projects further the relevant Section 11 policy objectives and precisely what local needs they will address.
(ii) The specific objectives and quantifiable targets to be achieved by the proposed projects.
(iii) The timescale over which objectives and targets will be measured.

(iv) Proposals for monitoring the results.
(v) The consultation procedures pursued with the involved communities and their responses to the proposals.

Purposes for Which Grant May Be Approved

11. The Government is anxious to ensure that grant is targeted at provision which will be effective in enabling members of ethnic minorities to participate fully in the economic, social and public life of the nation. The needs which a project is intended to meet must be either different in kind from, or the same as but proportionately greater than, those of the rest of the community. It is not enough that a project's client group are predominantly from an ethnic minority. Applicants must establish that there exists a need that requires special provision to redress. The policy document contains a statement of the functions in areas of local authority services which the Government considers may be appropriate for support through Section 11 funding. Those statements are not exclusive, but set out a policy framework for project bids. Projects may qualify for funding in areas to which policy statements do not specifically refer, nonetheless, if they comply with the general principles for the use of Section 11 grant laid down in the statements.

12. It is important that grant-aided provision should fall within a general strategy for meeting the needs of ethnic minorities.

The Voluntary Sector

13. The Government considers that the voluntary sector has an important contribution to make to the effective delivery of Section 11 provision. As part of this approach, the Government expects local authorities to include applications for projects placed in, and operating from, voluntary organisations. Such projects would remain under the overall control of the local authority who would continue to claim grant for them, but day to day responsibility for individual projects would rest with the organisation in which they were based. Examples of such projects can be found in the policy document.

14. To further the aim of greater voluntary sector participation, and in advance of legislation, a separate grant will be available to encourage projects from within the voluntary sector. The grant will be paid through the Training and Enterprise Councils (TECs) and will be available for voluntary sector projects addressing ethnic minority need in training and enterprise under the same *policy* principles (see

policy document) that apply to Section 11 grant but without some of the constraints of that grant. Where local authorities are proposing projects within the area of training and enterprise they must first consult with TECs or, where a TEC has not so far been established, Task Forces and City Action Teams where these exist. A copy of the guidance to TECs setting out their role in the administration of the grant, together with the scope of the grant, is enclosed.

Introduction of the New Arrangements

15. As indicated above, existing provision will cease when the new arrangements come into effect on 1 April 1992. To meet the requirement that all Section 11 expenditure conforms with the new policy, monitoring and targeting specifications, and in particular that ineligible expenditure is discontinued, existing projects and posts for which, in a local authority's view, there is a continuing need, will have to be bid for afresh under the new arrangements. Such applications will not be approved unless they meet the new criteria and monitoring requirements.

Enquiries

33. Enquiries about this Circular should be made to Ethnic Minority Grants (Section 11), I Division, Home Office, 50 Queen Anne's Gate, London SW1H 9AT.

Timetables

November 1991	— Final full quarterly payment in advance to local authorities.
May 1992	— Remaining quarterly payment for posts under previous system to local authorities.
July 1992	— Submission of first quarterly return for period Apr–Jun 1992 and projected costs for remaining 3 quarters of financial year 1992–93.
August 1992	— First quarterly payment under new arrangements (arrears) for period Apr–Jun 1992.
30 September 1992	— Deadline for receipt of audited returns on previous financial year's grant expenditure.

Full Operation

January 1993	— Notification of approved provision for year commencing 1 April 1993.
30 September 1993	— See 30 September 1992 – detail to cover period 1 Apr 1992–31 Mar 1993.
July, October, January, April	— Submission of quarterly returns.
August, November, February, May	— Quarterly payments made to local authorities

(The same annual timetable applies thereafter)

Introductory Timetable

October 1990 onwards	— Preparation and submission of project proposals under new arrangements for period 1 April 1992–31 March 1993.
	— Seminars/discussion by Home Office to explain new arrangements and assist in preparation of bids.
30 April 1991	— *Deadline for Receipt of Applications for April 1992 to March 1993.*
May 1991–October 1991	— Consideration of applications for April 1992–March 1993.
October/November 1991	— Applicants notified of decisions on project proposals for April 1992–March 1993.
1 April 1992	— *Funding under new arrangements commences*

Annual Operational Timetable

30 June (1992)	— Deadline for receipt of applications for year commencing 1 April (1993).
January (1993)	— Notification of grant available and project approvals for year commencing 1 April (1993).
1 April (1993)	— Continuation of existing approvals and new approvals take effect.
30 September (1993)	— Deadline for receipt of audited return of previous financial year's grant expenditure by recipient bodies.

Financial Timetable Introduction

30 September 1991	— Deadline for submission of final Fin From C1 to Home Office.

October/November 1991 — Notification of grant available and project approvals for year commencing 1 Apr 1992.

Notes on Contributors

Clem Adelman is professor of education at Reading University. He has published widely in evaluation and social and educational research. He has taught or researched in all phases of schooling and higher education. He has conducted research on accreditation of higher and professional education into bilingual schooling in the USA.

Contact address: Department of Education, University of Reading, Bulmershe Court, Earley, Reading, RG6 1HY.

Neil Burtonwood taught in comprehensive schools for thirteen years before moving to Bretton Hall College where he is senior lecturer. He was INSET tutor at Bretton Hall for several years and is now coordinating an M.Ed programme at the college. He has published a number of articles on various aspects of education in a culturally plural society. He is the author of *The Culture Concept in Educational Studies*.

Contact address: Bretton Hall College, West Bretton, Wakefield, West Yorkshire, WF4 4LG.

Andy Forbes is senior lecturer in race equality at the South Manchester College. He specializes in in-service training work with staff from a wide range of public and private sector organizations. As ex secondary-school teacher, he has worked particularly extensively with schools and colleges in the north-west of England.

Contact address: The South Manchester College, Fielden Park Centre, Barlow Moor Road, West Didsbury, Manchester, M20 8PQ.

Chris Gayford, head of the Department of Science and Technology Education at the University of Reading and consultant to the Council for Environmental Education is involved with initial teacher education and post-experience work with teachers. He has been involved with several projects involving environmental education in the school curriculum both in the UK and in other parts of the world.

Contact address: Department of Science and Technology Education, University of Reading (*v.s.*).

Elinor Kelly is a senior staff tutor in the Extra-Mural Department at the University of Manchester. She has maintained an active interest in equal opportunities for many years, currently through membership of the University's committees and the Association of University Teachers. Since carrying out research for the Macdonald inquiry into racism and violence in Manchester schools, she has developed analysis of name-calling, harassment and bullying and their relevance to the quality of school experience for pupils, both girls and boys, of different abilities, from various ethnic groups and social classes.

Contact address: Extra Mural Department, University of Manchester, Oxford Road, Manchester, M13 9PL.

Horace Lashley is a lecturer in the Department of Community Studies at the University of Reading. Before joining the University of Reading he was education officer with the Commission for Racial Equality in London. He has written and researched into the area of multicultural and antiracist education.

Contact address – Department of Community Studies, University of Reading, (*v.s.*).

Kanka Mallick is senior lecturer in educational psychology at Crewe and Alsager College of Higher Education. Her main research interests include personality and self-esteem. She has written and researched into the area of ethnicity and educational achievement, and cross-cultural psychology. She is an associate fellow of the British Psychological Society and a Chartered Psychologist.

Contact address: Crewe and Alsager Campus of Manchester Metropolitan University, Crewe Green Road, Crewe, Cheshire, CW1 IDU.

Ken McIntyre was born in Trinidad and has lived in the UK for the last twenty-five years. He has worked as a youth worker, teacher, and for the last ten years as an educational psychologist. He recently completed his Ph.D thesis on the needs of black pupils in secondary schools. He also continues to lecture and research these issues. Currently he is employed as a consultant psychologist to a private company, working in the field of childcare.

Contact address: Northern Child Care, 11 Eastway Business Village, Olivers Place, Fulwood, Preston, PR2 4WT.

Prabodh Merchant is an employment officer. He works for the Commission for Racial Equality (CRE) and has extensive knowledge of race relations legislation and its effect. Currently he is working in the north-west of England.

Contact Address – Commission for Racial Equality, Maybrook House, 40 Blackfriars Street, Manchester, M3 2EG.

Peter Mittler is currently professor of special education, director of the School of Education and dean of the Faculty of Education at Manchester University. His research interests include social and family influences on language and cognitive development and on educational achievement and more recently the implications of the National Curriculum for children and young people with special educational needs.

Contact address: School of Education, University of Manchester (*v.s.*).

Julia Pilling currently teaches in the Science Faculty at Mornington High School, Wigan. She studied at Manchester University (1985–91), and gained an M.Phil degree in health education. During 1987–8 she was appointed teacher fellow for Wigan LEA, working with Lancaster University and evaluating INSET teachers received for the GCSE.

Contact address: Mornington High School, Mornington Road, Hindley, Wigan.

Peter D. Pumfrey is professor of education and head of the Centre for Educational Guidance and Special Needs at the University of Manchester. His research and teaching interests include interethnic relationships, multicultural education, social psychology, and race-relations research. *Education Attainments: Issues and Outcomes in Multicultural Education* (1988) and *Race Relations and Urban Education* (1990) were edited, and contributed to, in collaboration with Gajendra K. Verma.

Contact address — Centre for Educational Guidance and Special Needs, School of Education, University of Manchester (*v.s.*).

Alex B. Robertson taught in secondary schools and a college of education before joining the University of Manchester School of Education, where he is currently senior lecturer and director of the Centre for Curriculum Policy. An historian by training he has widened his interests to include the formation of educational policy and educational administration. Current research is on the interrelation of social factors and change in higher education early this century.

Contact address: School of Education, University of Manchester, (*v.s.*).

Harry Tomlinson is principal of Margaret Danyers College, Stockport. He is treasurer of the Secondary Heads Association (SHA), chair of the

Manchester branch of the British Institute of Management (BIM), and national chair of the British Educational Management and Administration Society (BEMAS). He has recently edited books on '*Performance-related Pay in Education*' and '*The Search for Standards*', an examination of the impact of ERA.

Contact address: 13 Pleasant Way, Cheadle Hulme, Cheshire, Stockport, SK8 7PF.

Gajendra K. Verma is professor of education and director of the Centre for Ethnic Studies in Education, School of Education, University of Manchester. He has been responsible for directing over twelve national and regional research projects concerned with education, social, and occupational adaptation of ethnic minority groups. He was a member of the Swann committee of inquiry into the education of children from ethnic minority groups.

Contact address: Centre for Ethnic Studies in Education, School of Education, University of Manchester (*v.s.*).

Ann Webster until recently taught law and philosophy at Queen Mary 6th Form College, Basingstoke. Now partly retired, she has embarked on a Ph.D on the topic of 'Citizenship Education.' Her publications include *Law Matters*.

Contact address: Woodmans Cottage, Brambley Road, Silchester, Nr Reading, Berkshire, RG7 2LT.

Name Index

Subject Index